THE BEST BUSINESS STORIES
OF THE YEAR: 2003 *Edition*

Andrew Leckey, nationally syndicated investment columnist for the Chicago Tribune Company, is also visiting professor in Business and Economics Journalism at Boston University's College of Communication. He was previously a financial anchor on the CNBC cable television network, contributing editor of the Quicken.com financial Web site, and director of the Business Reporting Program at the University of California, Berkeley. He has been author or editor of eight financial books. Leckey received the National Association of Investors Corporation's Distinguished Service Award in Investment Education. He was a Knight-Bagehot Fellow in Economics and Business Journalism and a fellow of the Media Studies Center, both at Columbia University.

Allan Sloan, guest editor and *Newsweek*'s Wall Street editor, has had a distinguished 30-year business-writing career. A five-time winner of the Gerald Loeb Award, business journalism's highest honor, he also received the Loeb Lifetime Achievement Award and the Distinguished Achievement Award of the Society of American Business Editors and Writers. Sloan is a contributor to Public Radio International's *Marketplace* and frequently appears as a commentator on the PBS television program *Nightly Business Report*. Previously a columnist at *Newsday* and a senior editor at *Forbes*, Sloan has also held positions at *Money* magazine, the *Detroit Free Press*, and the *Charlotte Observer*. He was named an alumnus of the year in 1999 by the Columbia Graduate School of Journalism.

THE BEST BUSINESS STORIES OF THE YEAR: *2003 Edition*

THE BEST
BUSINESS STORIES
OF THE YEAR

2003 *Edition*

Edited by *Andrew Leckey*

with guest editor *Allan Sloan*

VINTAGE BOOKS
A DIVISION OF RANDOM HOUSE, INC.
NEW YORK

A VINTAGE BOOKS ORIGINAL, JANUARY 2003

Library of Congress Cataloging-in-Publication Data is on file.

ISBN: 1-4000-3145-1

Book design by Christopher M. Zucker
Photo of Andrew Leckey from Tribune Media Services
Photo of Allan Sloan © David Berkwitz

www.vintagebooks.com

Printed in the United States of America
10 9 8 7 6 5 4 3 2 1

To the memory of Daniel Pearl

CONTENTS

Foreword   xiii

Introduction   xvii

"Amid Global Turmoil, Wild Times
in Trading Afghanis" *by Daniel Pearl*   3

"Bidding War" *by James B. Stewart*   7

"This Little Slinky Goes to Market" *by Neil Irwin*   36

"Yes, We Have No Profits" *by Nicholas Stein*   47

"Corporate Veil"
by John R. Emshwiller and Rebecca Smith   62

"Portland Subsidiary Mirrors
Enron's Rapid Rise, Fall"
by Jeff Manning and Gail Kinsey Hill   74

"How Andersen Went Wrong"
by David Ward and Loren Steffy   87

"My Pro Forma Life" *by Rob Walker*   105

"The Iceberg Wars" *by Wayne Curtis*   109

"The Trucker and the Professor"
by David Diamond   114

"Telecom's Pied Piper: Whose Side Was He On?"
by Gretchen Morgenson   127

"License to Steal" by Roger Lowenstein   139

"Turning Red Ink into Gold" by Rob Kaiser   143

"The Incomplete Résumé" by Floyd Norris   147

"Restating the '90s" by Michael J. Mandel   156

"Smaller" by Malcolm Gladwell   166

"Agillion's Brief, Fast Life" by Lori Hawkins   177

"Is the S&P 500 Rigged?" by Jason Zweig   186

"The Rocket's Red Ink" by Brian Lawson   193

"A Race to the Top" by Johnnie L. Roberts   205

"Executive Women and the Myth
of Having It All" by Sylvia Ann Hewlett   216

"The CEO and His Church"
by Deborah O'Neil and Jeff Harrington   231

"The Economic Strain on the Church"
by William C. Symonds   250

"Nationalities of Convenience" by Hal Lux   261

"India Calling" by S. Mitra Kalita   270

"Hard Time" by Douglas A. Blackmon   277

"The $200 Billion Miscarriage of Justice"
by Roger Parloff 293

"The Empire Builder" *by Joseph N. DiStefano* 313

"Would You Pay $2 Million for This Franchise?"
by Carlye Adler 330

"Double Play" *by Kurt Badenhausen,
Cecily Fluke, Lesley Kump, and Michael K. Ozanian* 337

Permissions Acknowledgments 343

FOREWORD

Whom do you trust? Business journalism over the past decade prided itself on its quick turnaround of financial figures and instant analysis of them. This seemed the perfect melding of computer, communication, and financial savvy. Average investors became hooked on a daily fix of numbers capable of moving individual stocks, the markets, and ultimately the economy. It came as a shock and an embarrassment that many of those precious corporate numbers had been exaggerated or fabricated, while a great deal of pertinent financial information never saw the light of day. Making matters worse, many analysts who were relied upon for unbiased opinions had a personal financial stake in perpetuating myths about companies they monitored.

Since the "accounting-gate" scandals, business journalists have applied themselves to using analytical skills to more critically dissect corporate earnings reports, balance sheets, and government filings. Training in this important process has been admirably stepped up. But uncovering lies and fraud takes more than running numbers that may or may not give the total picture. Old-school "shoe-leather" reporting with its snooping around, persistent skepticism, building of sources, checking of every tip, and wariness about pundits is most likely to provide breakthroughs and rebuild trust in business journalism's role as a watchdog.

The Best Business Stories of the Year series has presented the stories behind the important trends of recent years from outstanding authors who did sweat the details, taking time to dig deeply into business and economic issues of local, national, or international consequence. The *2001 Edition* mused about the bursting of the technology bubble, while the 2002 *Edition* grappled with the emotional and economic fallout from the September 11 tragedy. In this 2003 *Edition,* trust is a major theme. Average individuals whose retirement savings dropped by one-third or more in value as companies confessed to "cooking the books" became wary of the financial system and much of the information received about it. What once seemed an exciting game to them became a dangerous no-win proposition. This makes trustworthy financial journalism important in helping individuals intelligently chart their future.

Consider the crash course that a new generation of business journalists has received. For example, Chris Gaither, a graduate student of mine from the class of 2001, as a summer intern wrote stories about twentysomething dot-com millionaires. Later, as a part-time correspondent, he interviewed CEOs of tech firms who insisted their financial woes would be short-lived. Now, as West Coast correspondent for *The Boston Globe,* Chris regularly hears CEOs admit to having no clue as to what's going to happen next.

"I've personally seen tremendous upside and downside, and must remember both so I don't get sucked into the next hype cycle," said Chris, 27, returning from a four-day assignment covering the Microsoft Corporation in Redmond, Washington. "Reporters have become much more skeptical about quarterly reports and what companies don't say about off-balance-sheet transactions, which no one really seemed to care much about before Enron exposed the fact that companies had been hiding things."

With unique styles and viewpoints, the accomplished writers of the stories in *The Best Business Stories of the Year: 2003 Edition* investigated, rethought what we assumed was obvious, introduced readers to new topics, and hurled darts at pretentiousness. Some took controversial stands and their editors and publications backed them, providing their readers and the readers of this edition with outstanding work. We applaud them and believe the quality within these pages offers great reason for optimism about business journalism's future.

There is no single description of a great business story and no single publication or Web site producing it. Some pieces have great human warmth and others have a plot like a detective novel. While many of these are longer stories, we have also included columns and shorter pieces. Few readers regularly see all the business and general publications whose stories are included here. Besides looking through hundreds of articles in print and on Web sites, we consulted editors, writers, and contest officials for additional recommendations. We especially appreciate those editors who accepted this challenge with gusto, proudly sending us their staff's best work. We hope that, with the publication of the *2003 Edition* of the anthology, even more people will join us in our goal and give further suggestions so that we can present as diverse a mix as possible.

My thanks to guest editor Allan Sloan, whose talent, knowledge of financial history, and irrepressible wit made our consultations a joy. He willingly took time out from writing deadline *Newsweek* cover stories and appearing on countless television and radio news programs to be involved in this project because he deeply cares about the quality of business journalism. Our lengthy discussions about stories were always fun, especially when we disagreed. Thanks to my literary agent, Nat Sobel, with whom the idea for this series began, and Edward Kastenmeier, the editor at Vintage Books who has deftly turned each of the first three editions into reality. Also appreciated was the assistance of Barney Calame, deputy managing editor of *The Wall Street Journal,* who helped compile articles by the late Daniel Pearl from which we made our selection; and the Society of American Business Editors and Writers (SABEW), which gave us access to the winning articles from its annual "Best in Business" competition.

The stories in *The Best Business Stories of the Year: 2003 Edition* were originally published between July 1, 2001, and June 30, 2002. Selections for next year's anthology will be made on that same "fiscal year" basis. Editors or writers who wish published or on-line business stories to be considered for next year's edition should throughout the year send copies to Andrew Leckey, c/o *The Best Business Stories of the Year,* Vintage Books, 1745 Broadway, New York, New York, 10019. We look forward to reading the next group of stories and heading to wherever the unpredictable financial world takes us in the coming year.

—*Andrew Leckey*

INTRODUCTION

When the *Charlotte* (N.C.) *Observer* sent me to the business desk in 1969, it was a form of internal exile. Business departments were at the bottom of the newspaper food chain in the 1960s. I became a business writer because I had just gotten married and I never got to see my wife because of the hideous night and weekend hours that I worked as a junior sportswriter. So I asked for a transfer. I wasn't good enough to be a feature writer, the job I wanted, so the *Observer* made me a business writer. Next to meeting my wife, that's the biggest break I ever got. No one had ever taught me that business was supposed to be dull, so I've had over 30 years of fun writing about it.

The very existence of this book—the third in what I hope will be an eternal series—shows how much things have changed since I was dumped into business writing. Business has gone mainstream. It's an academic discipline. It has cable TV channels and all sorts of specialized publications. And the ultimate blessing from the journalistic establishment: the last two Pulitzer Prizes for beat reporting—Gretchen Morgenson of *The New York Times* in 2002 and David Cay Johnson of the *Times* in 2001—have gone to business writers. Whodathunkit?

With over 40 million workers owning 401(k) accounts, which didn't exist until 1982, stock market news has a built-in mass market. That's a huge change: stocks used to be an esoteric investment for the elite or the venturesome, but now they're Everyperson's. Main Street has increasingly tied its fate to Wall Street—if our retirement portfolios don't do well, many of us who had counted on a caviar retirement are going to get cat food instead. People are being forced to take more and more control of their finances—not good for many of them but great for business writers, whose knowledge is more necessary than ever.

But business news is more than stocks and the stock market. Take the biggest pure business story of 2002: a three-headed beast consisting of the Enron scandal, the implosion of the stock market, and the calls for reform in the way that corporate America and Wall Street do business. The September 11 terrorist attack and its continuing aftereffects are vastly more important than any business story. But September 11 is a gigantic story with a relatively small business component. The Enron scandal and the 2002 market meltdown are business stories through and through.

The Enron story languished in the business pages after the scandal broke in the fall of 2001, but it leaped the species barrier in January 2002 and became a full-blown Washington story. There were televised congressional hearings. General-interest publications carried articles about accounting and "special purpose entities" and other esoterica that had previously had trouble making most business pages, let alone the front pages. TV hosts who had to be coached on the difference between a debit and a credit found themselves discussing the way that WorldCom snookered its accountants by hiding billions of dollars of expenses in plain sight.

Business-writing sensibility is starting to inform general coverage—marking its final move out of the business section. That's a trade that's good for both teams, to revert to my sports-writing days. Think of it as fusion. But rather than combining, say, Spanish and Japanese cooking, fusion journalism combines business-writing skills with general-interest topics. This infuses general-interest stories with a needed component—numeracy—while dragging business writers out of the business ghetto, where we have a tendency to sit around and whine about not being understood. Some fusion stories: federal, state, and local budgets; Social Security; Medicare; tax policy.

At their best, business stories are just that: stories. They tell a tale or make a point but don't beat you over the head with businessese. They just pull you along.

The stories that Andrew Leckey and I have picked show amazing diversity. You expect fine pieces from an eclectic magazine like *The New Yorker,* whose franchise is deep reporting and sprightly writing. You expect some first-rate business commentary and reporting from publications like *Fortune, Forbes, BusinessWeek, The New York Times,* and *The Wall Street Journal.* Business is their business. What struck Andrew and me was how smaller newspapers, niche magazines, and on-line publications, most of them without tremendous resources, had produced really fine business journalism since July 1, 2001, our starting date.

And the best part was that many of the articles, as you'll see, don't look like business stories. They're stories about business, and very good ones. To me, that's the highest form of business journalism.

And now to our selections.

It's only fitting to start with a memorial: a piece from Daniel Pearl, the martyred *Wall Street Journal* reporter who was murdered by religious fanatics for being a journalist, an American, and a Jew, not necessarily in that order. Given how Pearl died, some readers may find the final sentence of the article off-putting. I found it eerily prescient. For those interested, the nonprofit Daniel Pearl Foundation (http://www.danielpearl.org) 16161 Ventura Boulevard, #671, Encino, California, 91436, has been established to further the ideals of his life and work. Its mission is to "promote cross-cultural understanding through journalism, music, and innovative communications."

James B. Stewart's *New Yorker* piece about price-fixing in the auction business is an example of one of the very best business writers of my generation at the top of his game. You may not care about the auction business—I certainly don't—but his piece is compelling. As is the Slinky story that Neil Irwin wrote in *The Washington Post.* Rather than writing a light story about a child's toy or an abstract story about business practices, Irwin fused them.

Nicholas Stein's story about the fall of Chiquita Banana kicks off a corporate scandal and incompetence segment. It's a classic story of how a once great company blundered terribly. John R. Emshwiller and Rebecca Smith blew open the Enron story by chipping away at it in the *The Wall Street Journal* after Enron president Jeff Skilling resigned abruptly in August 2001. Many of their stories that were groundbreaking at the time don't read terribly well today—the curse of beat reporting. This one, though, holds up well, despite how much smarter we are about Enron and corporate shenanigans than we used to be.

Jeff Manning and Gail Kinsey Hill's Portland *Oregonian* article about an Enron subsidiary and *Bloomberg Markets*'s David Ward and Loren Steffy's analysis of Arthur Andersen's accounting lapses show how to convert liabilities into assets. *The Oregonian* produced a "local angle" story that's well worth reading even for those of us thousands of miles from Oregon. Ward and Steffy, operating more like a magazine than a specialized financial news service, put Andersen's Enron failings into perspective. And Rob Walker's send-up of accounting, published in *Slate,* shows that there's always a place for wit.

Wayne Curtis's *Atlantic Monthly* article about harvesting icebergs is a classic fusion story, as is the piece by David Diamond in *Wired,* showing how high tech affects truck drivers as well as computer geeks. These are classic examples of why you can write business stories about anything, if you understand the topic well enough.

Gretchen Morgenson of *The New York Times* and Roger Lowenstein of *SmartMoney* bring us back to hard-core business writing. If you meet either of these people—I've known them both for years—they seem so nice that you would never suspect how tough-minded they are. Morgenson's attack on Salomon Smith Barney's Jack Grubman gives you a taste of the coverage that has helped spur corporate reform proposals. And Lowenstein's piece, published in a magazine that flourished during the stock bubble, shows why I used to worry every Thursday, when his column would appear in *The Wall Street Journal.* I wrote on Fridays and had to see if he had preempted me—which he did far too often for my taste.

Rob Kaiser's *Chicago Tribune* article, part of a bankruptcy series, brings to public view what people knowledgeable about bankruptcy have always known: that in Chapter 11 proceedings, shareholders generally get trashed while creditors and professionals often do very well. It's not really news, because it's been going on forever. But people should keep it in mind when they're tempted to load up on the stock of bankrupts like Enron and Global Crossing, which almost always go to zero and stay there.

Floyd Norris of *The New York Times,* another longtime friend and competitor, shows in his "Chainsaw" Al Dunlap story why I dread seeing his byline. Norris actually has a memory and uses it. I love reading his stories. I just hate reading them when they cover something I had planned to write about and now have to abandon.

Michael J. Mandel of *BusinessWeek,* who lives in my neighborhood and is my occasional train companion, is a recovering academic who can break ground in ways that normal academics and general journalists can't. He invented the term "New Economy," but he never fell for the "endless boom" nonsense of the 1990s. I don't agree with his case here—but it's worth reading.

Malcolm Gladwell's analysis of the disposable diaper industry is another example of how you can write a compelling business story about almost anything. The success story of this mundane product is a natural contrast with Lori Hawkins's account, in the *Austin American-Statesman,* of the fall of a high-flying company that seemed to have it made.

Money magazine's Jason Zweig, one of my fellow members of the *Forbes* magazine diaspora, asks an irreverent question about the stock market's holy of holies, the Standard & Poor's 500 index. It won't make you feel any better about your S&P 500 index fund sucking wind, but at least you'll know why. Brian Lawson of *The Huntsville Times* takes on his local icon, the U.S. space program, and asks good, tough, interesting questions about it: classic local business writing.

Johnnie L. Roberts, my *Newsweek* colleague, is perhaps the only journalist who could ever have gotten three of America's top chief executives, all of whom happen to be black, to talk about how they got to be where they are. Johnnie is amazingly persuasive—and amazingly perceptive, as this piece shows.

Sylvia Ann Hewlett, writing in the *Harvard Business Review,* and Deborah O'Neil and Jeff Harrington of the *St. Petersburg Times* raise provocative and disturbing questions about subjects usually treated with kid gloves: family pressures on female executives and the place of religion, if any, in a publicly traded company.

Using financial analysis tools, William C. Symonds of *BusinessWeek* explains the cash squeeze that's hurting the U.S. Catholic Church, and examines why the church had money problems even before its sex scandal became public knowledge.

Hal Lux in *Institutional Investor* helped set off the current debate about the morality of U.S. companies opening file-drawer headquarters in the Bahamas to avoid paying U.S. income taxes. And S. Mitra Kalita in *Newsday* shows why you sometimes get such strange answers from customer service reps.

Douglas A. Blackmon's *Wall Street Journal* article about Alabama convicts combines business writing with a social conscience. And Roger Parloff's asbestos article in *Fortune* demonstrates how social justice can be perverted.

Joseph N. DiStefano, in *Inquirer,* the Sunday magazine of *The Philadelphia Inquirer,* explores how a once great businessman lost his touch. Carlye Adler, in *Fortune Small Business*, shows how shelling out $2 million for a Krispy Kreme franchise—which on the surface is an act of total lunacy—can be a very smart investment.

And, finally, to close the loop: returning to my sportswriting roots, we have a nifty sports story by Kurt Badenhausen, Cecily Fluke, Lesley Kump, and Michael K. Ozanian, explaining why the Boston Red Sox sold for so much and why its cable TV network is worth more than the team itself. After I moved to business writing from sports, I used to tell people that the main difference was that the numbers in business stories were bigger. This piece explains why that's no longer true.

—Allan Sloan

THE BEST BUSINESS STORIES OF THE YEAR: *2003 Edition*

Wall Street Journal reporter Daniel Pearl should be remembered not only for his courage and professionalism but for the clarity of his writing, his compassion, and his wit. In this story, Pearl gave his personal touch to a wild scramble by currency traders to play all financial angles—even in the midst of jihad.

Daniel Pearl

Amid Global Turmoil, Wild Times in Trading Afghanis

PESHAWAR, PAKISTAN—As a Muslim, and an ethnic Pashtun, Fazal-e-Maula has some sympathy for the ruling Taliban in Afghanistan. But on September 11, as he watched television replays of airplanes crashing into the World Trade Center in New York, he knew what to do: buy afghanis.

The afghani, Afghanistan's long-suffering currency, has the perverse tendency to go up whenever sitting governments fall. Mr. Maula, 32 years old, knew that from his 10 years of experience as a currency trader in Peshawar, one of the only places in the world with active trading of afghanis. So as soon as commentators labeled Osama bin Laden the prime suspect in the attack, Mr. Maula says, he figured the Taliban would become a target of the U.S., and "with attacks on the Taliban, the currency would go up."

So it has—94% against the Pakistani rupee, the other currency traded in the Faiz Market here. A small courtyard that functions as an informal afghani currency trading pit here, the market has become hyperactive in recent weeks as the Taliban have taken a pounding. Professional traders such as Mr. Maula, as well as amateurs with time on their hands, have turned neat profits. As Northern Alliance opposition troops approached Kabul, hundreds of dealers, many of them Afghans who fled U.S. bombing, have elbowed and jostled each other, slapping hands to make and accept bids, and cheering when the rate notched up on rumor of Taliban battlefield defeats.

"I have taken four aspirins, these people make so much noise," complained Mohammed Ilyas, who sells scarves from a courtyard shop. "I pray to Allah that the Afghanistan issue gets resolved, and these people go back to Afghanistan so I can have a normal business." One day recently, trading continued even as tear-gas fumes wafted over from a nearby demonstration. "They were crying, but they didn't stop trading."

Even more than currencies in other developing countries, the market in afghanis is unusual. For one thing, the currency hasn't been printed by the Taliban government since it came to power in 1996. Instead, the afghani actually comes from printing presses run by the opposition Northern Alliance, and there are two varieties. Afghanis printed under the auspices of the alliance's late Tajik commander, Ahmed Shaw Masood, are more widely accepted in Taliban areas than those printed by the alliance's Uzbek commander, Abdul Rashid Dostum, though only by the last two digits of the serial number can one tell them apart.

The market exchange rate also varies widely from the bank exchange rate. For example, according to the quoted exchange rate, it costs 4,750 afghanis to buy $1. In the bazaars where trading is done, the afghani is worth a lot less—it costs about 34,000 afghanis to buy $1 (albeit that means the afghani has risen 56% against the dollar since the conflict began, because then it cost 78,000 to buy $1 in mid-September). Similarly, after the recent run-up in the value of the afghani, a rupee is worth 606 afghanis, while the quoted bank rate has it worth only 74 afghanis.

It's in places like the Faiz Market where the real action is.

Nobody runs the market, and there are no written rules. In 1983, Pakistan's central bank declared that afghanis could be traded without a currency dealer's license. Dealers convene a "Loya Jirga," their version of a traditional Afghan tribal council, to resolve disputes. Like official currency exchanges, Faiz Market keeps regular hours, offers futures trading, and favors big dealers: They're the ones who can make occasional telephone contact with Afghanistan, and in case of shortages they order sacks of afghanis sent across the supposedly closed border.

The afghani's value has plummeted so far over the years that the highest note, 10,000 afghanis, has to be carried in thick stacks to be of any value. Traders quote the exchange rate as the number of Pakistan rupees it takes to buy 100,000 afghanis. That rate was 27,000 in the early 1970s, and fell to around 85 rupees under Taliban rule. Trading became so quiet that Mr. Maula and his brothers considered closing down their shop in 1998.

But September 11 galvanized the market, bringing prospects of a new government and, perhaps, economic development. Last Saturday's trading is typical. By the time the market opened at 8 A.M., the Northern Alliance opposition had captured the city of Mazar-e-Sharif, and the afghani started trading at 154 rupees for 100,000 afghanis, up 10 from the previous day. One of Mr. Maula's traders had been in touch with currency dealers in the Afghanistan capital, Kabul. "We have received news that the rate in Kabul is 160," he whispered. Mr. Maula, sitting cross-legged in his tiny shop, remained cool. "Don't panic. Take your time, we'll wait for the right moment."

Toward noon, as hawkers passed by with chewing tobacco and roasted corn, the currency crept up to 164 on the talk of further Northern Alliance gains. Suddenly, two traders near Mr. Maula's shop exchanged angry words, and fists started flying. "When the price fluctuates we have such problems," said a bystander. (The brawl was actually over a used-car deal.)

By 1 P.M., the afghan settled down to 160, amid market speculation Gen. Dostum had been arrested. By 1:30, it notched up on rumors the Northern Alliance had captured another town. By 2 P.M., settlement time, Mr. Maula had pocketed big profits for the day.

What moves the afghani market isn't always what's newsworthy from Western eyes. A headline quoting Osama bin Laden saying he had nuclear weapons had no effect. But rumors last month that exiled king Zahir Shah was coming to Pakistan to preside over a new Afghan government briefly pushed the currency above 300 rupees.

Yesterday, the afghani traded at 165 rupees for 100,000 afghanis, up from 155 the day before, showing traders like the Taliban's ouster from Kabul but want to see a new government take control.

Some traders acknowledge mixed feelings about profiting from the demise of the Taliban, which had its roots in Peshawar's religious schools. "It's not my regular job," Younus Khan, a 25-year-old cloth trader with a shaggy Taliban-style beard, says by way of apology, after gaining the equivalent of $1,500 in Saturday's trading. Then his face brightens. "I'll give this money as a donation for jihad purposes," he says.

An antitrust investigation into Christie's and Sotheby's aimed an unwelcome light on the business practices of those venerable auction houses for the first time. James B. Stewart in *The New Yorker* skillfully looks behind the scenes at the race to see who could betray whom, in the process revealing the unique personalities at each firm.

James B. Stewart

Bidding War

ON JANUARY 11TH of last year, the president and chief executive of Sotheby's, Diana D. (Dede) Brooks, and its chairman, A. Alfred Taubman, held a glamorous party to celebrate the renovation of the firm's Manhattan headquarters, on York Avenue, and the launch of an Internet auction site. "We believe Sotheby's is uniquely positioned for the twenty-first century," Brooks said, as a thousand guests admired works for sale by Sir Joshua Reynolds, Maurice Prendergast, and George Caitlin.

Taubman, a self-made real-estate and shopping-mall multimillionaire from Detroit, had acquired the international auction house in 1983, reportedly because of its social cachet. He and his wife, Judy, a former Miss Israel, quickly found themselves welcome in Manhattan, Palm Beach, and London society. But, as it turned out, Taubman resented Sotheby's aristocratic pretensions; in a speech he made shortly after the acquisition, he said that in all his years of art buying he had never been treated with such snobbishness as he had been at Sotheby's and at its chief rival, Christie's—everything from the cool appraisal of the white-gloved doorman to the suspicious "May we help you?" of the English-accented receptionist. Taubman's experience was hardly unusual. As one Sotheby's executive put it recently, "There were plenty of people here who could make you feel unwelcome."

Taubman set about changing that. In 1994, he replaced his chief executive, the patrician Michael Ainslie, with Diana Brooks. A graduate of Miss Porter's School and Yale, and a former Citibank lending officer, Brooks, who was in her forties, served on the board of directors of Morgan Stanley Dean Witter, Yale University, Deerfield Academy, and the Winterthur museum, in Delaware. Sotheby's employees were initially wary of her hard-charging manner and limited background in art, but most were soon won over by her energy and enthusiasm, and she became the best-known and most visible chief executive in the company's history. She oversaw the sale of Jacqueline Kennedy Onassis's estate, in 1996, in which a tape measure sold for forty-eight thousand dollars. She was featured in newsweeklies, and appeared frequently on morning television shows, extolling Sotheby's to a wider audience. She worked so closely with Taubman that some called it a father-daughter relationship.

Brooks and Taubman, working with the architects Kohn Pederson Fox Associates, had collaborated on the design of the new headquarters, a ten-story building sheathed in glass that was meant to embody the greater sense of openness that they had brought to the auction house. It had a rooftop sculpture garden accessible to the public, and, like many of Taubman's malls, an atrium. Christopher Tennyson, who works with Taubman in Detroit, said recently, "The whole effort was to bring more competition, more sunshine and visibility into the business."

But less than two weeks after the celebration Taubman received subpoenas from a federal grand jury investigating a criminal price-fixing conspiracy between Sotheby's and Christie's. Then, on January 29th, a headline appeared on the front page of the *Financial*

Times of London which said, "CHRISTIE'S ADMITS FIXING COMMIS-
SIONS: AUCTION HOUSE TELLS THE U.S. JUSTICE DEPARTMENT
THAT IT MADE DEAL WITH SOTHEBY'S." An accompanying article,
featuring a photograph of Brooks, noted that Christie's not only
had confessed to the scheme but had received conditional amnesty
for itself and its employees from the Justice Department. The
company would not be prosecuted.

A few weeks later, Brooks took a leave of absence and went into
seclusion at her house in Greenwich, Connecticut; she resigned
eight months afterward, abruptly ending a career as one of the
country's most admired executives. Taubman resigned as Sotheby's
chairman and didn't stand for reelection to the board the following May, though he remains Sotheby's controlling shareholder. On
May 2nd of this year, Taubman, who is seventy-six, was indicted,
along with the retired former chairman of Christie's, Sir Anthony
Tennant (who was not covered by Christie's amnesty), for antitrust
conspiracy. "These individuals mastered the art of price-fixing,"
the Justice Department declared in announcing the indictment.
Tennant denied the charges, but said he would remain in Britain,
outside the reach of United States courts. Taubman, too, insisted
on his innocence, and he is scheduled to go to trial next month.
The government's main witness against him will be his former
protégée, Diana Brooks.

The Sherman Antitrust Act was passed in 1890, when populist
outrage over the trusts and monopolists of the Gilded Age was at
its height. An agreement to fix prices at a level that would not pre-
vail in a competitive market means not only that consumers are
overcharged but that vast profits flow to a few people at the top,
and that productivity is dampened. The penalties for price-fixing
are severe; whereas a securities-law felon faces a maximum criminal fine of a million dollars, an antitrust conspirator faces a criminal fine that is twice the total amount of what he obtained in the
course of the crime. (In Taubman's case, conviction could mean
not only a three-year prison term but also a fine of hundreds of

millions of dollars.) Yet what surely galled Taubman and others at Sotheby's most was the fact that, as long as Christie's lived up to its agreement with the Justice Department, their chief competitor and its employees would face no criminal charges and no criminal penalties.

From Sotheby's point of view, Christie's wasn't just gaining an advantage over its chief rival; it was promising to destroy it. In addition to damaging press stories about the scandal and the extraordinary financial pressures of the criminal case, civil lawsuits were beginning to accumulate. The civil suits, unlike the criminal case, affected Christie's as well as Sotheby's. The art buyers and sellers who had commissioned one of the auction houses to handle their transactions were furious about being charged rigged prices, and by April, 2000, three months after the *Financial Times* article appeared, some forty civil suits had been filed against both companies.

Soon after the scandal broke, the government's chief antitrust prosecutor, John Greene, a mild-mannered but tenacious litigator, met with Sotheby's outside counsel, Weil, Gotshal & Manges. One of Sotheby's lawyers, Richard Davis, tried to impress upon Greene the irony that a policy meant to protect competition was likely to turn an auction-house duopoly into a Christie's monopoly, but Greene seemed intent upon a full-bore prosecution. He told the Sotheby's lawyers that the government could seek a fine of hundreds of millions of dollars, and the meeting ended.

The American law-enforcement system, especially the antitrust division, actively encourages the cooperation of informants like Christie's. Prior to 1993, a price-fixer who wanted amnesty for testifying against a co-conspiring competitor had to take his information to the Justice Department before an investigation was under way. But that year the department began offering amnesty even after an investigation was in progress—to whomever came in the door first and promised that all its employees would confess and cooperate against other conspirators. From a law-enforcement perspective, the program has been a success. Since it began, requests for amnesty, which under the old program had averaged one a year, jumped to more than one a month, and in the last four years the government has reaped fines of $1.7 billion. Many defense lawyers, mindful of the innate American distaste for informers, have argued that such incentives to cooperate are too generous, extravagantly rewarding testimony from people who are criminals and who tailor their testimony to what prosecutors want to hear. But so far none of the cases has generated a public outcry.

Christie's traces its origins to 1766, when James Christie, a friend and patron to Thomas Chippendale, Sir Joshua Reynolds, and Thomas Gainsborough, opened a London auction house that combined art, commerce, and social intercourse to an unprecedented degree. Christie's negotiated on behalf of Catherine the Great, whose paintings became the core of the collection of the Hermitage, and presided over the sale of Reynolds's studio. Gainsborough's portrait of James Christie hangs in the Getty museum, in Los Angeles.

In 1998, Christie's was acquired for more than a billion dollars by a French conglomerate owned by the billionaire financier Françoise Pinault. Like Taubman, Pinault built his own fortune, forging a luxury-goods empire that includes Yves Saint Laurent, Gucci, Balenciaga, and the Printemps department-store chain. At the time of the takeover, Pinault stressed that he didn't intend to interfere with the management of the auction house, then headed by Tennant, its chairman, and largely run by its chief executive, Christopher M. Davidge. Davidge, who had started as a porter with the company in 1965 and had worked his way up, secured his position as chief executive in 1993. He dressed fastidiously in bespoke suits, crisp white collars, and flashy ties. He had boyish features and blond hair that looked carefully blow-dried. Behind his back, many of his employees called him the "golden hamster."

Davidge had been steeped since childhood in the mores of the auction world—his grandfather had been the cashier at Christie's, his father had been the company secretary, and his mother had been a secretary to one of the partners in the firm before it went public, in 1973—but he lacked the pedigree required to climb the social ladder. He was ridiculed for telling a *Financial Times* interviewer that his favorite luxury was quilted toilet paper. As the derisive nickname implied, he would never be accepted as the social equal of many of Christie's directors and clients, a circumstance that gave his skillfully obsequious flattery of wealthy and aristocratic patrons an undertone of hostility and resentment. To some of his colleagues, it also accounted for the aggressive assault he made on Sotheby's dominant position as the leading art auctioneer.

Davidge worked closely with the president of Christie's North and South America, Patricia Hambrecht, who had been the firm's general counsel before assuming that position, in 1997. Hambrecht was often described as Christie's answer to Diana Brooks, though the two had little in common besides their occupations. Hambrecht had been educated at Yale and Harvard Law School and had spent most of her career at a Wall Street law firm. She was credited at Christie's for her part in persuading Bill Gates, the chairman of Microsoft, to pay more than thirty million dollars for the Leonardo da Vinci Codex Leicester.

Hambrecht was also known for her style and verve. *Town & Country,* in a 1997 article, described her as "petite, dark-haired and very soignée." A journalist for the London *Times* wrote admiringly, "When I last sat in her office, she removed her shoes, put up her stockinged legs and twiddled her toes under my nose for 45 minutes." She and Davidge had a close personal and professional relationship, which generated gossip in the company. According to the British press, she was named a co-respondent in Davidge's 1998 divorce in London, but both she and Davidge have denied that the rumors of an affair had any substance.

In April of 1999, Hambrecht presided over the opening of Christie's new Manhattan galleries, in Rockefeller Center. But later that year Christie's announced that Hambrecht would be taking a leave. A few months earlier, the company had paid more than two million dollars to settle a suit brought against her and the company by Michael Ward Stout, the executor of the estate of the photographer Robert Mapplethorpe. In 1989, Christie's had appraised the estate at two hundred and twenty-eight million dollars. Later, in sworn statements, Hambrecht attempted to explain the generous appraisal by claiming that Stout had misled her. He sued her for defamation. In the discovery process, however, virtually all of Hambrecht's representations, including her sworn statements, were called into question. An assistant vice-president who worked closely with Hambrecht, and had conducted the appraisal, contradicted her in an affidavit that supported Stout's version of events. Christie's lawyers pursued a settlement, and Hambrecht was told to resign.

Sotheby's was founded by Samuel Baker, a London book dealer, in 1744, and held its first auction that year. Its literary roots were later evident in its sale of Napolean's rare-book collection, in 1823, and its auction of the love letters of Elizabeth Barrett and Robert Browning, in 1913. Beginning with Queen Mary, the House of Windsor traditionally relied on Sotheby's for the discreet expansion of the royal collections. Sotheby's and Christie's dominated the world of rare art, books and manuscripts, and antiques, and they evolved into a genteel duopoly, in which Sotheby's traditionally maintained an edge in sales volume and profits.

Both auction houses suffered financially from the recession that followed the Gulf War, in 1991. To raise revenue, Sotheby's announced in November, 1992, that it was increasing the commission it charges buyers, from ten per cent of the first fifty thousand dollars of a purchase to fifteen per cent, effective January 1, 1993. A month later, Christie's announced that it would charge the same rates, beginning in March, 1993. The commissions were added to the winning bid, so that an item with a hammer price of ten thousand dollars actually cost the buyer eleven thousand five hundred.

When Davidge became the chief executive at Christie's, in

1993, the relationship between the two houses changed. Competition became increasingly ruthless, most of it occurring behind the scenes, over the right to sell the most prominent collections and prized masterpieces of the world's wealthiest collectors and major celebrities. Christie's landed the estate of Rudolf Nureyev, Princess Diana's dresses, and Barbara Streisand's art and collectibles, as well as the contemporary-art collection of the costume-jewelry magnate Victor Ganz and his wife, Sally, which in 1997 brought a record $206.5 million. Sotheby's auctioned Jacqueline Kennedy Onassis's estate and the Duke and Duchess of Windsor's personal effects, and sold a Renoir for a record $78.1 million and van Gogh's "Irises" for $53.9.

The big sales numbers and highly publicized celebrity auctions, however, masked deteriorating profits. Buyers' commissions remained fixed at fifteen per cent, but the auction houses, in their eagerness to attract new consignments, drastically cut the commission rates paid by sellers, in many cases to nothing. As a further inducement to sellers, they printed lavish catalogues to draw buyers and mounted expensive touring exhibitions to the world's art capitals; they made donations to the sellers' favorite charities; and, in the most extreme step, they extended financial guarantees to the sellers long before any bids were entertained. By the mid-nineties, Christie's sales had surpassed Sotheby's.

Davidge's open hostility to Sotheby's and his tactics to undermine its market share, even at the expense of profits, seemed to render unlikely the possibility of any collusion. Still, it's clear from many Christie's memos from the period that Davidge was aware of antitrust considerations. In one such note to Hambrecht, when she was still the company's chief counsel, he wrote, in a distinctive left-slanting script, "Let me know if it would violate any laws etc. Could it be considered collusion?" Memos from outside counsel contained warnings and analyses of relevant antitrust statutes in both the United States and the European Community.

In the spring of 1995—about the time that Christie's secured the Nureyev-estate sale—the fierce competition for consignments from sellers abruptly ended. That March, Christie's announced that it would charge sellers a fixed, nonnegotiable sliding-scale commission on the sales price. A month later, Sotheby's announced the same policy. Christie's, anticipating potentially hostile press inquiries, prepared hypothetical questions and answers for Davidge. One reads:

> Q: Isn't this the age-old tactic of trying to increase profits through price fixing? Do you have any antitrust concerns?
> A: We are instituting a new policy which we believe to be fairer and more straightforward than in the past.

Two years later, Christie's received its first grand-jury subpoenas. The company's lawyers diligently interviewed its top executives, including Hambrecht, Tennant, and Davidge. The executives reassured the lawyers that the firm had nothing to be concerned about. As the company's outside counsel concluded in a confidential report, "There were no admissions of contacts of an inappropriate nature between Christie's and Sotheby's, nor did any documents appear, either in the US or the UK, which contained references suggesting inappropriate contacts." They expected that to be the end of the matter.

Then, in 1999, the Stout defamation case was settled and Hambrecht resigned on August 6th. She did not go quietly. As she had told *Town & Country* in 1997, "As Christie's general counsel for seven years I dealt with absolutely every problem in every department. . . . The legal side is probably the single best place to get an overview of absolutely everything that goes on in this business—warts and all."

In the weeks after her resignation, Hambrecht met again with Christie's lawyers, and this time she revealed that Davidge—who had begun dating a Christie's curator of Asian artifacts, Amrita Jhaveri—had confided in her far more than she had previously acknowledged. What Davidge had told her, Hambrecht said, suggested than an antitrust conspiracy existed, and that it went to the top of the firm. (Hambrecht has not explained her motives for making these disclosures when she did. Like all the Sotheby's and Christie's principals mentioned in this account, she has refused to be interviewed.)

Armed with Hambrecht's allegations, Christie's lawyers questioned Davidge again, on October 20th. He remained unflappable, and "denied that inappropriate contacts with Sotheby's had taken place," as the lawyers later put it. But when they spoke to Davidge's secretary, Irmgard Pickering, she recalled that Davidge had met several times with his counterpart at Sotheby's, Diana Brooks, just before the 1995 announcement of the change in sellers' commissions. She also remembered the punctilious Davidge complaining that "he was more organized in keeping agendas" than Brooks was. Pickering didn't know exactly what the two had discussed at their meetings, but she recalled that Davidge had seemed "confident" that Sotheby's would follow Christie's action on sellers' commissions and match its new policy.

More serious allegations followed soon after, when the lawyers interviewed Lord Hindlip, who in 1996 had succeeded Tennant as Christie's chairman. At the time, Hindlip had brushed them aside, asking, "Do you know who I am?" (He is the sixth Baron Hindlip of Hindlip, an Eton-educated former Coldstream Guard.) But Hindlip now recalled that Davidge had come to him after the sellers' commissions were announced and confided that he had discussed the commission changes with Brooks. Davidge also told Hindlip that he and Brooks had exchanged so-called "grandfather lists"—names of clients who had been promised particular terms in sales that were scheduled to occur after the date of the new commission structure, and would thus be exempt from the new fixed-commission policy. Hindlip appears to have done nothing about these startling disclosures. On the contrary, after the grand jury began investigating, he sought to reassure Davidge. In December, 1997, Davidge told Hindlip that he was worried that his dealings with Sotheby's might cause him to be fired. He asked Hindlip to honor his contract in the event that he was forced to leave because of antitrust problems, and Hindlip obliged. Now Hindlip gave the lawyers a copy of a letter he had saved, handwritten on Christie's letterhead and dated December, 1997:

> Dear Christopher,
> I am writing to reassure you that, in the unlikely event that it should happen you are forced to resign your position because of the antitrust hearings in the U.S., Christie's will fully protect your position as per your contract. . . .

This was the first time that the Christie's lawyers had seen or heard of this letter. It had not been mentioned in connection with their earlier inquiry. When the lawyers tried to arrange another interview with Davidge, they were told that he was unavailable. He had stopped attending major auctions, was "losing interest in his work," as a Christie's lawyer later put it, and had all but disappeared from Christie's London headquarters, on King Street.

As the pressure on Davidge mounted, he hired a criminal lawyer, Joe Linklater, of Baker & Mackenzie, in Chicago. When Linklater arrived in London, he discovered that Davidge had kept numerous files at his apartment, which was next door to Christie's headquarters. One of them had belonged to Sir Anthony Tennant but had been taken over by Davidge when Tennant retired. Another contained Sotheby's "grandfather list" and handwritten agendas prepared by Davidge for a series of meetings with Diana Brooks. As his secretary had revealed, the two had met secretly on several occasions, including one in which Davidge reportedly flew to New York on the Concorde, drove around the airport in a limousine with Brooks, then returned to London the same day. Davidge maintained that he was only carrying out Tennant's orders.

The importance of the files, and the danger they represented to Christie's, was immediately evident. Linklater hinted at this to lawyers at Skadden, Arps, Slate, Meagher & Flom, in New York, who were representing Christie's in the United States, but the lawyers insisted that the documents be produced anyway. Meanwhile, Christie's was negotiating a generous severance agreement for Davidge. The company was willing to pay him, in installments, five million pounds in severance, as long as he agreed to state that he had committed no breach of fiduciary duty during his tenure at the company and that Christie's was free to terminate his remaining severance payments if it turned out that he had engaged in any conduct tending to bring himself or the company into "disrepute," including "breaching any requirement or requirement of law." Davidge initially refused; both sides knew such a claim was patently untrue.

On Christmas Eve, 1999, however, Davidge bowed to Christie's demands and signed the agreement, which included a non-disclosure clause. He gave his files to Linklater. In return, he was paid nearly two million pounds, the first installment of his severance. Davidge issued a statement saying that after thirty-four years at Christie's, ten of them as chief executive, "I have now decided to step down."

Linklater sent the documents to Skadden, Arps. Among the most devastating were the correspondence and the agendas of meetings between Davidge and Brooks. The lawyers concluded, "Generally, the documents appear to provide conclusive evidence that there was collusion between Christie's and Sotheby's. However, interpretation is needed."

The Skadden, Arps lawyers were shocked. They knew that the documents were subject to a grand-jury subpoena requiring that they be produced, and, now that they were in the United States, the lawyers had no option but to comply. The new evidence was so sensitive that they phoned John Greene, the prosecutor in charge of the case, that day, and the next day hand-delivered the documents to his office and sat there while he read them.

Edward Dolman, who had replaced Davidge as chief executive of Christie's, had instructed the lawyers to do the right thing and worry about the consequences later. In this instance, the consequences were potentially dire: almost certain indictment. Christie's only hope was to seek amnesty, but, given the advanced state of the government's investigation and the obvious culpability of at least one of its own employees, it was hardly an obvious candidate. Under Justice Department guidelines, Christie's had to meet several conditions to qualify for amnesty. It had to convince the government that it did not initiate the collusion and that it needed Davidge as a cooperative witness. Linklater had indicated that Davidge could testify to the most dramatic piece of evidence of all: that the conspiracy had been initiated at the very top—by Tennant and the chairman of Sotheby's, Alfred Taubman.

Davidge, of course, could have short-circuited the process by seeking amnesty only for himself, leaving Christie's to face indictment. Without help from Christie's, the Justice Department would be hard-pressed to gain Davidge's testimony, since he lived in London, beyond the reach of American courts. (Price-fixing is a civil, and not a criminal, offense in Britain, so extradition was unlikely.) But Christie's retained significant leverage over him, thanks to the remaining three million pounds owed on his severance contract.

Christie's simultaneously handed over the incriminating documents to the Justice Department and applied for amnesty, promising that it would try to secure Davidge's cooperation. A flurry of negotiations ensued. In an E-mail dated January 17, 2000, Christie's new chief executive reported that Davidge had agreed to cooperate as long as "nothing he says will be deemed to violate the settlement agreement and that he will be paid in full on his contract." Ten days later, on January 27th, the Justice Department conditionally agreed not to prosecute Christie's.

The government's policy of absolving antitrust criminals who betray their confederates has provided a windfall for lawyers, especially those who specialize in class actions. In January, 2000, a number of these lawyers, who had heard only sketchy reports that Christie's had agreed to cooperate with the government, began to scramble to reach possible plaintiffs—anyone who had bought or sold items through the auction houses since 1993—and sign them up. These lawyers, who often work for enormous contingency fees, are by nature risk takers, uncomfortable with, and sometimes contemptuous of, the staid hierarchy of established law firms. They are willing to hustle for clients in a way that some find unseemly, and often appear more interested in the size of their fee than in the well-being of their clients, who may number in the thousands. In the case of the auction houses, some twenty legal firms joined in what became a class-action suit on behalf of more than a hundred thousand clients.

David Boies, the New York-based litigator who successfully tried the government's antitrust case against Microsoft, and then led Al Gore's failed legal effort to gain the Presidency, is among the few class-action lawyers who bridge the gulf between swashbuckling trial lawyers and establishment law firms. Boies had been a partner at the New York firm of Cravath, Swaine & Moore, which represents many Fortune 500 companies and financial firms. In 1997, he resigned and, with two other lawyers, formed the firm of Boies, Schiller & Flexner. He also recruited a lawyer named Richard Drubel, who had worked in Houston with Stephen Susman, one of the country's best-known class-action lawyers. In early February of last year, a few weeks after the first civil suits were filed against the auction houses, Drubel got a call from a former partner at the Susman firm, asking if he wanted to join in one of its cases.

In class-action suits, the court usually chooses one of the plaintiff's firms to serve as lead counsel. That role is highly coveted, because the lead counsel reaps most of the legal fee. In the auction houses' suit, five law firms announced that the consensus among the lawyers involved was that they should share the role of lead counsel. Boies, still an outsider in the clubby plaintiffs' bar, was pointedly excluded. The judge who would decide was Lewis A. Kaplan, of the Southern District of New York. Kaplan, a 1994 Clinton appointee, was widely admired for his forthright manner and innovative approaches to complex legal questions.

Judge Kaplan was concerned about the number of class-action settlements in which the prime beneficiaries seem to have been the lawyers. Some of the most notorious examples have come from the auto industry, where plaintiffs in a 1996 settlement involving allegedly dangerous fuel tanks in G.M. pickup trucks received modest rebate coupons on future vehicle purchases while their lawyers received twenty-six million dollars in fees. In many such cases, it's hard to escape the conclusion that defendants were simply buying off the plaintiffs' lawyers at the expense of the plaintiffs. Or, as Judge Kaplan delicately put it, the "tension" between the best interests of the class and the highest attorneys' fees "can lead counsel to neglect the class' interests in pursuit of a higher fee."

A handful of judges in class-action cases had tried to address these issues by using, as it happens, an auction process, in which plaintiffs' lawyers compete for the role of lead counsel by bidding the percentage they would take from the plaintiffs in attorneys' fees in the event that damages were awarded. The lowest percentage wins, which leaves more for the victims. The approach eliminates an incentive to run up hours of make-work simply to increase the attorneys' fees, but it has been criticized for encouraging the winning bidder to avoid the time and expense of a trial by reaching a settlement beforehand—sometimes for far less than might have been realized had the case gone to trial.

Judge Kaplan decided on an even more unorthodox, all-or nothing approach—one that could be a significant precedent in future class-action cases. He ordered the competing lawyers to bid a number representing the minimum amount of damages they thought they could win for the victims. If the eventual settlement exceeded that amount, the lawyers would earn twenty-five per cent of everything over the amount of the bid. But if the victims were awarded less, the lawyers would forgo their fees. In choosing a winner, the judge would consider the amount of the bid—higher was obviously better, as far as the victims were concerned—and the reputation of the lawyers.

Boies, a poker enthusiast, was delighted by the secret bidding process, and he and Drubel began to discuss a bid: the number was based on the potential damages—an estimate that was complicated by the nature of the case. When Christie's had been granted conditional amnesty, Boies and Drubel inferred that both increases in the commission charged to clients—the 1993 buyers' commission and the 1995 sellers' commission—were part of a criminal antitrust conspiracy. Damages were easy to calculate for the buyers' commission: five per cent of sales up to fifty thousand dollars. But the sellers' commission was more difficult, given the sliding scale and the various exemptions. With the help of an economist, Boies and Drubel came up with an estimate of five hundred million dollars in total damages.

They thought that a good bid might be four hundred million, which meant that if the class received the full amount of actual damages the firm would still reap twenty-five million, or twenty-five per cent of the amount above their bid. Assuming that the other lawyers would bid in round numbers, they eventually decided on four hundred and five million dollars. It was a gamble, and Drubel told Boies that he was worried that the bid might be too high.

A few days later, Drubel got a call from Judge Kaplan's clerk. "Congratulations," she said. "You won the bid." The average bid of all the competing lawyers, it turned out, had been only a hundred and thirty million dollars. Boies and Drubel tried to mollify some of the other plaintiffs' lawyers by inviting them to help with the case, but when other firms heard that the winning bid was more than four hundred million dollars, they rejected the invitations out of hand. Drubel's former partner Stephen Susman remarked that "David Boies must be on some kamikaze pro bono mission."

Not long after, Drubel, accompanied by Philip Korologos, another lawyer at Boies, Schiller, met with lawyers for both auction houses. They were eager to begin discovery to see what Christie's had turned over to the government.

The documents that arrived at Drubel's offices contained the files of Sir Anthony Tennant, Christie's former chairman, which Davidge had inherited, and other written agendas and notes of conversations. Reading them, the lawyers realized that they had stumbled upon a remarkable trove of evidence. Few antitrust conspirators have been so reckless as to memorialize their conversations in writing and then save their notes.

One damning memo, in Tennant's handwriting, is dated April 30th. It begins with a catalogue of competitive measures that "we" have agreed to limit or eliminate, ranging from relatively minor ones, such as making "disparaging comments" about the other house, to major ones, such as refusing to guarantee sale prices to sellers or to offer buyers financing below a given rate.

It also outlines a schedule of sellers' commisions similar to the ones adopted by Sotheby's and Christie's in 1995—possible evidence of overt price-fixing. Tennant's notes suggest only the haziest grasp of antitrust principles. The commissions need not be "identical," but they "could be," the notes say. "With a sliding scale based on value, there should be no legal problems because you cannot price-fix a unique object." What was being fixed, of course, was not the price of an item at auction but the price of Christie's services—its commissions.

The measures detailed in Tennant's documents obviously reflected collusion to restrict competition. But the lawyers were puzzled by the memo's curious use of "we" and "you," and by the notation "This copied verbatim." If Tennant was essentially taking dictation from someone else, the question was, from whom?

The memo also contained references to possible co-conspirators. At one point, the memo reads, "DDB and MA know. Now to be DDB only. Given CMD home number to call this Tues. or Wed." The lawyers assumed that Tennant had privately told Brooks to call Davidge. ("MA" referred to Michael Ainslie, Brooks's predecessor as Sotheby's chief executive, who had resigned in November of 1993. Ainslie's lawyer said that Ainslie "knew absolutely nothing about any of the illegal conduct that has been alleged.") The document contained no explicit reference to Sotheby's chairman, Alfred Taubman, but concluded, "Everything should be monitored and checked back if need be. He and I should withdraw but stay in touch with a view to seeing how things go and intervening from on high if need be."

A second memo in Tennant's handwriting describes a conversation with another unidentified person, possibly Taubman. "Maybe we both shouldn't chase the same big stuff every time," Tennant suggested.

The notes in Davidge's handwriting were generally more cryptic, underscoring Davidge's value as a witness who could explain them. But some seemed to be agendas for discussion with Diana Brooks, with notes indicating the results of the discussions. Apart from price-fixing, the notes suggest that the two houses worked out a cozy arrangement to share the biggest estate sales. One memo indicates they would stop competing for the same business by making donations to a collector's favorite charity, often a family foundation. Sotheby's apparently gave to the Duke Foundation in order to "level the playing field" so that Christie's could, in turn, give to the Loeb Fund in its effort to win the collection of John and Frances Loeb, wealthy collectors who died in 1996. The Loeb sale at Christie's brought $92.7 million, one of the highest totals ever for a single-owner sale. Another memo discussed the sale of Rudolf Nureyev's estate, suggesting that landing the sale was the result of a prearranged understanding between the auction houses. Yet another memo expresses irritation that Sotheby's wasn't honoring all the terms of the agreement. "S&Co attending our parties recently in London. Not sticking to the rules."

Whatever the ambiguities of the documents, they provided compelling evidence of an antitrust conspiracy, and Boies felt certain that he and his colleagues would win their case at trial, at least with respect to overcharging the sellers. But, in preliminary settlement discussions with the lawyers for both auction houses, the Boies team was dismayed to learn that the damages in the case were far less than it had projected. The agreement to hold sellers' commissions to ten per cent hadn't always worked in practice, and when Boies and his colleagues reviewed the actual revenue figures they concluded that they could prove total damages of only three hundred million dollars, roughly two hundred million less than they had projected when they bid for the case. When Boies's team held its first serious settlement talks with lawyers from Sotheby's and Christie's, in late summer, the auction houses indicated that they might consider a total settlement of about a hundred million dollars and no more. Boies dismissed it out of hand. (The lawyers for the auction houses had no way of knowing that, under the bidding process established by Judge Kaplan, Boies and his partners would be paid nothing if that was all they recovered.)

Just as the Justice Department had gained Christie's cooperation by granting the company amnesty, Boies and his associates concluded that they had to drive a wedge between Christie's and Sotheby's, including one to cooperate with them against the other. Christie's was the obvious candidate. As a private company controlled by a billionaire, it had deeper pockets, and its conditional amnesty didn't protect it from a civil suit. But it had already resolved its possible criminal liability, which meant that it could provide helpful evidence against Sotheby's without further jeopardizing its own position. It might also be hard to collect a judgment against Christie's, since its headquarters and many of its assets were outside the United States. And it controlled Davidge, the star cooperating witness.

Drubel hit on the idea of offering Christie's what is known as a "Mary Carter agreement," named after a Florida case in which a plaintiff secretly agreed to split any damages with a defendant who testified against another defendant. Plaintiffs' lawyers love the spectacle of one defendant turning on another at trial, and Mary Carter agreements have proved to be so effective before juries that in many jurisdictions such agreements must be disclosed, since they might affect a witness's credibility. Boies and

Drubel would offer Christie's a chance to settle for a fixed sum, with the opportunity to reduce the amount by helping them in the case against Sotheby's and Taubman.

By early September, they were close to an agreement in which Christie's would theoretically pay two hundred and thirty million dollars—but that amount would be reduced to the extent that Christie's cooperation resulted in additional damages from Sotheby's. A draft of terms was ready to be signed, though negotiations continued on just how much Christie's would be rewarded for its cooperation.

Meanwhile, Drubel and a team of lawyers and paralegals took over a conference room and began poring through hundreds of boxes of documents from Christie's. They didn't have high expectations. All the talk in the case had been about the Davidge documents, which they'd already seen, and they assumed that Christie's lawyers at Skadden, Arps, in an effort to demonstrate their cooperation, would have alerted them to anything else that might be significant. Indeed, the material seemed irrelevant: press releases, correspondence on other matters—the routine if voluminous paperwork associated with any large, far-flung business.

Then, late one evening, a team member said, "I think I've got something." Drubel hurried over and saw that stashed in a folder in a box of accounting records was a handwritten memo from Stephen S. Lash, then vice-chairman of Christie's North and South America. Lash and his wife, Wendy, an heiress to the Lehman fortune, were fixtures in Manhattan society and art circles.

The memo, dated January 21, 1995, but addressed to no one in particular, seemed a curious attempt by Lash to record his own suspicions of an antitrust conspiracy as he struggled with what to do about them. Claiming that he had already taken his suspicions to a Christie's director, he wrote, "I couldn't confirm categorically that I knew but only that I detected some 'smoke' suggesting 'fire.' . . . I can recall A.T. [Anthony Tennant] constantly referring to the need to have a quiet word with the competition in a way that appeared dead serious and committed."

In a lengthy January, 1996, memo describing a conversation

with a Christie's board member, Daniel P. Davison, Lash wrote that he had strong reason to think that Davidge was continuing discussions with Diana Brooks over terms. Other memos and copies of letters suggest that both Lash and Davison made some efforts to raise antitrust issues with Tennant and Davidge, but that they proved ineffectual.

Lash's notes also named two other prominent Christie's executives who seem to have known of the scheme: Patricia Hambrecht, Christie's American president, who implicated Davidge when she was asked to resign, and Christie's well-known chief auctioneer, Christopher M. Burge. In one memo, Lash wrote that he had told Hambrecht, "I can't stand what's going on," and she had replied, "Neither can I." He added, "There was no ambiguity as to what we were discussing."

Boies's team was amazed that anyone would put such suspicions in writing. But the documents, apart from their immense value as evidence, raised some troubling questions. Why hadn't Christie's told the lawyers of their existence? Did Christie's actually think the documents could be buried in one of the boxes and not be found? Christie's maintains that its lawyers had never tried to hide the Lash documents; they had produced them as soon as they discovered them, and it wasn't their obligation to highlight them. But the discovery of the documents irrevocably changed the way the plaintiffs' lawyers thought of Christie's. The auction house suddenly seemed much less cooperative than it had purported to be.

The plaintiffs' lawyers weren't the only ones to have discovered the Lash documents. At Davis, Polk & Wardwell, the firm representing Taubman, an associate found copies of them, buried among other records, in one of the boxes of documents produced by Christie's. She took them to Scott Muller, who was in charge of Taubman's defense. Muller called Sotheby's lawyers; all were part of a joint defense agreement allowing them to share information that would otherwise be protected by attorney-client privilege.

Sotheby's and Taubman were in an increasingly precarious

position. The Lash documents, together with the original Davidge papers, were devastating evidence, especially against Brooks, since they contain so many references to her. (Taubman is never mentioned by name.) Muller assumed from converstaions with Brooks's lawyers that she was in talks with John Greene, the lead prosecutor. It was obvious that she had no defense. Indeed, from January 28th, when she was first confronted with the allegations, Brooks never denied the wrongdoing, and, friends say, she accepts full responsibility for it. She had hoped no one else at Sotheby's would be implicated; she had taken great care not to discuss it with anyone apart from Taubman, she said. She hadn't volunteered anything to prosecutors, even in seeking lenient treatment for herself. But her lawyers told her to answer prosecutors' questions truthfully, and in doing so she implicated Taubman. "She bears no malice toward Taubman," one friend told me, and only blames herself.

Despite the potential value of such testimony, Brooks was offered nothing but the possibility of leniency at sentencing— amnesty can be offered only to the first to confess. Under federal sentencing guidelines, she faced a maximum prison term of three years.

Sotheby's was in an even worse position, liable as a corporation for the actions of Brooks and Taubman. One of the more Draconian aspects of the antitrust laws is that each co-conspirator is jointly and severally liable for the entire amount of damages, trebled, and may not seek to recoup any of the damages from a co-conspirator. Even in the view of the evidence most favorable to the auction houses—that there was a sellers' conspiracy but not a buyers' commission agreement—the actual damages might be as high as a hundred million dollars. Trebled, that would be three hundred million, a sum that could plunge Sotheby's into bankruptcy.

Muller strongly suspected, and other lawyers in the case had confirmed, that Boies was secretly negotiating with Christie's to further isolate Sotheby's and its chairman. From Sotheby's point of view, this maneuver could not be allowed to succeed. Muller had recently worked with Boies on another antitrust case, and he knew how Boies liked to operate. He also feared that Christie's would take advantage of its better bargaining power to strike a deal that would essentially eliminate its chief competitor. It was bad enough that Christie's had escaped the criminal charges that Sotheby's and Taubman now faced—Sotheby's had no way of knowing how many clients it had already lost because of that— but failing to settle could "mortally wound" Sotheby's, as Muller put it. As the majority shareholder in Sotheby's, Taubman stood to lose his entire stake if Sotheby's went into bankruptcy.

So Muller called Boies. He tried not to sound desperate. "Let's resolve this," he said. "You've got to talk to Sotheby's." Boies indicated he might be interested in a deal in which Christie's, Sotheby's, and Taubman each paid one-third. "That's ridiculous," Muller insisted, arguing that, as a simple matter of logic and fairness, Sotheby's and its chairman could be no more than one-half responsible for a conspiracy between two auction houses. He also argued that Boies was "going after the wrong party," pointing out that it would be easier to try a civil case against a defender like Christie's, which had already admitted wrongdoing, than against Taubman and Sotheby's, which were still denying guilt.

Boies agreed to meet with Ira Millstein, Richard Davis, and Steven Reiss, who represented Sotheby's at Weil, Gotshal. At the age of seventy-four, Millstein commands great respect among other lawyers, and both he and Davis had worked closely with Boies. It was a critical meeting for Sotheby's, whose lawyers had to derail any settlement with Christie's but had very little evidence of their own to use as leverage. In contrast to the numerous documents that surfaced at Christie's, it appeared that no one at Sotheby's had been so foolish (or wise, as it turned out) as to memorialize a criminal conspiracy in writing.

For these reasons, Millstein and Davis attempted to convince Boies that it wasn't in the interest of his plaintiffs, many of whom were regular buyers and sellers of art, to drive Christie's only major competitor out of business; that Christie's failure to point to the

Lash document undermined the company's credibility; and that there were enough documents implicating people at Christie's that Boies didn't need the cooperation of people like Davidge and others at the firm to make his case. To back up their claims, the Sotheby's lawyers gave Boies some copies of documents pertaining to the critical issue of the 1993 increase in the buyers' commissions. One, for example, from late 1991, was a Sotheby's memo containing confidential terms of a proposed buyers' commission increase and what Sotheby's response was likely to be. With it was a cover sheet indicating that someone at Sotheby's had faxed it to Christie's: "FC will be in the NY jewelry dept until 4 P.M. Give him a copy." FC appears to be a reference to François Curiel, the head of Christie's jewelry department.

In a subsequent meeting, the plaintiffs' lawyers asked who might have known or discussed the matter of the buyers' commission. Sotheby's lawyers offered the names of Curiel and his counterpart at Sotheby's, John Block, and described them as "communicators." It was the first time the plaintiffs' lawyers had heard Block's name in connection with a possible conspiracy. Boies was so impressed by Sotheby's willingness to help, at a time when his doubts about Christie's were growing, that he decided to reconsider his deal with Christie's. Korologos called Shepard Goldfein, at Skadden, Arps, Christie's lawyers, and said that "things had changed," and the previous settlement agreement under discussion was now off the table. Instead, he was offering Christie's the chance to settle for a flat cash payment. Goldfein was apoplectic, rejecting the payment and arguing that Korologos and Boies were "walking out" on a deal. "How could we, when not all the terms had been agreed to?" Korologos responded. Boies later got on the phone and was blunt: there was no deal.

Soon after, Korologos was examining some timelines of Sotheby's and Christie's executives that had been pieced together from travel records. He was startled to see that Block, from Sotheby's, and Curiel, from Christie's, had been in Florida on the same date, in the spring of 1992—evidence that the increase in the buyers' premium could have been planned. Later, it was determined that Brooks had been there as well.

The Christie's lawyers pointed out that a Florida judge in an estate case had ordered both Curiel and Block to appear that day, an innocent explanation for their presence there. But the lawyers, too, probably knew that it was risky to let such evidence reach a jury. To do so would be betting the whole company.

At the same time, the Sotheby's lawyers were holding delicate negotiations with Taubman's counsel. They stressed that the numbers Boies had been talking about could bankrupt Sotheby's. And if Taubman didn't join in the settlement, he faced the prospect of a drawn-out civil trial on top of any criminal proceeding—one in which he might be personally held liable for the full amount of damages. Taubman was rich enough that he could, if he chose, pay the full amount out of his own pocket. With Brooks's negotiations proceeding, it seemed inevitable that she would cooperate with the government, making a defense at trial untenable. The case had to be settled, on both the civil and criminal fronts, if Sotheby's was to continue in business.

In September, Boies went back and forth between the two houses, trying to ratchet up the numbers, using the willingness of one to settle for a higher number as leverage against the other. Sotheby's board met and rejected one proposal; Boies warned that the number would go only higher. He offered to settle with Christie's for four hundred and sixty-five million dollars. When Christie's balked, he made it an even more unpleasant offer—five hundred and twelve million dollars.

He promised not to raise the figure again until the lawyers got back to him with a final answer. But the implication was clear: the longer they waited, the costlier the settlement would be.

But the proposed settlement would be meaningless to Sotheby's if it could not resolve the criminal charges as well. Greene, the chief prosecutor, had threatened the company with a huge fine, and it couldn't function for long with that level of potential liability on top of the civil settlement. Nor could

Sotheby's compete against Christie's, which was boasting to clients that it had resolved its problem while Sotheby's still faced criminal charges. As part of a large, private conglomerate, Christie's had the financial resources to weather an enormous payment, while Sotheby's, as a publicly traded company, faced a slumping stock price and curtailed access to public debt markets.

As plea discussions worked their way up the chain of command in the Justice Department, Sotheby's arguments that it made no sense to cripple one of only two competitors seemed to take hold. Sotheby's agreed to plead guilty to conspiring with Christie's to fix sellers' commissions. It agreed to pay a fine of forty-five million dollars, but, in an unusual recognition of Sotheby's precarious financial condition, the government agreed to let it pay the sum over five years, with no interest charges. With a deal with the government in hand, Sotheby's capitulated to Boies's latest demand, agreeing to pay two hundred and fifty-six million dollars.

On September 24th, both auction houses announced that they had settled the civil suit. Sotheby's also announced that it had reached an agreement to resolve the criminal investigation by pleading guilty. The auction houses would each pay two hundred and fifty-six million dollars. Of that amount, Taubman agreed to give Sotheby's a hundred and fifty-six million personally, which meant that Sotheby's would be responsible for just a hundred million of the total. Even that threatened to strain Sotheby's resources, and in the end Boies did not want to push it into bankruptcy. So he agreed that a hundred million of the total, to be paid by both houses, could be in the form of discount coupons offered to future sellers at the auction houses. (The face value of the coupons was subsequently increased to a hundred and twenty-five million.)

To the amazement of his colleagues in the plaintiffs' bar, Boies and his partners had exceeded their bid to Judge Kaplan by more than a hundred million dollars. Their reward for their work in the case was twenty-five per cent of anything over four hundred and five million—$26.7 million. Still, that represented just five per cent of the recovery—far less than the one-third lawyers often demand in contingency cases.

Of the two auction houses, Sotheby's seems to have borne the brunt of the scandal, but it has been stressing that everyone there tainted by the scandal has been asked to leave. John Block, Curiel's counterpart in the jewelry department and his alleged contact at Sotheby's, is now the chief executive for North America at Phillips de Pury & Luxembourg, which is trying to break into the auction-house duopoly with an aggressive push for major consignments. No one has been charged with fixing the buyers' commissions in 1993; the government said its evidence was inconclusive.

Diana Brooks, as the Sotheby's lawyers feared, pleaded guilty to one felony count of price-fixing on October 5, 2000, and promised to cooperate fully in the government's investigation. She had acted, she said in a prepared statement, "at the direction of a superior at Sotheby's." Brooks had hoped that her plea and the obvious reference to Taubman would help persuade him to plead guilty as well, bringing the criminal case to a close, and allowing her to be sentenced and begin putting the scandal behind her. But Taubman arranged a lie-detector test that he says proved his innocence, and "at no time has he ever considered pleading guilty," his colleague Christopher Tennyson insisted.

Brooks's crime carries a maximum sentence of three years in prison under federal sentencing guidelines, but her agreement to cooperate means that the judge will be free to evaluate her testimony and reduce her sentence, so it is possible that she will not have to serve any time in prison. While awaiting sentencing, she has been tutoring schoolchildren in Harlem. The nearest federal prison that houses women is at Danbury, Connecticut. A friend of hers told me, "She is not scared about the fact of jail. She's concerned about what life will be like in jail."

Alfred Taubman entered a plea of not guilty. Muller, his lawyer, has asserted Taubman's innocence. Opening arguments are scheduled for November 5th, and the trial promises to be one of the most closely watched antitrust trials in history. Boies, for one, believes that Taubman has a reasonable chance of being acquitted, in part because of his age, and also because the documentary evidence Boies reviewed suggests that Brooks, Tennant, and Davidge were more culpable. Taubman's main line of defense is expected to be that although he did not discourage Brooks from meeting with Davidge, he never authorized her to engage in an antitrust conspiracy. Further, he is expected to insist that, though he may have met Tennant and spoken with him, he warned the Christie's chairman that he could not discuss anything that would violate United States antitrust laws.

At trial, Taubman's main problems will be Brooks's and Davidge's expected testimony against him and Tennant's April 30th memo setting out the terms of an antitrust conspiracy. Although Taubman isn't mentioned by name, Davidge is expected to describe the memo as reflecting a conversation between Tennant and Taubman. As one lawyer put it, "If a jury believes Brooks and Davidge, Taubman has a problem." Given the importance of their credibility, the cross-examination by Taubman's lawyers is expected to be withering.

Apart from Taubman's guilt or innocence, one of the issues that may be resolved at trial is whether Christie's was in fact entitled to amnesty based on its representation that it didn't initiate the conspiracy and terminated it once it knew of its existence. Considerable evidence already suggests that top executives at Christie's—Hambrecht, Lash, Burge, Hindlip, Curiel—knew something about the scheme and did not stop it. Yet the Justice Department, in its eagerness to attract more informants, seems unlikely to take any action against Christie's. Under current policies, the government will be satisfied as long as Christie's didn't "coerce" Sotheby's into the conspiracy, even if Christie's was equally responsible for starting it. And the government will impute knowledge of the conspiracy to Christie's only if its directors or its inside or outside general counsel knew about it.

Despite the evidence that numerous high-ranking executives at Christie's knew or should have known of the illegal activity, many of them not only are still working at the auction house; they have been promoted. Lord Hindlip, whose conversations with Davidge should, at the very least, have aroused suspicions, remains chairman. François Curiel, head of the jewelry department, who is alleged to have communicated with his counterpart at Sotheby's, is now the chairman of Christie's Europe. Stephen Lash, the diarist who recorded his misgivings, was promoted to chairman of Christie's North and South America. Christopher Burge remains Christie's chief auctioneer and was named honorary chairman of Christie's North America.

Sir Anthony Tennant, who had retired as Christie's chairman before the scandal broke, was indicted along with Taubman on May 2nd. He failed to appear in court to answer the charges, and said that he will remain in England and refuse to enter the jurisdiction of an American court. Still, his status as an absent but indicted co-defendant will allow the admission of hearsay evidence about his role at Taubman's trial. In a widely circulated letter addressed to friends and former colleagues and clients, Tennant wrote, "I did not discuss price fixing with Taubman or anyone else."

Christopher Davidge received the second installment of his five-million-pound severance payment last December and is due to receive the rest at the end of the year, at which point Christie's will lose most of what leverage it retains over him. Taubman's lawyers have already said that they will attack his testimony by claiming it was bought. Shortly after Davidge resigned from Christie's, he and Amrita Jhaveri were married in a quiet ceremony in India, where Davidge now spends much of his time.

Patricia Hambrecht, who was in on the scheme and then betrayed her colleagues, is now president of the Fifth Avenue jeweller Harry Winston. She remains a member of the New York bar. She was featured on the cover of the September issue of *Quest* magazine wearing a prominent pearl necklace and earrings. The cover headline is "Women at the Top."

Most of us assume that the childhood Slinky toy is low-tech. Neil Irwin of *The Washington Post* carefully traces its modern manufacturing path, discovering that computers now play the pivotal role in this steel gadget that's been dutifully trudging down our stairways since 1945.

Neil Irwin

This Little Slinky Goes to Market

ON A LAZY SATURDAY AFTERNOON last fall, Mayra Gutierrez, a 15-year-old who lives in Gaithersburg, tagged along with her mother for a trip to Lakeforest Mall. They stopped in the KB Toys store to pick up a birthday present. As the cashier rang it up, Mayra picked up a toy she couldn't resist. A Slinky.

She ran it through her fingers, then plopped it onto the counter to add to their purchase—an extra $3.99. Mayra had never owned one before: an old-fashioned steel Slinky, the kind that clank and jangle and, as the famous commercial ditty goes, walk down stairs, alone or in pairs.

It was a whimsical purchase. She knew nothing about the software that figured out how to melt the steel in that Slinky, or the satellite tracking of the truck that carried that steel to the Slinky factory, or the Internet tools that let the manufacturer monitor sales at big retail chains.

Yet it was these and other uses of digital technology that turned junked cars in a Florida scrap yard into the 63 feet of flattened steel wire, coiled into 89 loops, now sitting on the desk in Mayra's room.

Over the past decade, as Internet companies attracted immense attention for their boom and bust, a quieter revolution has taken place in traditional businesses far from the glitz of Silicon Valley. All kinds of enterprises—steelmakers, trucking companies, Slinky manufacturers—have cut costs through technological advances rooted in the microprocessor.

Slinkys are among the most old-fashioned of toys. They are manufactured on the same machines built by the inventor in 1945; the only design change since then has been to crimp the ends of the wire for safety.

Nonetheless, a trip along the Slinky's production and distribution path offers a window into how digital technology has streamlined the way even the simplest children's toy is produced and distributed, which in turn helps illustrate how the United States achieved stunning economic growth through the late 1990s and into the start of 2000.

The current recession is in large part a hangover following the nation's wild enthusiasm for the new technology at the turn of the century, when eager investors pumped up tech stock values and enthusiastic business executives made or bought more high-tech products than the world could use.

At the same time, some economists believe that the widespread adoption of digital technology has made businesses more nimble and flexible, which has so far helped make the recession a relatively shallow one.

But the Slinky's journey also shows the possible limits of that technological revolution. In some situations, promising tech innovations are proving unworkable in practice. In others, the efficiency gains of the 1990s were one-time bumps, not ongoing improvements. And in some cases, potential benefits from new technology are outweighed by their high cost.

The making of the Slinky helps explain why, in some cases, the reality of the revolution lagged behind the hype.

The Slinky's journey to Mayra's shopping bag started about a year earlier in Tampa, on the dusty lot of North Star Recycling Co. Flatbeds rumbled in, carrying stacked hulks of junked cars. Dump trucks unloaded their tangled masses of steel rebar. Pickups brought in roadside trash. They came to sell their scrap metal for $39 a ton.

North Star employee Diane Hart, a thirtysomething blonde wearing hot-pink safety glasses and acid-washed jeans, drove her big yellow loader, which resembles a bulldozer, to the mountains of metal. She picked up load after load and deposited them into a shredder.

As she did so, a computer screen in her cab told her the exact weight of the materials she put in the shredder. In the old days, her employers never knew exactly how much steel came out of those big mountains; now they do.

"It's the difference between a dinosaur and a human," she said of her new loader, which has a variety of other computer-based touches to help her work more efficiently.

The steel came out the end of the shredder as a pile of "frag," which North Star Recycling shipped by barge to its sister company, North Star Steel, in Beaumont, Texas, where it was added to a mountain range of crankshafts, car doors and hubcaps, each pile dusted with paprika-colored rust.

In Beaumont, the frag was melted down in a massive furnace that roared with an apocalyptic blaze of fire, sparks and crashing metal as it heated the material to 3,000 degrees. The furnace is powered by artificial-intelligence software that makes sure energy is used as efficiently as possible.

Once melted, the steel was extruded as billet—six-inch-square logs of the stuff. To get it even thinner, more machines squeezed and rolled the billet, like a pasta machine shaping noodles, until it was steel rod just thinner than a pencil.

In the old days, workers had to use tongs to grab the steel rod as it zipped out the end of the machine, red hot, at 195 mph, and then measured it to make sure it was the correct thickness. Now a computer measures it with infrared sensors.

Across the economy, technological innovations such as those at North Star Steel have meant businesses waste less, have fewer goods sitting around in inventory and have a better understanding of what to make and how and when to make it.

But the next steps in the making of a Slinky show why changing the world turns out to be harder than many Internet visionaries thought.

Trucks carried steel rod, the thickness of a drinking straw, to Shelbyville, Kentucky, where Bekaert Corp. shift manager Brian Estridge turned it into galvanized wire that eventually would become staples, paper clips, the spiral coil of a notebook—and Slinkys. Rod is delivered at one end of the factory and wire comes out the other. In between, machines squeeze, heat, cool, acid-bathe, zinc-coat and spool the steel to prepare it for its ultimate destination.

The machines pull through more than a dozen strands of rod at a time; they run in parallel lines, looking like the inside of a piano. But on the day the wire for Mayra's Slinky was manufactured, only five lines were full, using less than half the machines' capacity.

"I really prefer having the lines full," Estridge said.

Technology visionaries would generally describe this inefficiency as ripe for an Internet solution.

The company, theoretically, could sell that extra wire-making capacity at discount rates on the Internet, just as airlines sell unfilled seats at reduced prices on the Web.

As much as Allan Hirsch, Bekaert's national sales manager, would like to be able to do that, however, it just wouldn't work. Manufacturers that buy his wire need long-term contracts so they can ensure absolute reliability. They need to buy wire with very precise chemical compositions and strength; if they skipped around and used a different supplier every time, they would be likely to meet big delays as wire that wasn't made just right tangled up their machines.

For an airline passenger, a flight from Washington to Chicago is always pretty much the same. But steel wire just doesn't work that way.

"The economics just aren't there," Hirsch said.

David Colby has graying hair, a mustache and a paunch acquired over the 3 million miles and 27 years that he's driven big-rig trucks. One bright morning he backed his truck to the loading dock at Bekaert to pick up 40,000 pounds of steel wire destined for the Slinky plant in Pennsylvania.

The spools of wire tucked into place, Colby pulled a small computer out from a sheath next to the driver's seat. He typed the number 22, then pressed "send." The message, code for "loaded at shipper," was beamed to a satellite and eventually made its way to Morton, Illinois, and the computer screen of Ray Stoner, a dispatcher at Colby's employer, Star Transport Inc.

Technology has revolutionized the trucking industry in the past decade. Trucks go no faster than they did 10 years ago, and drivers still need the same amount of sleep. But software and satellite technology allow truckers to spend more of their time hauling goods and less time sitting around or driving empty rigs.

In the old days, Colby would sometimes have to drive hundreds of miles between loads with nothing in his truck. Now Star Transport's computer system, connected to satellite-based devices that provide constant updates of where its trucks are, lets Stoner use them more efficiently, with minimum downtime between jobs.

The software also sets prices for different routes, so Star Transport charges enough to be competitive without losing out on potential profits. Company president Glenn Werry Jr. said that the software and wireless devices, installed in 1990, have increased the amount of hauling each driver does by 15 percent.

Driving through the Kentucky countryside at the beginning of his journey to Pennsylvania, Colby shifted through the gears, a cooler of Red Bull energy drink at his feet. He began a tirade, citing political writer and linguist Noam Chomsky, about the "corporate bean counters" of the world, whom Colby believes put profit above people.

But when it comes to the trucking industry, he is pleased with the changes those bean counters have wrought.

"I make a lot more money than a lot of people I went to college with," he said.

The high-tech success story of trucking, though, doesn't necessarily bode well for the future. Werry said that 80 percent of the productivity improvement at Star Transport came in the first two years after the tracking system was installed. Gains have been much harder to come by since.

The company is always improving its software, he said, but now the improvements are small and incremental. There are no revolutionary technologies around the corner that will offer efficiency gains of the scale seen in the 1990s, he argues.

The low-hanging fruit, he says, has been picked.

If many of the efficiency gains of the 1990s were indeed one-time bumps, as at Star Transport, there are big implications for the economy as a whole.

During the economic boom of the past decade, there seemed to be almost no limits to growth. A decade ago, most economists believed it was impossible for the economy to grow faster than 2 to 3 percent a year without spurring inflation, as too much money would be chasing too few goods.

The only way to grow faster than that without driving up the inflation rate, then, would be if productivity—the amount of stuff made for each hour worked—improved faster than it has historically.

Too much money wouldn't be chasing too few goods, because the nation would be making more goods.

Many economists believe that is exactly what happened in the 1990s, and that digital technology is a big part of the reason, though they are split on just how big a part. Manufacturing productivity increased by an average of 4.7 percent a year from 1995 to 2000, compared with an average increase of 2.8 percent over the past 50 years, according to Labor Department data.

That let the economy grow at an unprecedented rate—almost 4 percent annually from 1995 to 2000, compared with an average annual growth rate of 3 percent since the end of World War II.

That means the buoyant good times of the past decade—the booming stock market, low inflation, climbing personal wealth and the other benefits of a seemingly ideal economy—can be at least partly attributed to the technology advances so apparent in the making of a Slinky.

But if those gains are indeed starting to peter out, as the Slinky trail suggests, it would mean that the economy will grow from now on at something closer to the historical norm: 3 percent, rather than 4 percent. And that one percentage point is worth a lot of money and jobs when it is 1 percent of a $10 trillion economy.

Of course, none of that was on David Colby's mind as he plugged across Ohio, peering through a windshield thick with insect carcasses ("It's nothing compared to Arkansas," he said of the bug guts clouding his view).

He hosed off the bugs at a truck stop and grabbed dinner at a steakhouse in Bentleyville, Pennsylvania. He continued on and dropped off the wire at Poof Products Inc. in Hollidaysburg. While a forklift operator unloaded the wire, Colby tapped at his computer to read the address of his next pickup, a few towns over.

"I don't know that things can get much better than this," he said during the drive.

At Poof Products Inc., the company that makes the Slinky, workers hooked the wire up to the Slinky machines just a few hours after Colby dropped off his load. The machines pulled the round wire in, flattened it, coiled it and cut it, and then workers crimped the ends of the still-hot Slinkys and placed them on a conveyor belt.

The conveyor carried the Slinkys to the machine that boxes them, a fantastic device with arms that move as if dancing the herky-jerky. Each Slinky walked toward its own box.

First a Slinky hit a bar, flopped over and went down a step. At the same time, a mechanical arm pulled a box from a stack, opened it and placed the box down next to the Slinky, which was then automatically pushed inside.

The process isn't mere theatrics; it's a system of quality control that Slinky inventor Richard James devised in 1945. A Slinky wound too tight or too loose won't walk down into the box correctly.

As the boxes stacked up, they were driven on a forklift to the warehouse area, where Bertie Michaels, the shipping supervisor, took over.

Over the years, the company has received plenty of pitches from companies that want to make Poof Products' warehouse area more efficient. Bar codes, forklifts equipped with infrared scanners, handheld computers for warehouse workers: They've been offered the works.

Instead, the company has used carbon paper stuck on the side of boxes to keep track of its warehouse contents.

One might think the fancier inventory tools would let Poof Products save money, letting the company use warehouse space more efficiently, better track workers' use of their time and juggle inventory more skillfully.

Nice as it might be, Michaels said it just wouldn't make sense at Poof. "Our people know exactly where our inventory is. We just draw our own little maps."

In other words, no need to spend thousands of dollars for fancy equipment when carbon paper, employee memory and paper maps do the job just fine.

At 3 P.M. one day, a truck carrying, among other things, 98 cases of Slinkys pulled up to Door 44 of K-B Toys' Clinton, New Jersey, distribution center. One worker unloaded the merchandise on wooden pallets and attached a bar-code sticker to each pallet.

When another worker pulled up in his forklift, a scanner on the machine read the bar code. His handheld computer flashed information on which slot in the massive warehouse the Slinkys should be placed in; because Slinkys sell moderately quickly, the computer knew to put them on a moderately accessible aisle. When the Gaithersburg KB Toys store ran low on Slinkys, the company's inventory-tracking system fed the order to New Jersey. Another warehouse worker's handheld computer told him to pick a case of Slinkys from the shelf, slap a bar code on it and throw it on a conveyor, which whipped it down a chute toward a Maryland-bound truck.

Most of the innovations that let KB Toys get the Slinkys on their way to Gaithersburg with barely a human hand touching them were installed in the past five years, as the company invested hundreds of thousands of dollars in such systems.

But in early September, when the facility's then-manager, Louis J. Nacke, discussed his wish list, it was decidedly nontechnical. (Nacke died in one of the planes hijacked by terrorists on September 11.)

He said he wanted more standard bar coding from his various suppliers; in companies' rush to outfit themselves with the latest technology, they have ended up with different standards, resulting in more work.

He spoke of finding new ways to recruit workers. With the market for low-skilled labor tight in recent years, he had to come up with new ideas to recruit for the holiday season.

And those conveyors could use higher-horsepower motors to speed things along.

Nacke and other KB executives said that computer technology has paid big dividends, and that the firm will keep making such investments. But making those investments work has proven to be harder and slower than a software sales brochure would suggest.

The digital tech revolution of the late 1990s was not the first time that the nation, enamored of the Next Big Thing, had gotten a little ahead of itself.

In 1880, there were 93,267 miles of railroad track in the United States. Developers saw expanding rail lines as the secret to the country's growth—and a way to make big bucks. By the end of the decade there were 163,597 miles of track, according to Clemson University rail historian Roger Grant.

The first new lines were very profitable. Not so latecomers. "The traffic just wasn't there," said Bob Post, a senior fellow at the

Dibner Institute for the History of Science and Technology. "These things were promoted as kind of an 'If you build it, they will come' theory. But there just wasn't the business.

"The image was that what had succeeded can succeed over and over and over again. And it can't."

Some railroads went bankrupt. Almost all of them retrenched. The collapse of the railroad investment bubble drove the economy into a deep recession that lasted well into the 1890s.

But by the beginning of the 1900s the American economy had recovered and its industrial base expanded at unmatched rates. The economy could grow quickly in part because there was enough rail capacity to move around all the goods that needed moving. Lines that went unused in the 1890s suddenly became essential, as the nation's population density increased and industry grew.

John Staudenmaier, a professor at the University of Detroit Mercy and editor of the academic journal *Technology and Culture,* sees something of a pattern in that experience. From railroads to the telegraph, the automobile to the Internet, Americans tend to get so excited at the promise of an innovation that it gets hyped beyond any sense of reality.

"The original hype of these things is that this is the second coming of Christ. It's crazy, people invest in ridiculous dimensions, and then everybody goes broke. Then there's an irrationally depressed time. But little by little, the new technology gradually finds its place in the larger world," Staudenmaier said.

But while that attitude can get the nation in trouble now and again, that very enthusiasm has helped make the United States, over time, an economic superpower. The rail boom of the 19th century laid the foundation for 40 years of awesome industrial development.

The most recent tech boom is less than a decade old, and its legacy has only begun to take shape.

Slinky's inventor, Richard James, left the country and the toy company he created in 1960, putting his wife, Betty, in charge of James Industries Inc., which later was sold to Poof Products.

Under her successful management, the toy company was cautious about the new technologies it embraced.

"We started out with one computer, to manage our inventory and payroll and things," said Betty James. "They came to me a few years later and said, 'Mrs. James, we need a new one.' I didn't understand. Most things, you buy them and they last a while. But when you first go into something like a new computer, it's natural to be skeptical."

But ultimately she realized that despite the hassles and the upfront cost, these temperamental machines that needed to be replaced every few years could do the company some good.

"We continued with the computers," she said. "It worked for us, in the long run."

The banana may be the perfect fruit, but it, too, can fall prey to flawed business practices. This compelling tale of the rise and fall of Chiquita Banana, written by *Fortune's* Nicholas Stein, chronicles a string of blunders by a seemingly infallible American brand that sullied its reputation and sent it on the road to bankruptcy.

Nicholas Stein

Yes, We Have No Profits

MY FIRST GLIMPSE of the Chiquita banana plantations in Bocas, Panama, comes through the window of *Sweet Bocas,* the twin-engine company plane transporting me across the Costa Rican border to this remote swath of northwest Panama. As I look below, the lush rain forest, which creeps inland from the Caribbean coast, gives way suddenly to the manicured plots of the banana plantations. These symmetrical squares seem the ultimate triumph of man over nature—a dark green quilt stitched from the surrounding jungle.

When you enter the plantations, the calm and order that seem so apparent from 20,000 feet disappear, and the tidy plots morph into rolling jungle. The tropical air is heavy with humidity, the muddy ground strewn with the tangled remains of fallen leaves and stalks. Banana plants sprout from the earth like magic beanstalks. Red twine used to stabilize the plants dangles in intricate cobwebs. Stems laden with cascading bunches of green bananas, wrapped for protection in pale blue plastic, hang just out of reach. And the banana workers—their tattered clothes and dark skin covered with the gooey latex that drips from the plants, their machetes constantly in motion—dart from one plant to the next, harvesting and pruning.

The scene probably looks much as it did a century ago, when Chiquita Brands International—then the United Fruit Co.—first hauled bananas from this area. Though harvesting and packing and shipping techniques may have changed, the essence of Bocas remains the same. This is Chiquita country, and the interests of the company are indivisible from those of the people who live and work here.

That may change later this year, when Chiquita is expected to file for Chapter 11 bankruptcy protection—an act that could result in layoffs at the plantations. Over the past decade, the company has lost more than $700 million and has watched its stock price plunge from a high of $50 in 1991 to a low of 48 cents. In January, after a dismal 2000 in which the company lost $112 million on revenues of $2.3 billion, Chiquita announced that it could no longer pay the interest on its $862 million debt.

How could a company with a brand name recognized the world over and nearly a third of the market for one of the globe's most popular foods find itself in such a precarious position? According to Chiquita, the answer is based on a single circumstance: the European Union's decision in 1993 to enact a restrictive quota system, which limited the access of Chiquita (and other non-European companies) to what was then its largest and most profitable market—the 15 member states of the EU. Overnight, the company says, its share of the European banana trade was cut in half. For the past eight years, Chiquita has engaged in an expensive and well-publicized trade dispute with the EU to force it to reverse its position, a battle Chiquita says has cost the company hundreds of millions of dollars and left it without the resources to service its debt. Though the feud was resolved this summer in Chiquita's favor, the reprieve may have come too late. "We had a good business," says CEO Steven Warshaw. "Then the [EU] quota system came into effect, and we had eight-plus of the most trying years you could imagine."

At first glance, Chiquita's explanation for its decade-long slide seems both logical and clear. But like an aerial view of the banana plantations, it only hints at the deeper, more complicated story that lies beneath. After dozens of interviews with former Chiquita executives, independent banana producers, industry analysts, and other experts, that story begins to emerge. It is a chronicle not simply of unfair quotas and bad luck, but of poor management—of an executive corps that placed risky bets, made poor decisions, and alienated customers and supporters on Wall Street. The company's dispute with Europe did not cause these problems. It merely exposed and exacerbated them.

In 1998, after years on the periphery of the national consciousness, Chiquita once again found itself in the spotlight. An 18-page section of the *Cincinnati Enquirer*—headlined CHIQUITA SECRETS REVEALED—charged the company with perpetrating a host of political, environmental, and human rights abuses in Central America. Then, eight weeks later, after learning that the story's lead reporter had illegally hacked into Chiquita's voice-mail system, the newspaper issued a front-page apology, fired the reporter, and agreed to pay Chiquita $14 million in damages. The *Enquirer*'s mea culpa made headlines across the globe, but Chiquita, happy to talk about how it had been violated, never addressed the validity of the newspaper's claims. Jeff Zalla, Chiquita's corporate responsibility officer (yes, the company now has one), dismisses most of the newspaper's charges but acknowledges that it was a mistake to remain silent. "It left some people with an unsavory impression of our company," he says.

Throughout its history, the company, long referred to as "the Octopus" for its broad reach and influence, has often left such an impression—on employees, competitors, politicians, and anyone else who got in its way. To grasp the significance of Chiquita's recent decline, you need to understand what the company once was: an enormously powerful player in the banana industry, the American corporate establishment, and the Latin American countries in which it operates. So entwined were these nations with the company's business that the term "banana republic" was coined to describe them.

When United Fruit first opened its doors for business in 1899, such prospects would have been hard to imagine. At the time, the banana business was in its infancy. Though traders had been bringing small quantities of the fruit from the tropics to the U.S. and Europe since the 1860s, it wasn't until the development of the steamship that large-scale transportation of such perishable cargo became possible. Created by the merger of two of the largest operators, United Fruit quickly came to dominate its industry. In only its second year of operation, the company accounted for 75% of the 20 million banana stems sold in the combined U.S. and European markets.

As demand grew, so did United Fruit. By 1955, banana sales in Europe and the U.S. had risen sixfold, and United Fruit's share of those markets was 40%. The company employed more than 60,000 workers, operated the world's largest private shipping fleet, and owned more than 1.7 million acres of land and 1,100 miles of railroad in Guatemala, Honduras, Costa Rica, Panama, Colombia, and Ecuador—the republics responsible for 60% of world banana experts. United Fruit's $288 million in sales that year would have placed it at No. 106 on the first *Fortune* 500 (back then, the list included only industrial corporations).

The company was not simply a beneficiary of changing consumer tastes. Rather, United Fruit's own innovative practices were responsible for much of its growth—and by extension the growth of the entire industry. The company was a pioneer in the use of pesticides and herbicides; the first to ship its cargo in refrigerated vessels; and the first to brand bananas by labeling them with stickers. Its 1944 advertising campaign—featuring the Carmen Miranda–esque Miss Chiquita and the popular "Chiquita Banana

Song"—was one of the most memorable in history and helped make the banana the world's most widely consumed fruit.

The labor, technology, and infrastructure required to get a box of bananas from the plantations of Latin America to supermarkets in the U.S. is truly astounding. Bananas grow year round, in 13-week cycles, and need to be harvested daily. Because the stems have to be cut by hand, the process is highly labor intensive. Once the stems are harvested, workers take them to packing plants, where they are separated into bunches, sorted, cleaned, labeled, and placed in cardboard boxes. The boxes are stacked in refrigerated containers, transported to the nearest port, and loaded onto refrigerated ships. The cool atmosphere keeps the bananas from ripening until they reach their destination. Most large supermarket chains have ripening rooms, which introduce small amounts of ethylene gas, prompting the bananas to reach their optimal level of ripeness. All this for a fruit that, in North America, sells for less than 50 cents a pound.

Since most of United Fruit's assets and workers were based in Latin America, the company became a major force in the economic, social, and political fabric of the region. United Fruit recognized early on that infrastructure would be critical in delivering bananas to market on a reliable basis, and it was responsible for building many roads and train tracks. It also built entire villages with homes, schools, medical facilities, and factories that made cardboard boxes and other ancillary products.

But as its power in the region grew, United Fruit sought to control the workers it employed and the leaders of the republics in which it operated. "Through bribery, fraud, chicanery, strong-arm tactics, extortion, tax evasion, and subversion [United Fruit] grew to be a swaggering behemoth," writes Stephen Schlesinger, whose book *Bitter Fruit* details the involvement of United Fruit and the U.S. government in the 1954 overthrow of Guatemala's democratically elected president. "America smuggled guns on banana boats and trained an army of mercenaries on [United] Fruit Co. plantations," writes Thomas McCann, a former vice president of public relations, in his book *On the Inside*. "Companies like United Fruit . . . became political instruments. The government got what it wanted through the use of the company, and the company got what it wanted as well."

For years, rumors circulated about United Fruit's nefarious activities. Then, in 1975, the Securities and Exchange Commission uncovered a $2.5 million bribe the company had agreed to pay a Honduran official in return for reducing his country's banana tax. At the time, corporate raider Eli Black led the company. Black had gained control of United Fruit in 1968 and had merged it with his own public company, AMK—made up principally of meatpacker John Morrell—under the name United Brands. But when the bribery scandal surfaced, Black was no longer in control. A few weeks earlier he had jumped to his death from the window of his 44th-floor office in midtown Manhattan.

The company Black left behind, though still among the largest in America (No. 84 on the 1975 *Fortune* 500 list), was not the same as the one that had dominated its industry and Latin America for so long. Its reputation was sullied, its finances were in shambles, and its competitors—Standard Fruit (now Dole) and Del Monte—were making inroads into many markets, especially North America.

One member of the United Brands board at the time was a 55-year-old high-school dropout-turned-corporate-raider named Carl Lindner. Lindner had built his reputation—and a sizable fortune—reviving distressed corporations. (He had also left behind a trail of SEC consent decrees relating to stock-manipulation charges.) Intent on doing the same for United Brands, he slowly accumulated a majority interest and, in 1984, installed himself as chairman and CEO. And for the next eight years, it appeared as if he might succeed.

Europe's restrictive banana quotas did not emerge suddenly after the formation of the EU in 1993. They began at the end of World War II, when many European nations decided that banana production was fundamental to the social and economic health of their former and current colonies and territories in Africa, the Caribbean, and the Pacific. To encourage St. Lucia, Dominica, and others to grow the fruit, many European nations gave preferential treatment to bananas grown in those territories and granted European traders exclusive rights to sell them.

The countries most protective of their former territories, including Britain, France, and Spain, kept strict quotas on Latin American bananas and imposed steep tariffs on the fruit that did get in, limiting the access of United Fruit and other Latin American producers. Denmark, Belgium, and others levied tariffs but allowed significant Latin American imports. And Germany, Europe's largest consumer of bananas, maintained a free market. So in spite of the barriers, United Fruit had access to many European markets. Moreover, growing conditions in the former European territories were vastly inferior to those of Latin America, meaning the territories' combined output could fill only a third of Europe's demand, leaving plenty of room for United Fruit and other Latin American producers to supply the rest.

The quotas also resulted in greater profits for Latin American producers. Since much of Europe was obliged to purchase fruit from inefficient and expensive producers in its former territories, retailers in Europe had to charge twice as much as their counterparts in North America, enabling efficient producers like United Fruit to rake in twice the profits.

The company began to focus more of its attention and marketing dollars on Europe, especially the continent's less protected markets. By the late 1970s, even as the company lost ground to Standard Fruit and Del Monte in North America and other parts of the world, Chiquita remained Europe's dominant Latin American brand.

When Carl Lindner took control of the company, he sought to increase its market share in Europe even further. Lindner wasted little time putting his stamp on the company. He moved United Brands' corporate headquarters from New York to his native

Cincinnati, where his $16 billion holding company, American Financial Group, is based; changed its name to Chiquita; and replaced many of its seasoned banana men with younger executives, including his son Keith, whom he installed as president in 1989. Recognizing Europe's potential as a cash windfall, the elder Lindner began to reconfigure the company's supply chain—from its mix of production regions to the deployment of its ships—to better serve the European market. Under the Lindners' guidance, Europe became Chiquita's primary engine of growth. Between 1987 and 1991, European sales grew an average of 8% per year and soon made up more than half of the company's $1.8 billion in annual banana sales and an even larger portion of its earnings.

Around this time, the European Community finalized plans to form a single trading block and began to consider what to do about banana quotas. They debated whether to adopt the highly restrictive policies of Britain and France, the free-trade approach of Germany, or something in between. Convinced that post–Cold War Europe would develop a relaxed regulatory environment, Chiquita embarked on an ambitious and expensive expansion of its European operations. "We were led to believe by people throughout the governments of Europe that there would be a gradual liberalization of trade policy," says Warshaw, at the time one of the company's senior executives. The Lindners outlined their aspirations in Chiquita's 1990 annual report: "The European Community, which is poised to become a single market in 1993, may offer Chiquita access to previously restricted countries, including the United Kingdom, France, and Spain. The Company continues to make strategic investments . . . to enhance its prospects in these countries, where almost 200 million potential customers live." Chiquita also believed banana consumption would escalate in the newly liberalized economies of Eastern Europe and the former Soviet Union.

The expansion efforts focused on two areas: banana production and shipping. Between 1989 and 1993, Chiquita increased its production capacity in Latin America by 32,000 acres. To handle the transportation of all those bananas, the company took delivery of 14 custom-made refrigerated ships that at the time were the largest ever built. The total cost of these initiatives exceeded $1 billion. Since the majority of that cost was financed with debt, the expansion left the company in a highly leveraged position. (In 1989, Chiquita's debt was 96% of its equity; by 1993, the debt had ballooned to 270% of equity.)

In 1991, Chiquita had its best year in decades, posting an operating income (earnings before interest and taxes) of $226 million on revenues of $4.6 billion. More than 80% of those earnings came from its European division.

Management gurus say you can't really judge a corporate leader until he or she is tested. For Keith Lindner, the youngest of Carl's three sons, that test came in 1992. Keith had taken over as president and COO in 1989 at the age of 29 (his father retained the CEO title) and had shepherded the company through two years of growth. Then, in April 1992—well before the EU quota system took effect—Chiquita reported that its first-quarter earnings would fall 85% short of the consensus analyst estimate. The company ended up posting losses that year of $284 million.

The sudden shift in fortunes was largely a result of the company's own miscalculations: The increase in Eastern European demand that Chiquita anticipated never materialized, resulting in a supply glut and depressing prices worldwide. But instead of accepting any responsibility for the company's poor earnings, the Lindners blamed the results on "a decline in product quality resulting from an extraordinary outbreak of disease and unusual weather patterns."

The earnings shortfall shocked analysts, who had been assured by Lindner less than a month earlier that Chiquita would hit its targets. "Not only do we now have no confidence in the earnings, but we have serious doubts about the abilities of management to deal with the company's problems," wrote C. J. Lawrence food analyst Timothy Ramey in a report accompanying his "sell" recommendation.

A few months later the EU announced that its new banana

quota and licensing system would go into effect July 1, 1993. Rather than the loosely regulated model upon which Chiquita had wagered its billion-dollar expansion plans, the new system resembled the highly restrictive policies of Britain and France. Prior to the implementation of the new system, 70% of the bananas sold in Europe came from Latin America. Chiquita was responsible for 40% of those sales, giving the company a 22% share of the Continent's banana market. Once the quotas were put in place, Chiquita says, its market share was sliced in half, costing the company close to $200 million a year in lost earnings.

Chiquita suddenly found itself in a precarious position. Its most profitable market had been obliterated. It had a surplus of bananas and nowhere to sell them; a fleet of ships and nowhere to sail them; and a mountain of debt and no way to pay it. "If an angel had come to us and said, 'Trust me, Europe is going to be thoroughly regulated, the size of the market is going to be smaller, and you are going to have your market share illegally taken away,' the plan for Chiquita would have been completely different," says Warshaw. "And the enterprise value of Chiquita would be many billions of dollars higher."

Chiquita was not the only banana company to misread the EU's intentions. In the late 1980s, Dole had also ramped up its operations with the expectation that a united Europe would mean a less regulated Europe. Yet a decade later Dole's balance sheet is clear, while Chiquita's is awash in red ink. True, Dole had a smaller share of the European market and less to lose. But the difference between the two rivals comes down to how each of their management teams handled the crisis.

While Dole continued to protect its non-banana-related assets—its pineapple business accounted for much of the company's success in the 1990s—Chiquita focused almost exclusively on bananas. Perhaps the company's biggest blunder was its decision in 1992 to sell John Morrell, the meatpacker that contributed nearly half of the company's revenues. After languishing on the block for three years, Morrell was purchased by Smithfield Foods in 1995 for about $58 million. With much of the same management team still in place, Morrell now contributes earnings of between $40 and $50 million a year to Smithfield. "The company pretty much paid for itself in two years," says Smithfield's Jerry Hostetter. According to one former Chiquita executive, the protracted sale and low selling price were a result of panic: Chiquita, spurred by concern over its mounting debt, had announced its intention to sell Morrell prematurely, before properly calculating its value or gauging the market conditions.

Keith Lindner declined to comment about the Morrell sale, or any other aspect of the company's business, but Warshaw says Chiquita felt pressure at the time to reduce its debt. It also unloaded Numar, its edible-oils business, in 1995. "It was an excellent business," says Warshaw. "And it has done very well since. But we needed to reduce debt and deleverage to survive."

In the early 1990s, Chiquita also made several smaller mistakes that exacerbated the company's financial woes. It bought 43-foot containers to ship its fruit—rather than the standard 40-foot size—only to discover that when filled they exceeded the weight restrictions for U.S. highways. It made an expensive foray into the frozen-fruit-bar market, only to abort when profits failed to follow. And, on a whim, it purchased a tilapia breeding company. When the fish business faltered, Chiquita was forced to turn to Morrell (then still part of the company) to help unload the fish.

As it struggled with the fallout of the trade dispute, Chiquita faced serious labor problems in Latin America, forcing it to curtail production, lay off thousands of workers, and incur millions of dollars in losses.

These developments weren't well received by Wall Street analysts. Nor was the discovery of Honduran court documents claiming that a Chiquita executive had been involved in a kidnapping attempt of an executive at rival Fyffes. Though the executive protested his innocence, and the case was later dismissed, it provided analysts with another reason to distrust the company. "That [incident] really sealed the stock's demise," recalls one analyst.

"We just thought this company was not only fundamentally dishonest but also stupid. Increasingly, people just stopped covering them."

After years of dominance in the U.S., Chiquita lost ground to Dole and Del Monte. "The Lindners got rid of a lot of old-school people," says a former Chiquita executive, "people who had relationships on the produce side. And the new managers they brought in didn't understand the business." In 1995, the Cincinnati division of the Kroger supermarket chain announced that it was switching from Chiquita to Dole. The move was especially embarrassing for Carl Lindner, who was a major shareholder of Cincinnati-based Kroger and is an influential member of the city's business community.

"If a secretary on the 27th floor of the Chiquita building got pregnant out of wedlock," jokes a former Chiquita executive, "the company would blame it on the European Union." Indeed, in each year that the company posted a net loss—as it did in eight of the past nine years—it attributed its poor performance to the EU regime. "As a result of government legislation," says Bob Kistinger, president of Chiquita's fresh food division, "what took us years to develop was wiped out, without any ability on our part to deal with the issue."

Similarly, Chiquita says that its weakened position in Europe made it vulnerable to the mid-1990s rise of the U.S. dollar, which the company blames for its current cash crunch. "Ultimately," says Warshaw, "we reached the point where we had to restructure the parent company's debt because of the weakening of European currencies." (Of course, Chiquita didn't credit strong European currencies for bolstering its earnings in the late 1980s.)

It was this attitude that led Chiquita to challenge the EU. Where other corporations might have resigned themselves to the new quota system, Chiquita was determined to regain the market share it felt had been stolen. Faced with what it considered a hostile foreign act, the company turned again to the ally that had helped it in the past—the U.S. government.

But much had changed since the days of the Cold War, when the Octopus and the CIA collaborated to keep Latin America free of communism and profits flowing to the company. Besides, the U.S. was reluctant to antagonize its European allies to protect a product that wasn't even produced in America. Internal memos from the U.S. Trade Representative (USTR) suggest that, in 1993, the banana issue was a low priority. Yet the following year, the USTR joined Chiquita in an all-out trade war with the EU. At first, the U.S. battled cautiously within the courtrooms of the World Trade Organization. But in 1999, with the EU refusing to replace its quota system even after two separate WTO panels found it "illegal," the USTR went a step further, imposing prohibitive sanctions on select EU products, including coffeemakers and bath oils.

Some have suggested that the change in the USTR's position was influenced by the more than $5 million donated between 1993 and 1999 by Carl Lindner, his family, his companies, and his executives to the Republican and Democratic parties. In 1992, the year before the EU announced its quota system, Lindner and his associates donated a combined $67,500 to both political parties, a number not unusual for the head of a large multinational corporation. Yet in 1993, the year Chiquita approached Washington for help, Lindner's contributions rose to $484,000. They continued to climb for the duration of the trade war, reaching a peak of $1.4 million in 1998, the year before the U.S. imposed sanctions. By the mid-1990s, Lindner had become one of the top donors in the nation, warranting invitations to the White House and even a night in the Lincoln bedroom. (The USTR did not respond to requests for an interview, but it has denied any link between Lindner's contributions and its actions.)

This summer, in response to the USTR's sanctions, the EU finally relaxed its quotas. A new system, which went into effect July 1, returns import volumes to levels similar to those existing prior to the EU regime, when Chiquita dominated the competitive landscape. In 2006, the EU plans to move to a tariff-only system. While the new system gives Chiquita the license to import more bananas, it doesn't restore the market share the company lost over the past eight years. Chiquita now faces the formidable task of convincing customers that its financial woes will not affect its performance.

Acre by acre, the reddish-brown mud that covers the Bocas plantations is being transformed into green. Slowly, ivy-like plants are taking root at the base of the banana plants, reducing Bocas's reliance on herbicides by 75%. Plastic sacks hang at regular intervals so workers can dispose of waste. Nearby, rotting bananas lie neatly in landfill pits. These projects are part of a six-year, $20 million environmental improvement campaign. Chiquita's plantations are now certified according to the dictates of the Rainforest Alliance, an American nonprofit organization. And last year Wal-Mart named Chiquita its most environmentally conscious supplier—quite a departure for a company that long battled charges of environmental and labor abuse.

Chiquita recently released a corporate responsibility report acknowledging the company's troubled past and promising a more open future. "Times have changed," writes Warshaw. "Our stakeholders expect more of us. We expect more of ourselves. Our understanding of . . . what it means to be a responsible corporate citizen is quite different than it was not long ago."

One of those changes was the elevation of Warshaw this summer to the position of CEO. A trim, square-jawed 48-year-old, Warshaw came to Chiquita in 1987 and replaced Keith Lindner as president and COO a decade later. (Lindner moved to the parent company, American Financial, where he and his brothers are co-presidents.) In fact, since the *Cincinnati Enquirer* imbroglio, the Lindners have taken a more hands-off approach to Chiquita. The family stake in the company, once 55%, now sits at 36%, and with Chiquita shares trading at under $1, their investment is insignificant relative to their other holdings. Company executives say Chiquita's newfound openness is not unrelated to the Lindners' diminished role.

Since Chiquita announced in January that it could no longer pay its debts, Warshaw has had to guide the company through one of the most challenging periods in its long history. Chapter 11 is a costly process. To move through it as quickly as possible, Warshaw has worked diligently over the past year to orchestrate a prearranged bankruptcy, in which Chiquita bondholders agree to relieve the company of its debts in exchange for equity. Though Chiquita has already realized cost savings of $150 million over the past three years from layoffs and streamlining, more of these measures are likely to follow.

Ironically, the company's weakened condition seems to have quelled any threat of a takeover or a breakup. In fact, a Latin American company that had amassed nearly 10% of Chiquita's shares and was considering a takeover will be left with a diluted stake once Chiquita's bondholders swap their debt for equity.

The end to Chiquita's eight-year trade dispute with the EU also leaves the company in a stronger position. But it removes the crutch the company has used to explain away its problems. Chiquita has owned up to its spotty environmental record and is taking steps to improve it. If it wants to emerge from Chapter 11 with a chance to succeed, the company similarly will need to acknowledge its corporate missteps.

Investors have learned that what they don't know about companies hurts them. The unraveling of Enron, poster child for nondisclosure and hidden deals with officers, is skillfully traced in this story by John R. Emshwiller and Rebecca Smith of *The Wall Street Journal*. It's indicative of the *Journal*'s excellent ongoing coverage of events behind the scandal.

John R. Emshwiller and Rebecca Smith

Corporate Veil

HOUSTON—Around the beginning of October, Enron Corp. executives visited credit-rating-agency officials for talks about the company's third-quarter results. Those results contained what turned out to be a bombshell.

Enron mentioned in the talks that shareholders' equity, the difference between the company's assets and its liabilities, would be reduced by $1.2 billion because of transactions with certain partnerships, says a person familiar with the matter. Some of the credit analysts, regarding this as so significant it needed to be disclosed, privately urged Enron to report it to the Securities and Exchange Commission, this person says.

But Enron didn't do so, nor did the company explain it in its nine-page earnings announcement in mid-October. The only public inkling came during an earnings-report conference call, in a reference by the company chairman so fleeting that some analysts say they missed it.

It was vintage Enron: minimal disclosure of financial information that, in retrospect, was central to understanding the complex company. Only a few months ago, Enron was wowing Wall

Street with its growth and innovation, racking up large, steady earnings gains as it pioneered the global trading of everything from power to weather contracts. But virtually unseen until the end was an Enron culture that contained the seeds of its collapse, a culture of highly questionable financial engineering, misstated earnings and persistent efforts to keep investors in the dark.

Senior Enron executives flouted elementary conflict-of-interest standards. The company hired legions of lawyers and accountants to help it meet the letter of federal securities laws while trampling on the intent of those laws. It became adept at giving technically correct answers rather than simply honest ones.

One senior Wall Street official recalls recently asking Enron officials whether the company had retained bankruptcy counsel. He was told no. He later found out that while Enron hadn't formally retained such representation, it had met with bankruptcy lawyers. "If you don't ask the absolute right question, you don't get the right answer," he says. "Enron does that a lot."

Yet public trust, above all, was what Enron had to have, in order to conduct its business as a trader and party to thousands of contracts. Once doubts began to seep into the public realm, thanks partly to that mysterious hit to equity and Enron's waffling about what it meant, other suspicious Enron moves began to emerge.

The company had transactions with certain partnerships that were run by its own officers but treated by Enron as separate. It offered only murky and fragmented information about these partnerships. One partnership, whose existence Enron didn't reveal for four years, was part of an arrangement that inflated earnings by several hundred million dollars during that period.

And the company's debt level was much higher than it revealed, thanks to the partnerships, which allowed Enron to keep some debt off its books. Meanwhile, executives made repeated public assurances that Enron's finances and business operations were healthy, only to have those statements refuted by subsequent revelations. Ultimately, these disclosures created a crisis at Enron, sending its stock plunging and its partners and clients fleeing.

While Enron has acknowledged that a loss of investors' confidence was at the root of its woes, company officials have consistently defended their actions as legal and proper. An Enron spokesman reiterated yesterday that the company made every effort to put out accurate information. When something was found to be inaccurate, Enron took prompt steps to correct it, the spokesman said.

On Sunday, Enron filed for bankruptcy-law protection in New York federal court—the biggest such filing ever. It simultaneously filed a multibillion-dollar suit against a company that last week backed out of a rescue pact, rival Dynegy Inc. Enron's stock, which touched $90 a share last year, closed yesterday on the New York Stock Exchange at 87 cents.

Top officials now are the targets of some two dozen shareholder suits. They face a formal SEC investigation, a Justice Department criminal probe and congressional inquiries. The company, now struggling to avoid liquidation, has tapped existing credit facilities and lined up fresh capital exceeding $7 billion in recent weeks, and is looking for more.

Not every detail of this tangled tale has yet been fully unraveled. It's still not clear whether concealment and financial engineering were a central strategy at Enron for years, or just a last desperate resort when earnings were falling short. Questions also still surround the sudden midsummer resignation of Chief Executive Jeffrey Skilling, whose role in Enron's collapse remains uncertain.

What is clear, though, is that rarely in the annals of American business has an enterprise so mighty and so highly regarded fallen so far so fast.

Led by its chairman, Kenneth Lay, Enron during the 1990s morphed from a nondescript gas-pipeline company into the nation's biggest energy trader, matching utilities, power suppliers and other investors in a vast unregulated marketplace. It gradually turned into a trading juggernaut that increasingly disdained long-term ownership of hard assets.

Moving far beyond energy, Enron pioneered hundreds of different types of trading contracts, ranging from commodities such as water to exotic new financial instruments. The company assembled an immense pool of financial and trading talent among its 21,000 employees.

As Enron concentrated on trading of complex instruments, it came to resemble a vast financial-services empire, handling billions of dollars of other people's money. But to analysts and investors seeking to understand it, Enron wasn't very informative. Officials could be dismissive of inquiries, even rude. Closely questioned during a conference call last spring, Mr. Skilling called one company critic an "a—h—."

Many Wall Street analysts admitted to not fully understanding chunks of Enron, a company that had 3,500 subsidiaries and affiliates spread across the globe. During the booming 1990s, as Enron delivered plump earnings and stock gains, this didn't matter. Investors "were scared not to be in it," says Paul Patterson, an analyst at ABN Amro.

The confluence of events that changed perceptions began in August with the sudden resignation of Mr. Skilling.

The former McKinsey & Co. consultant, who is 48, had become president in 1997. Last February he became CEO as well. Remaining chairman was his mentor, Mr. Lay, a friend and financial backer of President Bush and Vice President Cheney. In the early days of the Bush administration, Mr. Lay, who is 59, had been widely expected to take a cabinet post.

Messrs. Lay and Skilling made a formidable team. The courtly and amiable Mr. Lay had wide-ranging experience in government, academia and business, and his opinion was frequently sought in the energy world. Mr. Skilling, a Harvard M.B.A., was a brash, fiery figure who spoke rapidly and peppered his conversations with financial jargon.

Without warning, Mr. Skilling resigned on August 14. He initially cited "personal reasons." But in an interview the next day he said his own frustration over Enron's weakening share price—

then about $43—played a major role in his decision. "I don't think I would have felt the pressure to leave if the stock price had stayed up," he said.

The abrupt departure forced Mr. Lay to retake the reins. He was reassuring to the public. "I can honestly say the company is in the strongest shape it's ever been in," Mr. Lay said at the time. He also promised that in the future, Enron would be more open and accessible to investors. Mr. Lay acknowledged that the company had "lost some credibility" with investors.

The day of the announcement, Enron filed its report with the SEC for the three months ended June 30. Tucked in the 36-page document were several paragraphs describing deals involving hundreds of millions of dollars between Enron and unnamed partnerships headed by and partly owned by an unnamed "senior officer" of the company. The filing added that the officer had sold his partnership interests in July and "no longer has any management responsibilities for these entities."

But it wasn't Mr. Skilling who ran the two partnerships, known as LJM Cayman LP and LJM2 Co-Investment LP. It was Chief Financial Officer Andrew S. Fastow, a Skilling protégé who was still very much with the company. The "LJM" came from the first initials of Mr. Fastow's wife and two sons. A company spokesman said the dealings between Enron and Mr. Fastow's partnerships were perfectly proper and had been done to help Enron protect its assets against fluctuating market prices.

The partnerships had been around for two years and appeared in Enron SEC filings during that time. But the manner in which they were disclosed, with different pieces of information appearing in different filings, made it difficult to learn such basics as which senior executive was running the partnerships.

Worse, there was no way from the available information to understand just what the partnerships were doing or what impact they had on Enron's finances. Some stock and credit analysts say they had never heard about the LJMs until they read about them in the newspapers in recent weeks.

Mr. Fastow's LJM dealings were, however, well-known within Enron and a magnet for criticism. Part of LJM's activities involved buying Enron assets, and some officials balked at doing deals that could enrich a senior executive at the company's expense, say people familiar with the matter. At least two senior officials complained internally about the potential conflicts of interest. The concerns were turned aside by top management, say the people familiar with the events.

The anger might have been greater had those who complained known the extent of Mr. Fastow's financial gains from LJM. Internal partnership documents show that the CFO made millions of dollars a year from LJM, far more than his corporate compensation.

One private document for LJM2's successful effort to raise nearly $400 million boasted of "preferred access" to Enron deals and said that Mr. Fastow's economic interests would be "aligned" with the partners'. Late last year, Mr. Fastow and Enron were laying plans for a $1 billion LJM3 fund, though it never came to fruition. Enron later estimated that Mr. Fastow made more than $30 million from the LJM partnerships.

Mr. Fastow has declined repeated requests to be interviewed. His attorney points to Enron statements saying that all of the company's dealings with the partnerships were proper and thoroughly vetted by the board and top management.

In September, Enron faced questions from *The Wall Street Journal* about the partnerships. According to a person familiar with the matter, there were sharp internal disagreements over whether to make top officials available for interviews. This person says that at one point, Mr. Fastow shouted that he saw no "upside" to talking.

Then came Enron's October 16 report of its third-quarter earnings. Although a $1 billion write-off for telecommunications and other ventures produced a big net loss, the company trumpeted a 26% increase in "recurring earnings" due to "very strong results" of its "core" businesses. The stock posted a gain for the day.

The news release contained a cryptic reference to a charge relating to the "early termination . . . of certain structured finance arrangements with a previously disclosed entity." This seemed to be Enron code for LJM. In response to questions, the company said the LJM-related charge was $35 million.

Mr. Lay himself tried to put the LJM matter to rest. "I don't think we need to say anything more about that," he said in an interview at the time.

Later, however, an Enron SEC filing on November 8 disclosed that the actual charge related to LJM dealings was $462 million. The $35 million figure represented cash paid to LJM in the termination, company officials now said, with the other hundreds of millions reflecting declines in the value of Enron assets held by LJM-related entities.

"It was not our intent to mislead," said Mr. Lay's chief of staff, Steve Kean, in mid-November.

On October 17, the *Journal* revealed some of the partnerships' inner workings, their dealings with Enron and the fact that Mr. Fastow stood to make millions from his participation. Shortly afterward, Enron's stock began tumbling.

That same day, word of the $1.2 billion reduction in shareholders' equity started rippling through Wall Street. On October 18, the *Journal* reported for the first time that the equity reduction stemmed from transactions related to the LJM partnerships.

During the earlier discussions with credit-rating agencies, Enron had attributed the equity reduction to an "accounting error," says the person familiar with those discussions. However, in an October 17 interview with the *Journal,* Enron Chief Accounting Officer Rick Causey didn't mention an accounting error. He said that as part of its dealing with the partnerships, Enron had put up 62 million of its own shares. In return, it gained a $1.2 billion note receivable from the partnerships. When the arrangements were terminated, he explained, Enron simply canceled the note and retired the stock. The retirement of so many shares accounted for a $1.2 billion reduction in shareholders' equity.

A spokesman added that Enron didn't see this as a material transaction that needed to be publicly disclosed. The spokesman yesterday said that he had been told by company officials at the time that it was "a balance-sheet issue" and didn't need to be included in the third-quarter earnings discussion.

However, in a November 8 SEC filing, Enron declared that the equity reduction was largely due to an accounting error—one that required the company to restate prior-year financial reports.

The SEC within a few days started an informal inquiry. It soon grew into a formal investigation, which meant the agency had power to subpoena witnesses and documents. At the same time, credit-rating agencies were beginning to put Enron on review for possible downgrade.

That was worrisome. Keeping an investment-grade rating was vital for the health of the trading operation, which produced more than 90% of Enron's third-quarter operating earnings. More-over, a fall to "junk" status would trigger accelerated repayment of billions of dollars of obligations.

In an effort to stanch the bleeding and restore confidence, Mr. Lay and other top officials, including Mr. Fastow, held a confer-ence call on October 23. Sparring with analysts and investors, the executives seemed defensive and even hostile at times. Mr. Lay wouldn't let Mr. Fastow answer questions about the partnerships, but expressed his "highest faith and confidence" in his chief finan-cial officer.

The next day, the company announced Mr. Fastow was no longer Enron's CFO. Mr. Lay said the about-face was necessary to "restore investor confidence."

After the conference call, Enron top brass retreated from the public arena. Behind the scenes, Enron was frantically looking for a rescue strategy, approaching both competitors such as Dynegy and wealthy investors such as Warren Buffett for a cash infusion. So intense was the quest that one Enron attorney, a member of the Weil, Gotshal & Manges law firm, flew from Dallas to Houston for a planned two-hour meeting and didn't get back for two weeks.

Dynegy was intrigued by the notion of taking over a company that was five times its size and had long overshadowed it. Dynegy President Steve Bergstrom, an Enron alumnus, had a scheduled social lunch with an old friend, Stan Horton, who runs Enron's pipeline business. Mr. Horton asked if he could bring Enron Vice Chairman Mark Frevert and President Greg Whalley. In a private room at Houston's Plaza Club, Mr. Whalley popped the question: Would Dynegy be interested in buying Enron? "I was flabbergasted," says Mr. Bergstrom. "We were like the little kid on the block to them." He remembers thinking, "They're in worse trouble than I thought."

Mr. Bergstrom suggested having Mr. Lay call Dynegy Chairman and founder Chuck Watson, and within hours the two talked. Then they met face-to-face and privately October 27 at Mr. Lay's home in Houston's exclusive River Oaks neighborhood, hammering out major points of a deal.

Dynegy's biggest shareholder, ChevronTexaco Corp., approved a $2.5 billion investment in Dynegy that Dynegy would use to give Enron a cash infusion. The first $1.5 billion would come right away and the rest at the closing. J.P. Morgan Chase & Co. and Citibank arranged a further $1 billion of credit, so that on November 9, the two sides were able to announce a $9 billion all-stock betrothal. Mr. Lay, deflecting questions about Enron's woes, said the combination "is all about the future."

But amid the optimistic talk, new bombshells were exploding at Enron. Its November 8 SEC filing disclosed for the first time company dealings with an entity called Chewco Investments LP. Just four days before the filing, the company had refused requests by *The Wall Street Journal* to discuss the entity or even acknowledge its existence.

As it turned out, Enron had plenty of reason to be sensitive about Chewco, named for the *Star Wars* character Chewbacca. Chewco had been set up in late 1997 during a rocky period for Enron, when the company was missing its quarterly earnings targets and losing a bit of its Wall Street credibility. Prudential Securities analyst Carol Coale recalls a meeting with Mr. Skilling during this period when, she says, he promised "some strong earnings growth" in the coming quarters.

Now it's known that between 1997 and the end of last year, Enron's dealings with Chewco and a related partnership known as JEDI (for Joint Energy Development Investments) kept hundreds of millions of dollars of debt off Enron's books. Moreover, business deals with the partnerships also allowed Enron to book $390 million in net income, roughly 13% of reported profits for the period, according to the November 8 SEC filing.

Although Enron treated Chewco as an independent third party, there were lots of indications to the contrary. Chewco was managed by Michael Kopper, an Enron officer who later helped Mr. Fastow run the LJM partnerships. Early Chewco funding of $383 million came almost entirely via Enron through loans it arranged or guaranteed.

In its November 8 filing, Enron said that Chewco and JEDI never should have been treated as separate parties. Retroactively folding them back into Enron was the principal cause of a restatement that slashed Enron earnings for the prior four years by $586 million, or 20%. The company said its financial statements for those years could no longer be relied upon.

These disclosures further rocked an already shaken investment community. If Enron officials knowingly created and controlled Chewco as a sham third party to boost profits, they could be in violation of federal fraud statutes, says Jacob Frenkel, a former SEC attorney and federal prosecutor. At the very least, says Ronald Barone, head of Standard & Poor's energy and utility group, Chewco represented "financial engineering on the razor's edge."

Mr. Kopper, who last summer left Enron to run the LJM operation, declines to be interviewed. According to Enron, he bought out Mr. Fastow's partnership interests. A recent visit to LJM's offices, across the street from Enron's Houston headquarters, found no one willing to talk.

During the years in which Enron was issuing earnings statements it now says were incorrect, Mr. Lay, Mr. Skilling and other top executives of Enron sold hundreds of millions of dollars in

Enron stock. Partly as a result, they and others face a raft of share-holder suits. Some Enron traders complained angrily at a company meeting last month about $62 million in severance the Dynegy deal would bring Mr. Lay. After a day of giving out conflicting signals, Mr. Lay announced he wouldn't take the severance.

Revelations about Chewco and LJM fueled concern about other surprises that might be hidden in dozens of other partnerships with which Enron did business. One problem: Millions of shares of Enron stock provided the underpinnings for at least some of those partnerships.

As Enron's stock price fell, the stability of those structures was threatened, says one Enron insider, who speculates that Mr. Skilling's decision to resign might have been influenced by this development. "When he saw the stock price falling, I think he knew a crisis was coming," this person says.

Mr. Skilling won't talk about Chewco or anything else having to do with Enron. On a recent morning, outside his newly built mansion in Houston's River Oaks neighborhood, Mr. Skilling reiterated his desire to be left alone but didn't seem angry about being approached. "I understand it's a big story," he said in a soft voice.

On November 19, Enron revealed more bad news. In another SEC filing, it said it could be forced to take a further $700 million pretax hit to earnings because of a plunge in the value of assets at yet another investment partnership. In addition, Enron said its declining credit rating had triggered $690 million in accelerated payments to investors.

Trading partners began to back away. The stock plunged anew, falling to about $5 a share by Thanksgiving.

Dynegy executives say the November 19 filing was pivotal in changing their thinking about the merger. Enron appeared to be burning through cash at a frightening rate, says Mr. Bergstrom, Dynegy's president, and it kept coming up with unpleasant surprises. "I think they knew more than they were telling," he says. Enron spokesman Mark Palmer replies that "if they had done their due diligence, they would have known about" Enron's condition.

The companies made one last stab at saving the deal over the Thanksgiving weekend, huddling at a resort in Westchester County, N.Y.

They slashed the deal's price to $4.17 billion. But in an ominous sign for Enron, neither of Dynegy's top two executives attended. And the revised deal was never made final. Analysts estimated that at least $4 billion more cash was needed to bolster trading partners' confidence, and no one was willing to put up that kind of money.

A week ago, Enron's world caved in. Standard & Poor's, tired of waiting for the negotiations to produce a new rescue of Enron, dropped its credit rating below investment grade.

Other rating agencies followed. Later the same day, Dynegy formally called off the acquisition, and Enron traders walked away from their screens. About 4,000 Enron employees already have been laid off, with $4,500 in severance pay.

Many face a further hit as retirement accounts, heavy with Enron shares they weren't allowed to sell, are decimated. After the collapse of the merger, some of the 7,500 headquarters employees headed to Houston bars to blow off steam.

One took the time to remove Dynegy's stock symbol and stock price from the electronic tote board in the Enron lobby. Left behind was Enron's stock price, by then measured in dimes, and the constantly replaying message at the bottom of the board: "Enron . . . endless possibilities."

The subsidiary Enron Broadband Services in Portland, Oregon, was to be a jewel in the crown of its ambitious parent company. Unfortunately, most employees were eventually laid off, their 401(k) stock at rock bottom. *The Oregonian*'s Jeff Manning and Gail Kinsey Hill probe the cultlike following of a firm that made promises it couldn't keep.

Jeff Manning and Gail Kinsey Hill

Portland Subsidiary Mirrors Enron's Rapid Rise, Fall

JEFFREY SKILLING, Enron's brilliant and sharp-tongued president, came to Portland in June 1999 and delivered a bombshell to employees of a small telecommunications company Enron had inherited when it bought Portland General Electric.

Skilling promised to open Enron's immense treasury to throw more than $1 billion at the establishment of a national fiber optic cable network.

In return, Skilling said, he expected nothing less than for the Portland operation to dominate the pipes carrying digital information, a commodity that in the information age might be more valuable than all the gas and electric lines Enron already controlled. Skilling ended his pitch with: "We're all going to make a lot of money together, aren't we?"

The meeting launched Portland employees of what would become Enron Broadband Services on a 2½-year odyssey marked by the highest of hopes, the lure of vast wealth, a liberal dose of

Houston-based Enron's swaggering style and a stunning, humiliating crash to earth that left most of the employees without jobs and struggling to comprehend what had happened.

"They were dreaming great dreams," said Barry Lavine, a former programmer for Enron Broadband. "As we listened to these people and their plans of world domination, it was intoxicating."

The dreams became a nightmare this fall as Enron, which last year was the nation's seventh largest company with a stock price as high as $90, collapsed into bankruptcy court. Its stock fell as low as 26 cents. Three federal agencies and Congress launched investigations into the staggering investor losses. Now a growing number of lawsuits claim that Enron Broadband was part of an elaborate campaign by Enron management to mislead investors about the true financial condition of the company. Enron disclosed in October that a quarter of Enron Broadband's 2000 revenue came from LJM2, one of the controversial partnerships the company in filings with the Securities and Exchange Commission has admitted had the effect of concealing Enron's debt.

"There was no real business there," said Carol Coale, a Prudential Securities analyst who covered Enron Broadband. "They generated cash by selling to affiliated partnerships."

In the past month, *The Oregonian* interviewed dozens of former Enron employees as well as regulators, consultants, analysts, competitors and business associates. The newspaper also reviewed the company's filings with the SEC.

The interviews and filings reveal a hugely ambitious place, where executives wanted nothing less than to build "The World's Leading Company." It was also an impatient company with a short attention span. If an idea didn't work, Enron shoved it aside and moved on to something else. But the cost of those failures, obscured by unusually complex financial reports, mounted. When the problems surfaced this year, the company imploded.

Enron Broadband was one of those problems, though not the biggest. Still, the human toll of Enron's collapse in Portland is obvious.

Enron laid off the bulk of its roughly 300 Portland broadband employees. The workers, many of them paper millionaires at the company's peak, saw their stock options become worthless, much as PGE workers saw Enron stock in their 401(k) accounts plummet in value.

The embattled company declined to respond to *The Oregonian*'s questions about its telecommunications subsidiary.

1996 THROUGH 1997

IN SEARCH OF MARKETS

Enron had one resolute purpose when it first came to Oregon in July 1996—to use PGE, Oregon's no. 1 supplier of electricity, as a launching pad into deregulated markets in the West.

"They had an almost cult-like belief in markets," said Ron Eachus, then-chairman of the Oregon Public Utility Commission, the state agency that regulates utilities. "They were like Marco Polo in the energy industry—they'd go anywhere to find a market. And if there wasn't one, they'd create one."

When the PUC staff criticized the deal, Chief Executive Officer Ken Lay and President Jeffrey Skilling demanded a face-to-face with commissioners.

Commissioner Joan Smith remembers the February 14, 1997, confrontation well.

"They treated us like country bumpkins," she said.

Smith became so angry, she interrupted them.

"I said, 'We're not simpletons, we're not children. . . . We didn't just fall off a turnip truck.'"

Lay immediately toned down the condescension, Smith said. Skilling was a different story.

"He was just on another planet," Smith said. "He's very smooth, very bright, and to him, we just weren't very interesting."

The PGE deal closed July 1, 1997, with Enron paying $3.1

billion in stock and assumed debt. Enron barely noticed that the acquisition included a tiny telecommunications unit called First-Point Communications, which later became the high-flying Enron Broadband.

Despite Enron's initial enthusiasm, it quickly grew bored with PGE. The electricity market free-for-all in which the burgeoning trading company intended to thrive bogged down in state legislatures and regulatory caveats. An impatient Enron turned its attentions elsewhere.

While Enron was focusing on energy markets, FirstPoint was building a fiber optic loop around Portland and its suburbs. The network would provide an underground grid for high-speed Internet travel and tap a growing demand from businesses and consumers.

Ken Harrison, then PGE's chief executive officer, handpicked Chief Financial Officer Joe Hirko to lead a more aggressive push into telecommunications.

"Ken said, 'Go look at this company. See what you can do,'" recalls Hirko, a PGE insider who initially balked at heading up such a pint-size enterprise.

As Hirko took over as FirstPoint's chief executive in December 1997, workers were steadily building a regional network that would stretch across the Mount Hood pass into central Oregon across to Boise, Salt Lake City, Las Vegas and Los Angeles.

The venture leased enough of the fiber optic cable to pay for the network before the final lines hit the ground, a rapid-fire payback that drew Enron's attention.

"Enron liked us," said David Leatherwood, FirstPoint's first employee and the one in charge of building the network. "This was good money, and they like money."

1998 THROUGH 1999

GETTING HOUSTON'S ATTENTION

In March 1998, Hirko and Harrison jetted to Texas to make a pitch to take their fiber network national.

The two men met with Skilling in Enron's sleek Houston high-rise and enthusiastically explained their plan. Skilling practically yawned in their faces. What did he want with cables and switches? He thrived on complex financial dealings and what he called "intellectual capital."

"Jeff just wasn't interested," Hirko said.

Skilling even suggested selling FirstPoint, which had been renamed Enron Communications after the PGE purchase.

A lot of convincing later, Skilling gave his OK, provided that the business immediately made money.

Even so, "Jeff saw it as an investment opportunity, not a core business," Hirko said. "He made it clear we couldn't be a drain on Enron—and we weren't."

Enron put its resources behind the project, both laying cable and trading fiber for existing lines. By 1999, it had parlayed a 5,000-mile network into a 15,000-mile national network, Leatherwood said.

As the network grew, so did the enthusiasm of Portland employees.

"I called myself a glorified ditch-digger," said Kevin Kohnstamm, then the company's vice president for network development. "It was a dream job. You weren't cutting down old-growth forests. You weren't exploiting anyone."

But Skilling didn't like traditional hard assets. Nudged by Hirko, Skilling decided trading bandwidth as a commodity, just as Enron already traded gas and electricity, was the road to riches.

In May, the company announced that bandwidth trading would begin. It will "supercharge the entire Internet industry," gushed Tom Gros, Enron's vice president of global bandwidth trading.

Now Skilling was ready to come to Portland and anoint Enron Communications. In the early summer of 1999, he met with employees at the company's offices above the beer vats of the Rock Bottom Brewery and told them the news.

"Jeff decided we were a core business and not just an investment," Hirko recalled.

Core.

The designation catapulted Enron Communications to the top of the corporate hierarchy. No longer were telecommunications and broadband an afterthought. They were the thought. They were a commodity, capable of big trades and big money, just like natural gas and electricity.

Or so Enron thought. The concept sounded simple enough: Offer contracts that allowed customers to quickly buy or sell space on fiber optic lines in the United States and, eventually, all over the world. Dot-com mania was building. Potential customers included Internet providers, telephone companies and corporations intending to use the networks for high-speed data transmission.

Broadband was among many products, including weather derivatives and water futures, that Enron decided it could trade profitably.

To emphasize its intent, Enron renamed the Portland subsidiary Enron Broadband Services and called for a wildly successful 2000.

2000

TRYING TO FULFILL THE PROMISES

At a stock analysts' meeting on January 20, Enron announced a $350 million alliance with Sun Microsystems to improve the quality and speed of video and Internet traffic on the Enron network. Lay was so enthusiastic about broadband's potential that he predicted bandwidth trading would "dwarf" Enron's gas and power trading.

The news, along with the apparent success of the entire company, ignited the stock. Enron shares on the New York Stock Exchange started out 2000 at $43.44. The day of the analysts' meeting, the stock shot to $67.38 a share, a 26 percent jump from the preceding day's close.

By early summer, financial reports also suggested Enron's epic bet on the telecommunications business was paying off. Enron Broadband's revenue reached a record $151 million in the quarter ended June 30, 2000.

Publicly, Hirko sounded a bullish note. "We are pushing the technology envelope and setting new standards daily," he said at that spring's National Association of Broadcasters show.

Behind the scenes, Enron Broadband was experiencing growing pains. As its parent company de-emphasized certain international investments, hundreds of employees were "redeployed" to Enron Broadband, which by then had offices in Houston and Portland.

Many of these newcomers knew next to nothing about telecommunications. But they were steeped in the Enron attitude and seemed determined to tell the Portlanders what they were doing wrong, said Kohnstamm, the Enron Broadband vice president.

In Portland, the employee count had approached 300, and workers were ensconced in three floors of an office tower just south of the city's tony RiverPlace development.

They reveled in the attention and in the stock's meteoric rise, but not the direction their subsidiary had taken—a decided shift to Houston and a commodity-driven mentality.

"It was an invasion of the traders," said Leatherwood, who tagged late 1999 as the time the balance of power began to tilt.

What really irked Leatherwood and his colleagues was the apparent neglect of the network. Though Enron had spent hundreds of millions of dollars laying fiber optics, the company left portions of the network idle.

In some cases, Enron had already purchased the electronics needed to make a segment operational. Yet the gear remained in the warehouse. They were hard assets. No one in Houston much cared.

Leatherwood traveled to Houston on an unsuccessful quest to get the network turned on. "I built the thing, I at least wanted to light it up," he said. "They saw the price of bandwidth dropping, so they wanted to limit what was available. . . . That's the short-term trader mentality."

The price of bandwidth was falling because of a market glut. It seemed that every electricity company, natural gas operation and railroad with established rights of way decided to build their own national fiber optics network.

Privately, Hirko was having doubts of his own, not because of the competition or broadband prices, but because of an awkward dual CEO arrangement, which pitted him against Enron insider Ken Rice. Hirko was fed up with sharing the top spot with Rice, not to mention all the travel time to Houston and back.

Hirko says he went to Skilling and told him to choose between the two of them. Skilling told Hirko he could run Enron Broadband as long as he moved to Houston. Hirko took the offer as a none-too-subtle hint to resign and left the company in June 2000.

Hirko could afford to walk. He began selling Enron stock in large blocks beginning in January 2000, unloading $35 million worth by May 2000. Also in June, Enron Broadband cut a deal that casts doubt on whether the company was ever financially viable.

As later SEC filings would reveal, Enron Broadband sold $100 million worth of fiber optic to LJM2, one of the controversial partnerships headed by Andrew Fastow, the Enron chief financial officer who later was forced out of the company. Enron Broadband received $30 million up front and a $70 million note from LJM2.

Why LJM2 needed fiber is unclear. What is clear is that $100 million, nearly a quarter of Enron Broadband's 2000 sales, came from a partnership run by an Enron insider. Employees said they didn't know any details about the LJM2 deals.

More than a year later when Enron disclosed the write-downs and accounting irregularities that hastened its collapse, LJM2 was described as one of the limited partnerships that took debt off Enron's balance sheet and concealed the company's true financial condition.

Enron Broadband continued to build momentum in July 2000 with its announcement that it would hook up with video rental giant Blockbuster Inc. With Blockbuster providing the content, Enron Broadband intended to make the long-held dream of movies on demand over its fiber optic network a reality.

On August 23, 2000, the stock hit a high for the year of $90 a share. It would be the company's all-time high. Analysts predicted Enron stock would reach $100, even $115, within 12 months.

In September 2000, Enron said it would invest as much as $1.9 billion in its broadband operations between 2000 and 2001.

JANUARY I, 2001 THROUGH DECEMBER 2, 2001

A SPECTACULAR COLLAPSE

At a memorable employee meeting in January 2001, Skilling went even further than analysts. He predicted Enron's stock would go from $80 to $85, where it was then trading, to $120 within 12 months. He'd guessed wrong before on the stock price, Skilling told employees, but always on the low side.

Enron Broadband's Portland employees, gathered at the Alexis Hotel at RiverPlace to observe the proceedings via video feed, watched with glee. "The place went wild," Lavine said.

Like many of his co-workers, Lavine owned thousands of Enron stock options. For every dollar the stock increased over $38—the exercise price for his options—Lavine's holdings would jump in value about $30,000. "It was very exhilarating—going home and telling the wife, 'Guess what, we're $60,000 richer,'" Lavine said.

Yet for all the hype and hoopla, by early 2001, Enron Broadband was in deep trouble. The dot-com bubble had burst. Companies that Enron Broadband counted on as customers and trading partners closed their doors.

Enron Broadband disclosed in March that it had lost $64 million in 2000 on disappointing revenue of $408 million.

Worse yet, the trading that was supposed to be at the heart of Enron Broadband never materialized in the expected volume.

"We never believed in bandwidth trading," said Husein Kumber, a spokesman for Orlando, Florida-based EPIK Communications. "We just felt the market hadn't matured enough."

In addition to the disappointing financial numbers, Enron Broadband disclosed in March 2001 that it was terminating its 20-year agreement with Blockbuster. It also quietly began cutting costs, laying off as many as 200 of Enron Broadband's 300 Portland employees that spring.

Talk began circulating that Enron was going to shut down its broadband operations altogether, which Skilling emphatically denied. "In contrast to the rumor last week that we were backing out of this business, we are pedal to the metal," he told analysts in a March quarterly conference call.

Skilling, named Enron's CEO in February, and Ken Lay, Enron's chairman, returned to Portland in the spring to reassure anxious employees: Yes, the market was tough, but Enron was in the broadband business to stay, they said.

The broadband rank-and-file weren't so sure. "We were developing the network anticipating this huge growth surge, and you basically had a market that went off a cliff," said Chris Shirkoff, a contract engineer.

The company's quarterly revenue nose-dived to $16 million in the company's second quarter, down from $150 million in the same quarter a year earlier. In July, the company told Wall Street it would cut its subsidiary's expenses "to correspond to slower market development and the associated lower revenue outlook."

Later that month, Enron Broadband announced it was closing its Portland office and eliminating another 100 jobs. Since the beginning of the year, Enron's stock had fallen from more than $80 a share to $44.96 on July 25. Skilling criticized stock analysts who lowered their earnings predictions for the company. He admitted the broadband market was in "meltdown," but vowed to wait out the turmoil.

Within weeks, however, Skilling was gone. Shocked analysts and employees were told only that Skilling was leaving for personal reasons.

The final nail in the coffin of Enron Broadband, and Enron itself, came in October, when the parent company delivered the now infamous earnings report stating that it was reducing shareholders' equity by $1.2 billion, taking significant charges—$180 million for Broadband alone—against certain money-losing operations.

Later, Enron also disclosed that it was consolidating the financial results of LJM2 and several other partnerships into Enron's results, which had the effect of reducing earnings for four years by nearly $600 million.

The news sent Enron's stock into a tailspin from which it couldn't recover. Shares fell from $34 the day of the third-quarter earnings announcement to 26 cents by mid-November. On December 2, the company filed for bankruptcy protection.

DECEMBER 3, 2001 THROUGH TODAY

A PAINFUL AFTERMATH

Today, some former employees see a fitting justice that this company of "hard-core capitalists," who never hid their scorn for government regulators, was brought down not by a government agency but by the market itself. Investors, the ultimate free-market arbiters, felt misled and shunned Enron. "Clearly, Wall Street's expectations were for a rapidly evolving business," said Steve Elliott, Enron Broadband's former chief financial officer. "The business grew too fast, too many people, too many ideas. Our leadership was fractured with the move to Houston. It's sad. It was a fun place to work."

Enron Broadband did not bring Enron down. On that question, most employees agree. Enron's forays into the water market and mammoth power plants in India and Brazil did more harm to the company than the relatively tiny telecommunications arm.

But some former insiders also argue that Enron Broadband's failure did expose Enron's vulnerable underbelly. When the company was finally forced to admit that its much-hyped broadband arm was falling woefully short of expectations, it resulted in the first blow to Enron's credibility.

"All of a sudden, everything they had told everyone was open for question," said Stan Hanks, Enron Broadband's former vice president for engineering. "When outsiders realized the emperor was wearing no clothes, it turned into an analyst and media feeding frenzy."

A horde of lawyers has since jumped on Enron's carcass, accusing the company of gross deceit. Enron Broadband "was a daisy chain," said Paul Howse, a San Diego lawyer representing shareholders suing Enron. "They had no real customers and no real trading partners."

Others argue that Enron Broadband was simply too far ahead of the curve. "I happen to believe that their only fault was being too early and too aggressive," said Seth Libby, a senior analyst with Yankee Group.

The company's collapse cost workers their jobs and, in some cases, their financial security. Lavine's stock options, once worth $1.04 million on paper, became worthless.

"I was dumb, I was gullible," Lavine said. "I had a lot of depression for a while."

Lavine jokingly said he is doing "penance" for his time at Enron by working as a contract programmer for The Nature Conservancy.

Jim Hoekema, a broadband engineer who moved from Portland to Houston just to qualify for stock options, also is far out of the money. He reckons his 8,300 stock options were worth about

$431,600 at the market's peak. "If I had just dumped everything, I would have been rolling in cash," Hoekema said. "But I didn't because upper management—Jeff Skilling and Ken Lay—were telling us the stock would easily hit one-ten, one-twenty. . . . And it did—Skilling just had the decimal in the wrong place."

The ugly accusations of fraud have made Enron's collapse all the more painful. Said Kohnstamm: "I've gone from feeling good about making a contribution to a widely respected company to feeling stigmatized by my association with Enron."

"Accounting-gate" forever changed the way we look at number crunchers, yet the problems of Arthur Andersen & Co. didn't just start with Enron. David Ward and Loren Steffy of *Bloomberg Markets* uncover examples of past legal challenges, auditor-consultant conflicts, and greed.

David Ward and Loren Steffy

How Andersen Went Wrong

DUANE KULLBERG, then chief executive of Arthur Andersen & Co., says that as he read the three-page memo back in 1988, one word flashed in his mind: mutiny.

The document revealed that Gresham Brebach, head of Andersen's consulting business, had held a secret meeting at New York's 21 restaurant that April with a dozen of the firm's top consultants.

The consultants were furious at a noncompete clause placed in their contracts that would have prevented them from working for other consulting firms for a year if they left Andersen. They discussed the value of the consulting business if it split from Andersen, and they plotted strategy with a lawyer and an investment banker they'd invited to the meeting.

Kullberg, who ran Andersen from 1980 to 1989, says he realized that the meeting could mean only that Brebach was planning to lead an exodus of consultants from the accounting firm.

Three days after he was leaked the memo by a partner who'd attended the meeting, Kullberg summoned Brebach to his office and fired him.

A long-simmering internal battle between Andersen's auditors and consultants was about to boil over.

"MATCH IN THE TINDERBOX"

"I had fired one of their crown princes, and that was the match in the tinderbox," says Kullberg, 69, who retired at the end of that year. He's now lead plaintiff in a lawsuit aimed at protecting pension rights for former Andersen executives.

Brebach's firing sparked an internal war between consultants and auditors that more than a decade later, in 2000, would rend the firm in two—and help bring down the original enterprise.

From the early 1980s on, the firm's partners had become increasingly dependent on lucrative consulting fees. Once much of that revenue had disappeared from Andersen because of the split, all bets were off, say former company executives. Andersen's top managers, they say, struggled to find new revenue sources and often allowed auditors to overlook shoddy accounting by clients.

Evidence of those problems isn't hard to find. During the past five years, Andersen has been named as a defendant in 146 federal cases brought by clients and their shareholders, about 50 of which involve Enron.

ANDERSEN'S RECORD

That's more than double the number brought against PricewaterhouseCoopers LLP, the largest U.S. accounting firm. In the past five years, Andersen has paid four of the five largest settlements for audit failures.

"Senior officials at Andersen have trouble reconciling their duties to investors with their business interests," says Richard Breeden, who was chairman of the U.S. Securities and Exchange Commission from 1989 to 1993.

The U.S. Justice Department cited those trends when it indicted the firm in March for allegedly impeding an investigation into Enron Corp.'s collapse by shredding relevant documents.

On April 17, talks with the Justice Department aimed at settling the charges broke down, and the government is preparing for a May 6 criminal trial. A guilty verdict probably would prohibit Andersen from auditing U.S. companies.

"BIG PROBLEMS"

"Arthur Andersen had big problems before we indicted this case," Assistant U.S. Attorney Samuel Buell told a federal judge in Houston during a hearing on March 20.

Andersen spokesman Patrick Dorton says all accounting firms are common targets in shareholder lawsuits.

In July 1997, Andersen paid $90 million to settle shareholder claims against Colonial Realty Co., which went bankrupt in 1990. Colonial, based in Hartford, Connecticut, had used financial projections prepared by Andersen to raise money for real estate tax shelters.

Connecticut's attorney general, who investigated the firm's collapse, found it had corrupted an Andersen executive with $200,000 in cash payments, hotel stays, cruises, cars and assistance in getting loans.

"It was a systematic failure at Andersen," says Harold Williams, who, as SEC chairman from 1977 to 1981, was an early critic of allowing auditors to do consulting work. "Something is fundamentally wrong."

In May 2001, Andersen paid $110 million to settle claims that it had approved fraudulent audits at home appliance maker Sunbeam Corp.

ANOTHER $100 MILLION

One month later, in June 2001, it paid almost $100 million more to settle similar claims involving Houston-based Waste Management Inc., the biggest U.S. trash hauler, which had been acquired by USA Waste Services Inc. in 1998.

In March 2002, it agreed to pay $217 million to settle charges brought by investors who lost millions when the Baptist Foundation of Arizona, a nonprofit religious group that invested in real estate on behalf of elderly churchgoers, went bankrupt.

It backed out of the settlement on March 29, after its insurer—a subsidiary of Andersen's parent company, Andersen Worldwide—refused to pay.

In all, Andersen paid almost $400 million from 1997 to 2001 to settle claims related to audit failures, according to industry newsletter *Public Accounting Report.* Settlements involving the Baptist Foundation and Enron could double that figure.

RIVALS

None of Andersen's rivals have paid as much. Only Ernst & Young LLP paid a larger settlement for a single failure, shelling out $335 million for its work for Cendant Corp., owner of the Avis rental car company and Days Inn hotel chain.

Andersen has lost about 200 clients this year. The company's partnerships are voting to join rivals, and a special committee led by former Federal Reserve Chairman Paul Volcker recommended Andersen shed its tax operations and remaining consulting business to focus solely on auditing.

Chief Executive Joseph Berardino resigned in March, and the firm named Aldo Cardoso, a Paris-based partner who ran the firm's worldwide umbrella organization, to replace him.

Andersen told partners in a conference call on April 4 that it would cut 6,500 jobs to preserve cash and transfer much of its U.S. tax practices to Deloitte & Touche LLP.

LAWSUITS

Andersen also faces lawsuits by Enron shareholders seeking billions in damages. Those claims could leave the partnership unable to rebuild, even under the protection of a bankruptcy filing.

The firm's fate is particularly stunning because of the stellar reputation it once enjoyed. Arthur Andersen, a Northwestern University professor who founded the firm in 1913, was the first industry executive to hire only professionally trained accountants.

Under former Chief Executive Leonard Spacek, who took over after Andersen's death in 1947, the firm served as the conscience of the accounting industry.

When he was named to Andersen's oversight board, Volcker referred to Spacek's tenure as a time when Andersen was the "gold standard" for accounting firms.

Spacek, who retired in 1973 and died two years ago, exhorted auditors to champion investors by resisting clients' efforts to cut corners.

ANDERSEN'S PAST

He helped create the Accounting Principles Board, an organization that set accounting and ethical standards. SEC officials still quote from Spacek's speeches calling for greater oversight and more public accountability for auditors.

"Arthur Andersen historically has been the type of firm that would stand up to its clients," says Scott Whisenant, a University of Houston accounting professor.

Spacek did something else with lasting implications for the accounting industry: He introduced it to consulting. In 1954,

Andersen auditors, working with International Business Machines Corp., convinced General Electric Co. to install a Univac I, the first mainframe computer.

The computer system was designed to help GE streamline its payroll and help its auditors better monitor expenses.

Within two years, Spacek was making speeches warning that accounting firms' burgeoning consulting businesses could compromise their independence and undermine the integrity of audits.

CONSULTING CONTRACTS

The warnings didn't slow Andersen's own pursuit of consulting contracts. By 1978, Andersen's consulting practice led the industry and accounted for 21 percent of the firm's $546 million in revenue, according to a Harvard Business School study of Andersen.

By 1984, consulting had surpassed auditing in profitability, the study found.

While consulting was boosting profits, former executives say, it was tearing Andersen apart. Consultants at Andersen had been complaining for years that they were underrepresented in the firm's management. They wanted their pay to reflect the success of their business, which was driving Andersen's growth.

In 1986, two years before Kullberg quelled the consultants' mutiny, Gresham Brebach's predecessor, Victor Millar, left to form a consulting group at Saatchi & Saatchi Plc.

Later, Kullberg rejected an overture from the British advertising firm to buy Andersen's consulting operation outright.

HOLDING ON

Then CEO Maurice Saatchi flew to Chicago to meet with Kullberg at Andersen's headquarters. "We had no intention of getting rid of our consulting business," Kullberg says. "When I said it wasn't for sale, he abruptly got up, turned around and walked out of my office."

Saatchi didn't return a call seeking comment.

In order to stem future defections after Millar's departure, Kullberg forced through changes designed to keep more consultants from leaving. Andersen amended its bylaws to require that consultants sign one-year noncompete agreements.

Brebach and other consultants got furious and began demanding greater control. "We were getting a disproportionately small piece of the income, given what we were contributing," Brebach says.

Brebach, now chairman of Seurat Co., a Waltham, Massachusetts-based consulting firm, says he never intended to lead a rebellion within Andersen.

SECRET MEETING

He called the secret meeting in April 1988 to determine the value of Andersen's consulting business as part of a plan to demand a larger role in running the firm, he says.

The uprising nonetheless sparked changes within Andersen to keep its consultants happy. After firing Brebach, Kullberg created an internal panel that studied how to deal with the consultants' mounting discontent.

The group recommended splitting the firm into two units under one worldwide organization.

At the end of 1988, the partners voted to form Andersen Consulting—now known as Accenture Ltd.—and Arthur Andersen LLP and to christen the new global entity Andersen Worldwide, which would be based in Geneva and serve as a parent company for Andersen partnerships around the world.

Andersen Consulting would focus on large consulting projects, while Arthur Andersen would bid on consulting work for smaller companies to make up its lost revenue.

RESIGNATION

Kullberg resigned voluntarily after the vote. The firm's partners voted to elect Lawrence Weinbach as Kullberg's replacement.

George Shaheen was appointed head of Andersen Consulting, and Richard Measelle, who would be involved in two of Andersen's biggest audit failures, would run the audit business.

Weinbach, now chairman of Unisys Corp., declined to comment. Shaheen, who ran online grocer Webvan Group Inc. before it filed for bankruptcy in July 2001, also declined to comment.

Under the agreement, Arthur Andersen was supposed to handle consulting contracts with firms that had a market capitalization of $2 billion or less, while Andersen Consulting focused on larger firms. The two would not share revenue, and that division created an immediate disparity between auditors and consultants.

AVERAGE BASE SALARY: $600,000

Consultants were earning $50,000 to $100,000 a year more than their audit colleagues, the Harvard study estimated. Partners currently earn an average base salary of about $600,000 a year.

Soon, each side was accusing the other of encroaching on clients. The differences became irreconcilable, and in December 1997, Andersen Consulting filed for divorce, asking the International Chamber of Commerce's Court of Arbitration in Paris to allow it to split from Andersen Worldwide.

"The agreements that we reached provided for separate but complementary businesses, but since that time, Arthur Andersen itself has embarked on a strategic intent to build its own separate and distinct consulting practice," Shaheen said in a Bloomberg News interview at the time. "For three or four years, we've been in internal discussions to resolve that, and we have been unable to do that internally."

$100 MILLION BREAKUP FEE

In August 2000, the court ruled that Andersen Consulting could separate. Andersen Worldwide had earlier rejected an offer from the consulting arm to pay more than $1 billion to split.

In the arbitration, Arthur Andersen received a $100 million breakup fee and overnight went from annual revenue of $16.3 billion to $7.3 billion.

With its revenue lopped in half by the split, Andersen set out to bolster its own consulting business by seeking more clients. That drive for fees caused Andersen to cut corners, say regulators investigating its work.

For example, Andersen didn't change its audit policies or discipline key personnel in the wake of the Sunbeam and Waste Management cases.

Several top managers who oversaw the Waste Management account also were involved in approving Enron's accounting after some partners questioned it, according to internal Andersen memos.

"GRIT THEIR TEETH"

"They don't want to lose the account, so they grit their teeth and go along with it," says Roderick Hills, a former SEC chairman and Waste Management board member who led the company's internal investigation into its accounting. "The more fees, the more danger."

The seeds of the company's later woes had been planted almost two decades before, as consulting and other services began to overtake auditing as revenue producers.

In one of the earliest examples, creditors blamed Andersen when automaker John DeLorean's car company collapsed in 1982. DeLorean had left General Motors Corp. and started DeLorean Motor Co. in 1975, vowing to spawn an auto-making revolution.

His 12-cylinder sports car with gull-wing doors and stainless steel skin became best known for its role in the *Back to the Future* movies. It was never a commercial success.

Creditors, including parts suppliers and the British government, claimed Andersen auditors knew or should have known that DeLorean, through a shell business he controlled in Panama, had diverted $17.6 million from the car company to accounts in Europe.

IGNORING FRAUD

Andersen ignored the fraudulent accounting because DeLorean was a top client of Andersen at the time, says Michael Hess, an attorney who led the 1998 trial against the firm to recover losses for DeLorean creditors.

"Andersen didn't have an automotive company as a client, and there was a big desire to get a foothold into that market," Hess says. "It would mean both prestige and revenue for them."

A Manhattan jury found Andersen guilty of negligence and breach of contract, ordering it in March 1998 to pay as much as $110 million. Andersen settled the case a year later for about $27.8 million, according to David Allard, a lawyer for the DeLorean trustees.

Andersen also agreed to pay $35 million to the British government, which had helped finance DeLorean's factory in Northern Ireland. The firm settled the case without admitting wrongdoing.

SCAPEGOAT

Andersen spokesman Robert Hubbell said at the time that the firm had been made a scapegoat for DeLorean's schemes. The DeLorean audits were handled by Measelle, the future head of Andersen's auditing unit.

Measelle didn't return phone calls seeking comment.

Andersen's relationship with Commercial Financial Services Inc. provided another early warning sign.

Andersen began auditing CFS's books in 1988, and by the mid-1990s, it was providing a host of consulting services for the company as well, generating fees of $3.8 million from 1995 to 1998.

CFS started as a family-owned business in Muskogee, Oklahoma, in 1986. Its founder, William Bartmann, had gone bust selling oil field equipment and was angered by what he considered the shabby treatment of debtors by collection agencies.

DEFAULTED LOANS

He bought a portfolio of defaulted loans and, working with his wife, Kathy, from their kitchen table, made a profit by using polite persuasion to collect the debts, according to a lawsuit filed last year against Andersen by the company's bankruptcy trustee.

By 1998, when the company collapsed, the Bartmanns were among the 400 richest Americans as listed by *Forbes* magazine, with a net worth of $1.4 billion.

At Andersen's urging, CFS began to concentrate on the riskier businesses of collecting bad credit card debt and packaging and selling bad loans to investors—a move that contributed to CFS's demise, the lawsuit says.

The company overestimated its ability to collect overdue loans and filed for bankruptcy in December 1998, two months after Bartmann resigned amid allegations that, to boost profit, CFS sold some of the bad loans to another company it controlled.

INAPPROPRIATE ADVICE

"Andersen, as a counselor and an auditor, did not appropriately advise CFS and was partially responsible for its demise," says Harley Tropin, an attorney representing CFS's bankruptcy trustee.

Andersen hasn't responded to the lawsuit. Andersen spokesman Dorton declines to comment on CFS or any other lawsuit involving the firm.

Even as it allegedly overlooked accounting lapses at CFS, Andersen was ignoring even bigger problems at Waste Management, according to the SEC.

Waste Management paid Andersen almost $20 million from 1991 to 1997 for audit and consulting work. At the same time, according to SEC investigators, Waste Management was overstating revenue and fraudulently representing the financial state of its business so it could meet Wall Street expectations.

According to the SEC investigation, the company undervalued the depreciation on its trucks and equipment, failed to record expenses on its balance sheets and postponed costs.

"COOKED THE BOOKS"

"For years, these defendants cooked the books, enriched themselves, preserved their jobs and duped unsuspecting shareholders," SEC Enforcement Director Tom Newkirk said when the agency filed civil charges against Waste Management executives in March.

For four years, Andersen's auditors, backed by senior executives in the firm's Chicago headquarters, approved the practices.

Robert Allgyer, known as a "rainmaker" inside Andersen for his skill at winning business by pitching consulting, tax and other nonaudit services, was named lead engagement partner. Waste Management became one of Andersen's "crown jewel" clients.

Allgyer first brought the accounting problems to senior Andersen executives' attention in January 1994, saying the trash hauler had overstated 1993 earnings by $128 million, or 21.5 percent of net income, according to internal SEC documents obtained by Bloomberg News.

WASTE MANAGEMENT

Senior executives, including Steve Samek, then head of the firm's commercial audit business, agreed that Andersen would approve the fraudulent audits and urge Waste Management to correct the situation, the SEC report says. Then–Chief Executive Measelle was briefed on the decision, according to the report.

Waste Management didn't address the issue, and the following year, Allgyer again met with senior Andersen executives, identifying $163 million in accounting errors, the report says. Again, Andersen approved the trash hauler's financial statement.

In 1995, Waste Management attempted to cover up past misstatements by using profits from the sale of its stake in Service-Master LP's ServiceMaster Consumer Services subsidiary, the documents say. Allgyer approved that in January 1996.

In October 1996, Samek was told about the improper accounting and was told it was "an area of SEC exposure." Neither man ordered the problem corrected, the report says.

ALLEGED FRAUD

The alleged fraud was exposed in 1998, when Waste Management was purchased by USA Waste Services and the new management restated earnings by $1.7 billion.

A subsequent SEC investigation found Andersen responsible for approving audits it knew were fraudulent, and in June 2001, regulators fined the firm $7 million, the largest SEC penalty ever assessed against an auditor. Samek, who was by then U.S. country managing partner and on the firm's executive committee, was not named in the settlement—at Andersen's insistence, according to two people familiar with the case. Measelle also wasn't named.

Andersen settled the case without admitting or denying wrongdoing. During the investigation, Allgyer was asked by SEC investigators whether the millions Andersen had been paid by Waste Management clouded the firm's judgment. He replied, according to the SEC report, "We are in the business to make money."

FIRM'S BIGGEST CUSTOMER

No client made more money for Andersen than Enron, which by 2000 was the firm's biggest customer. Enron paid $52 million in auditing and consulting fees in 2000, and Andersen partners openly discussed the prospects that those fees could double.

"They were getting paid too much money, and they were enchanted by the success of Enron," former SEC Chairman Hills says.

Andersen was aware of accounting snares at Enron more than a decade ago. The firm helped unravel a 1987 scandal involving Enron's oil trading division in Valhalla, New York.

Traders sold short millions of barrels of oil in a bet that prices would fall. Unraveling the transactions, which were uncovered by Enron's internal auditors, ultimately cost the company about $140 million, says Michael Muckleroy, former Enron vice president in charge of the cleanup.

QUESTIONS ABOUT ENRON

By 2001, questions about Enron's accounting prompted Andersen partners to discuss whether it should continue auditing the Houston energy trader.

In February of that year, eight Andersen partners in Houston met to discuss the Enron account via telephone with seven senior firm officials, according to a memo written by Michael Jones, one of the Houston partners.

The auditors were concerned about private partnerships set up and run by Enron Chief Financial Officer Andrew Fastow. Fastow was using the partnerships to buy Enron debt, poorly performing power plants and other weak assets, effectively hiding huge losses from shareholders.

The Andersen partners discussed Fastow's compensation for running the partnerships, which Enron later would reveal was more than $30 million, the memo says.

Auditors questioned Enron's use of an accounting process known as mark-to-market, which allowed the company to book immediately all of the revenue from a multiyear trading contract.

"INTELLIGENT GAMBLING"

One of the partners referred to mark-to-market as "intelligent gambling," Jones writes.

"Ultimately, the conclusion was reached to retain Enron as a client," Jones says in the memo.

Two sentences after that, he says the Andersen partners discussed the possibility that Enron's fees—$25 million for auditing and $27 million for consulting in 2000—could double. They questioned whether such large fees would appear to compromise Andersen's independence as an auditor.

"We discussed that the concerns should not be on the magnitude of the fees but on the nature of the fees," Jones writes.

Six months later, Andersen got another alarm signal. James Hecker, a partner in the Houston office who wasn't assigned to the Enron account, got a call from Enron Vice President Sherron Watkins.

MASKING BIGGER PROBLEMS

Watkins told Hecker she believed Fastow's partnerships masked widespread accounting fraud at the company, according to a memo Hecker wrote detailing the conversation.

Hecker forwarded her concerns to three other Andersen partners, including David Duncan, who was in charge of the Enron audit, he says in the memo. Andersen fired Duncan on January 15.

A day after talking to Hecker, Watkins wrote a letter to Enron Chairman Kenneth Lay, warning that accounting improprieties could destroy the company. Watkins's memo became the focal point of U.S. congressional investigations into Enron's collapse.

The warnings—and Andersen's refusal to act on them—factored into the Justice Department's decision to indict Andersen on March 14 for shredding Enron audit documents after the SEC had begun an investigation into $586 million in earnings restatements related to the partnerships.

FACTORS DETERMINING
CRIMINAL CONDUCT

"In determining whether to charge an entity with criminal conduct, we consider many factors, including the seriousness of the alleged offense, the firm's history of wrongdoing, the pervasiveness of the wrongdoing and the need to deter others from similar activity," Deputy Attorney General Larry Thompson said at a press conference the day the indictment was unsealed.

The indictment said Andersen had also engaged in a systematic program to purge its computer hard drives and electronic mail system of Enron files.

Andersen maintains that the document shredding was the fault of a few partners and employees and says the firm and its management are blameless.

The case marks the first time the government has prosecuted a firm of Andersen's size. Jacob Frankel, a former SEC enforcement lawyer who's now in private practice, says government prosecutors probably weighed Andersen's previous audit failures before deciding to seek an indictment.

"PERVASIVE WRONGDOING"

"They have to feel they have come across pervasive wrongdoing or such egregious conduct that criminal prosecution is the only way," Frankel says.

For Andersen employees, the indictment punctuated the firm's slim chance of survival. "The indictment was a deathblow," says Anthony Gutierrez, a partner in Andersen's marketing division in New York.

Clients began to flee. Apache Corp., a Houston-based oil and gas producer, decided to switch in late March, after using Andersen for 47 years. "It was difficult," spokesman Tony Lentini says. "We worked with a lot of good people, but there's a taint."

In some cases, Andersen isn't even trying to keep clients. When insurer Argonaut Group Inc.'s board met to consider whether to keep Andersen as its auditor, the firm decided not to make a presentation, says David LeFlore, Argonaut's vice president and general counsel.

"They were scheduled to appear and at the last minute chose not to," he says.

LESSONS FOR THE INDUSTRY

Andersen's troubles hold lessons for the entire accounting industry, experts say. Firms too often use audit work as a loss leader to attract consulting clients, says Wayne Shaw, an accounting professor at Southern Methodist University in Dallas.

He adds that accountants are too reluctant to stand up to clients for fear of losing lucrative contracts.

"The standards aren't demanding enough to provide sufficient information to investors," says Shaw. "We've set up a system where creativity is rewarded. I'm not sure you want an auditor to be creative."

Former SEC Chairman Arthur Levitt, who's now a director of Bloomberg LP, campaigned unsuccessfully for several years to force audit firms to shed some of their consulting businesses. The agency in 2000 settled for a requirement that companies list in SEC filings how much they pay their accountants for audit and nonaudit work.

"LOST THE ABILITY"

Now Congress is weighing new ways to ensure auditors remain independent from their clients. "We've lost the ability of these firms to come out and tell people bad things," Shaw says.

That's a concern Spacek, Andersen's revered CEO, voiced in 1956: Accountants, Spacek said, are too reluctant to prevent financial improprieties and too willing to shirk their responsibility to the public.

"The most serious problems in our profession are caused by our own self-indulgence," he said. "We must wait for the catastrophe, because we do not have a sufficiently strong or self-appraising accounting profession to right this public wrong before—not after—serious injury results."

Those words, almost 50 years later, may serve as Andersen's epitaph.

If you were a company, how would your financials look? Rob Walker in *Slate* becomes a spin doctor for his own life, burying his personal shortcomings deep in the small print. He provides a unique, humorous new look at an era in which the term "pro forma" has become synonymous with deception.

Rob Walker

My Pro Forma Life

XEROX HAS AGREED to restate several years' worth of its financials and pay a record-shattering $10 million penalty. Meanwhile, the SEC now seems likely to go after Qwest. Months after Enron, in other words, accounting scandals flourish. But while others may criticize, and seek restrictions on, the clever ways that public companies have found to polish up reality on a quarterly basis, I choose to embrace those practices. Consider "pro forma results." Pro forma literally means "for the sake of form," but *The Wall Street Journal* sheds light on what the phrase means to corporations in America when it explains that "a growing number present their earnings on a 'pro forma' basis, 'as if' certain expenses didn't exist." This is not a scandalous idea; it's a delightful one.

On a pro forma basis, I'm having an outstanding year. In calendar 2002 I've gone to the gym on a regular basis and expect this trend to continue and to have a material impact on my health going forward. Year-to-date, my health has improved by a solid 15 percent on an annualized basis.

These results do not reflect certain items. Loss of good health and potential mortality stemming from 62 consecutive quarters of above-plan intake of assorted spirits, tobacco and other substances reliant on mouth-to-lung delivery systems, and miscellaneous off-book chemical and pharmaceutical substances, are addressed in a onetime write-down. Results also include the application of "goodwill" regarding those days, and in some cases weeks, when actual gym attendance was negatively impacted or curtailed by visits to the racetrack, where I ate oysters and drank Budweiser. Finally, a recent post-workout lunch of a 22-ounce bone-in rib steak at Smith & Wollensky and three shots of bourbon is treated here as a nonrecurring expense. I'll never do that again! I encourage you to focus on these pro forma results as a truer portrait of the state of my health than "traditional measures," which suggest that I have been dead for at least a year.

In an unrelated onetime charge, pro forma results do not include a restatement of costs associated with the acquisition during the last calendar year of a SlamMan computerized boxing workout partner. My revised forecast includes no expectation that previously anticipated benefits to cardiovascular function or muscle tone will materialize in the foreseeable future, apart from those that may result from transporting SlamMan, ideally by aerial means, from my second-floor office to the sidewalk. However, there is a current lack of visibility regarding the timing of that event.

Next I'd like to address the "work" portion of my life. Again, results are gangbusters, pro forma-wise, and are in line with recent guidance. Basically, I've never been so productive, and all key internal efficiency metrics are through the roof.

These work results include certain items not recognized by traditional standards of accounting for what it is I do all day. Hours and full days previously recognized as losses due to apparently "wasted" time have been recategorized. In some cases (staring off into space, quietly weeping with the office door closed), these activities now count toward "research and development," and their cost will be depreciated over a span of 79 years. This adjustment recognizes a shift in market conditions (and a recent rise in the number of years that have elapsed since my birth) affecting the time horizon for an anticipated "big success." The 79-year time frame assumes that I will continue working, productively, until I am 112 years old. (See health results above.) I remain confident that the market is undervaluing my "work" and that additional, carefully targeted R&D efforts (including a "guerrilla" rebranding campaign conducted aggressively at parties, bars, and other gathering points of key "influentials," such as various editors who tend not to return my phone calls) over the course of that revised time frame will stoke demand and help unlock this hidden value.

The remaining "wasted time" losses have been recategorized as unrealized, noncash gains, associated with the anticipated completion, at an undetermined time, of a comic novel on the theme of procrastination, which certain indicators suggest should have massive upside potential. Current regulations offer little guidance and give much leeway in placing a value on contracts for books that have not been written, pitched, or even mentioned to an agent. This is a relief because I have a feeling that strict oversight might have discouraged me.

That brings me to the final item on the agenda: my love life. I remain in a long-term relationship with a significant other, and as in prior quarters, my love grows and grows.

To address some concerns regarding transparency in this area, I wish to disclose at this time that I have in recent years, as a hedge against the volatile nature of love, entered into approximately 913 discrete partnerships with entities. A number of these relationships were formed "offshore" in the Caribbean, where they are less taxing to maintain. The details are complex (see footnotes), but each of my "special purpose entities" (as I like to call them) is distinct. Extensive measures have been taken to prevent their recognition by my significant other and our pro forma relationship.

Some of these ventures may be categorized as high risk, and indeed I am currently in the process of unwinding a number of them, as quickly as I possibly can. If everything works out, the impact on affection flow and the day-to-day operations of my love life (and indeed my health) should be immaterial. Knock wood.

In summary, then, everything is great, and the future is full of limitless possibilities. However, please note that some of the statements made by me in this report are forward-looking in nature, and actual results may differ materially from those projected in forward-looking statements. On the other hand, these pro forma results have been reviewed and certified by my longtime accountant, so there's probably nothing to worry about.

A financial story can transport you to a new place and provide a tutorial on something you'd never even thought about. This story by Wayne Curtis in *The Atlantic Monthly* takes us to Newfoundland for the harvesting of ice from icebergs to be melted for use in bottled water, beer, and vodka. As in far less exotic businesses, competition is fierce.

Wayne Curtis

The Iceberg Wars

"IT'S RIGHT OVER THERE where it happened," Cecil Stockley told me as we motored out of the Twillingate harbor aboard the M.V. *Iceberg Alley.* Located on Newfoundland's northern coast, Twillingate not only has a name seemingly borrowed from *The Hobbit*—it has the landscape as well. The treeless hills are woolly with mosses and lichens; in the late afternoon light they appeared as if draped in chenille. All that was lacking was a cloaked figure holding a crooked staff and gazing enigmatically off into the middle distance.

What happened is this: in the summer of 1998 an iceberg floated into the harbor and ran aground. That was not in itself unusual—some summers hundreds of icebergs drift just offshore from Twillingate, and occasionally one or two find their way into the harbor. But what happened next *was* unusual: a barge equipped with a crane loomed from around the headlands, tethered itself to the iceberg, and started noisily and methodically chipping away at it with a device designed for dredging rock. "I think everybody in town was kind of peeved off," said Stockley, who has been running iceberg excursions since 1985. "Here we were, trying to do a boat-tour operation, and people were stealing the iceberg right in front of our eyes."

Iceberg tourism is one of the few new growth industries in Newfoundland, an island still reeling from the collapse of the cod fishery a decade ago. Icebergs are becoming to Newfoundland what wines are to Napa Valley: tourists can be overheard talking about individual specimens in precise yet lofty terms, discussing the cragginess of towers and the sapphire radiance of blue streaks as if comparing rare vintages. Island gift shops sell framed photos of especially charismatic icebergs; the shots have the gauzy, soft-focus feel of cheesy studio photos.

But as the incident in Twillingate suggests, icebergs have lately attracted the notice of another business: the extractive industry, which harvests floating ice for processing into vodka, beer, and drinking water. Although commercial harvesting began only in the past decade, iceberg products are rapidly evolving from a novelty to a commodity, and the business is gearing up for greater industrialization. Sipping iceberg beer at a hotel bar in St. John's the next evening, I chatted with Ron Stamp, the vice-president of sales and marketing at Iceberg Industries, a firm he co-founded in 1996. "We have," he told me with satisfaction, "gone beyond the pet-rock stage."

The possibility of towing icebergs to the Middle East and other arid regions around the world was studied and widely discussed during the 1970s. Nothing much came of the idea, for a number of reasons, chief among them being that it was stupid. (One report noted that it would take 128 days to tow an iceberg from Antarctica to the Middle East—twenty-four days longer than it would take for the iceberg to melt.)

Although towing icebergs proved impractical, harvesting ice at sea did not. The first commercial efforts, by the Canadian Iceberg Vodka Corporation, were modest. Fishing boats would edge alongside an iceberg, and workers wielding chain saws lubricated with vegetable oil would lop off a manageable section and hoist it aboard with large nets. A more ambitious harvesting technology was later developed by Iceberg Industries, the company responsible for the Twillingate caper. This involved a crane and an eight-claw grapple installed on a salvaged barge (originally used to transport molasses on the Great Lakes) equipped with heated storage tanks.

The harvesting of ice is tricky but not terribly sophisticated. During the season, which runs from April to late November, Iceberg Industries sends spotter planes in search of bergs that have drifted into coves, away from the swells of the open ocean. The barge then chugs in, secures itself to its prey, and begins chomping away. Each bite of the grapple picks up about half a ton of ice, which is fed into a crusher and conveyed into the tanks for melting. When the barge is filled to capacity (about 1,200 tons), it returns to the firm's tank farm, on Newfoundland's Avalon Peninsula, where the meltwater is stored for bottling, brewing, and making vodka. "It's not rocket science," Stamp admits. "You hang on, chew it up, hope for the best, and get out of there before the damn thing rolls over."

Stamp says that his company has already completed much of the engineering for its next project—essentially a floating bottling plant. This operation will be centered on what Stamp calls a "mother ship," where the meltwater is to be filtered and bottled. A seventy-five-foot-long iceberg excavator will do the actual harvesting ("It's basically like coal mining," Stamp says), and ice fragments will be suctioned back to the mother ship by a sort of pneumatic tube. "We got the idea from central vacuuming," Stamp says.

The Canadian Iceberg Vodka Corporation is also gearing up for a major expansion. Before the end of the year the company hopes to start construction on a 240,000-square-foot drinking-water bottling plant near the tip of Newfoundland's Great Northern

Peninsula, close to productive iceberg fields. "We've developed a conveyor-and-auger system, and we'll use mining techniques to carve into the side of the iceberg," Gary Pollack, the company's president, told me. "It's very similar to open-pit mining." Pollack envisions a fleet of "maybe thirty ships" that will eventually prowl the seas in search of icebergs, making frequent trips back to the plant.

Talk of these projects inevitably raises the question, Why go to the considerable expense and hassle of capturing and melting icebergs? Why not, say, just back a tanker truck up to a garden hose?

The answer, not surprisingly, has to do with marketing. "A lot of people want pure water, and they'll pay the price," Pollack says. Proselytizers are quick to point out that the water in these icebergs fell on Greenland as snow 10,000 or more years ago and has been bound up in glaciers ever since, safely sequestered from modern contaminants. Pollack and Stamp claim that their product is purer than spring water (which is merely filtered naturally) and more natural than distilled water (which is mechanically processed). "It's great that a large inland city can clean its drinking water and strip out impurities," Stamp says. "But ten million people pee in it on a daily basis. And you know what? Nobody peed in mine. Isn't that worth an extra ten cents a bottle?"

"We're talking about a major, major pure product—it's the purest water on earth," Pollack says. Iceberg water is so pure, he claims, that the vodka produced from it can be consumed in quantity with little or no risk of hangover. "I've seen people drink a whole bottle and not have any problem," he says. "Not that I'm recommending that to the general consumer."

Although no environmentalist opposition has arisen to the mining of icebergs, the impact on tourism has yet to be fully gauged. After Stockley and others made the press aware of the Twillingate iceberg grab, Iceberg Industries untethered itself from the local attraction and moved up the coast, where other icebergs awaited safely out of view of tourists. "Tourism has its place," Stamp admits, although he insists that his industry's expansion offers an entrepreneurial opportunity for the tourist trade: "People do factory tours all the time."

About a dozen tourists were aboard Stockley's boat the day I took the harbor tour. Most stood at the bow, some doing that annoying Kate Winslet splayed-arms thing from *Titanic,* others quietly scanning the horizon with binoculars, as if tracking a wily quarry. In time an iceberg was spotted in the distance, an event that triggered much excited gesturing.

I peered through my binoculars and saw it, a white apostrophe punctuating the hazy line between sky and sea. It looked uncommonly small—not only physically but metaphorically as well. What was once a terror of the sea, inciting awe in landscape painters of the nineteenth century, balefully stalking shipping lanes in the twentieth, now seemed captive and defeated—destined to end up in dreamy snapshots or decanted into plastic half-liter bottles.

Getting from point A to point B in an 18-wheeler is all about high-level mathematics and logistics, not garbled messages from dispatchers on CB radios. David Diamond in *Wired* introduces us to the creator of the modern system. It's the kind of story well off the beaten path to which that magazine's readers have grown accustomed.

David Diamond

The Trucker and the Professor

FOR A BRIEF, shining moment of national obsession in the Ford and Carter administrations, America's truckers ascended to heroic cultural status—they were the cowboys or dotcommers of their day. Americans glorified the risk-taking and self-reliance and independence of these peripatetic heroes by adopting their colorful CB lingo (referring to motorcycles as "crotch rockets" and rest areas as "pickle parks") and praising them in song. Who could forget those lines from the 1976 hit "Convoy": "Yeah, them hogs is startin' to close up my sinuses. Mercy sakes, you better back off another 10."

The romance is gone. Today's trucker is likely to have a lot in common with Orlando Mitchell, the man to my left, a genial, contemplative guy in a plaid shirt who is hauling 42,000 pounds of batter from Cleveland, Ohio, to Gloucester, Massachusetts, as an employee of Marten Transport, a $260 million national carrier. From the second Mitchell starts his engine in the morning, a dispatcher tracks his exact location and sends him regular instructions, keeping him on a tight electronic leash that makes liberty and leisure a thing of the past.

In the freewheeling days of the CB craze, a trucker like Mitchell would deliver his load in Gloucester, amble to the nearest truck stop, reach for a pay phone to contact a dispatcher or broker, and ask for a new load. In some cases, he might search for shipment requests on a truck stop corkboard. The process, called "dialing for diesels," typically allowed the driver to lounge around and kill time until a load could be rounded up—it might have involved an overnight stay—and he would then "deadhead" (drive an empty truck) to his next pickup.

That sort of rambling life is unimaginable today. Like the routing of IP packets on a communications network, the routing of trucks on the nation's 42,794-mile interstate highway network is handled systematically by satellites and software. Mitchell rarely uses the CB inside his 17-ton Peterbilt Model 379; instead, his main connection with the outside world is what he refers to as his "Qualcomm," a laptop-sized device that serves as a satellite link to Marten's corporate headquarters in Mondovi, Wisconsin.

When a red light appears on the dashboard in front of us, Mitchell pulls over the first chance he gets and reaches back for the gadget—Qualcomm's Omni Tracks—to check his new LCD message. It tells him that after he drops the batter at 10 A.M., in a warehouse grafted onto the offices of seafood purveyor Gorton's of Gloucester, he is to adjust the refrigeration unit to minus 10 degrees Fahrenheit and wait for a load of fish sticks at 2:30 P.M., which he will haul 1,086 miles to a warehouse in Lithia Springs, Georgia. It tells him where in Raphine, Virginia, to fuel up during that trip, how much fuel to get (63.8 gallons of diesel), and what it will cost. As he rumbles northward on the New Jersey Turnpike toward Massachusetts, he could at any moment get a message detailing where he should head after Lithia Springs.

Independence? The closest Mitchell ever gets to that is passing exit 12 on Interstate 70—the turnoff for downtown Independence, Missouri.

Truckers like Mitchell are the pawns in the burgeoning logistics industry, a vast economic heartland that includes the shipping and warehousing of goods. A term once generally limited to the military, logistics is now viewed as a brass ring for business. When consultants talk about "squeezing efficiencies" from the supply chain that stretches from raw material to consumer, much of the opportunity for the squeezing lurks in logistics, a field so broad it accounts for an estimated $1.06 trillion of the U.S. gross domestic product—more than defense. Despite the slowing national economy, total revenue of third-party logistics companies like Penske Logistics and FedEx Logistics rose 24 percent in 2000 to $56.4 billion, according to Cass Information Systems.

But within logistics, nowhere is the potential for savings as great as it is among the 2.5 million Class 8 trucks that, at any one time, are driving America's highways. Transportation is the largest individual component of logistics costs, and trucking is the primary means of conveyance. Of each dollar spent on moving freight in the U.S., 80 cents is devoted to trucks. When companies outsource transportation procurement—as they are doing today in record numbers—they rely on software companies like Logistics.com, i2 Transportation, and Manugistics to squeeze efficiencies out of the hard-to-forecast areas of route planning and carrier bidding. In the game that is trucking logistics, scheduling, planning, and route mapping are increasingly determined without human intervention.

To get a firsthand look at modern trucking, I've arranged to hitch a ride with Mitchell and his 50-pound sacks of batter. To get a firsthand look at modern logistics, I visit Yosef (Yossi) Sheffi, a balding 53-year-old Israeli who has spent the past three decades bringing high-level mathematics to America's highways. Currently director of the MIT Center for Transportation and Logistics Studies, Sheffi has drawn from general mathematical insights into optimization to create decision-making systems that change the way trucking gets done. He has teased out algorithms and put them into practice both in companies he's owned and in those he has advised. He has founded five logistics-related companies since the late 1980s—so far he has sold four of them for a profit—and has consulted for some of the nation's largest shippers and carriers. David Closs, professor of logistics at Michigan State University, calls Sheffi "one of the few gurus" in the field, and Ted Farris, a professor of logistics at the University of North Texas, says simply, "In terms of linking the thinking to practice, Sheffi is the leader."

Sheffi's office is oversize for an academic's, containing no fewer than eight flip charts and a whiteboard. Perched on a bookshelf that runs for maybe 20 feet is his collection of model trucks bearing the names of various carriers. "Which truck goes where and how it is routed are very difficult questions," he explains, "because you have to simultaneously consider millions of possible movements. The number of decisions grows exponentially as you consider not only how the trucks go or how the freight is routed but all the possible combinations. And every time you change one variable, everything else has to change to achieve optimization."

The fundamental problem facing transport companies boils down to finding the best route between points A and B. Carriers come in two flavors: less-than-truckload and truckload. In the less-than-truckload sector, one rig carries goods for a variety of shippers just like FedEx carries packages. Less-than-truckload companies have a set of terminals and consolidate their shipments as they go along. As in the business of commercial air travel, locations and schedules are essentially fixed. The challenge for companies in this sector is to keep trucks full as consistently as possible. For example, when transporting goods from Philadelphia to Chicago, a carrier will determine which truck to use, at what time, and following which route—through Pittsburgh, Cleveland, or Detroit. (Or should the truck unload the goods it's hauling to be picked up by a different Chicago-bound conveyance and instead grab a new load bound for, say, St. Louis?) A single less-than-truckload carrier may have hundreds of terminals. "If you have four terminals you may have 10 decision variables," explains Sheffi. "If you have 400 terminals you might get 400 million." And like that butterfly in Beijing flapping its wings, each decision affects the entire network.

The so-called truckload world—the one in which Mitchell and his batter live—has its own set of daunting decisions to make. If a truckload company with a fleet of 10,000 vehicles is called upon to haul Pine-Sol from Boston to Detroit, should it take the job? And if so, what should it charge? Which driver should it use? If the rig goes to Detroit, what happens when it gets there in two days— will it have to wait three more days for another load? If the truck is already in Boston, is there a better arrangement that would mean hauling goods to Atlanta, instead of Detroit? Or should it just hang in Boston for a day to see if a better job comes along?

The cost of shipping one particular load of goods is not the only consideration. A carrier must also work around a truck's maintenance schedule, for example, or try to position trucks favorably for future trips, or deal with a driver who wants to end up at his kid's wedding in Santa Fe on Friday.

This last point has become particularly vexing in the scheme of logistics. The era of deregulation has brought with it not only increased competition but increased employee dissatisfaction. Trucking is plagued by a 100 percent annual turnover rate—on average, an entire workforce quits each year. In response, carriers have resorted to a host of enticements. They have increased their reliance on "drop 'n' swap" routes, for instance, in order to accommodate drivers who don't want to venture too far from their homes. A driver leaving San Francisco, say, may be hauling freight that's bound for Seattle, and another driver leaving Seattle may be hauling freight bound for San Francisco. Instead of going the distance, the drivers meet in Portland, unhitch, swap trailers, and head back to their originating cities.

And there are other ways of improving driver loyalty. When assigning variables for optimizing routes, carriers will factor in such previously unheard-of considerations as whether a route takes a driver in the vicinity of his girlfriend's house or past the truck stop that has his favorite video games. The challenge for Yossi Sheffi is to input *every* concern on a carrier's wish list—and output the most profitable solution.

It would be a stretch to use the words "truck stop" to describe the location in Newark's edgy Downneck neighborhood where I arrange to meet Orlando Mitchell's 18-wheeler. The place consists of a fuel pump and a spot to park a few trucks set amid barbed-wire fences and car junkyards and the fumes of a nearby refinery. An hour after our agreed-upon time, Mitchell's truck glides by, a pure gem in this trash heap. It is stately in appearance—from its blue, square-nosed hood to the door on its white trailer, the freshly washed vehicle stretches regally for 53 feet and stands 13 feet, 6 inches tall.

Together we traverse the Jersey Meadowlands, the George Washington Bridge, the Cross-Bronx Expressway. He talks in a high voice, explaining that, if he were alone, he would be listening to jazz or blues or maybe inspirational leadership tapes from a college basketball coach or a lecture on postmodernism. And shortly after New York gives way to Connecticut, we pull off the road for dinner, parking behind other trucks whose engines are still groaning. We are in McDonald's at a state-of-the-art truck stop. Mitchell ingests two cheeseburgers and a banana milk shake and explains the rules of the road. Marten Transport pays him 35 cents a mile. Truckers are entitled to one day off each week. Or they can opt to continue driving for three or four weeks in order to take a single three- or four-day break at home. Mitchell himself hasn't been home in three months.

But Mitchell doesn't actually have a home. A Milwaukee native who has held a succession of factory and janitorial jobs, he moved to Sacramento, California, in 1993 on a whim. He learned to drive a truck and worked for a host of companies before settling with Marten. He drove long routes, returning every couple of months to his apartment in Sacramento. Eventually, to avoid the risk of break-ins while he was gone, he gave up his lease and put his belongings in storage. Now, the rare times he goes "home" to Sacramento, he deposits his trailer at a Marten facility in nearby Stockton, and then drives without the trailer—that's called "bobtailing"—to a truck stop near Sacramento, where he lives out of his cavelike cab.

Sheffi is at the whiteboard, professor-style. I have asked him to explain the algorithms that are involved in routing trucks like Mitchell's. Each day, more than 60,000 trucks rely on the optimization software provided by Burlington, Massachusetts-based Logistics.com, where Sheffi stepped down as CEO this year, selling his majority stake to Internet Capital Group in September. In addition, hundreds of thousands of trucks benefit from Logistics.com services like OptiBid, an online auction for shippers and carriers that is based on Sheffi's core technology.

"Structured optimization is basically an elimination process," Sheffi begins. "It's a combination of stepping through a solution space and discarding as I go the large part that I don't have to deal with. Throughout the process, I'm focusing on where possible good solutions lie, rather than actually checking each one." As an algorithm continually tests a small number of solutions, it uses the properties of those solutions, and some characteristics of the problem, to discard whole groups of other possible solutions without explicitly evaluating them. The system then repeats, testing some solutions and discarding many others until, from among all the possibilities, the best have been adopted. Says Sheffi, "The fastest computers would take years to solve just one of these problems if they had to check every solution."

But what is the space that this algorithm metaphorically creates? This notional area—also known as the feasible region—is best understood as a polysided, multidimensional box. Optimization problems involving two variables (such as two trucks picking up some portion of a shipment from separate warehouses) can be represented geometrically on a standard x-y axis, and the feasible region—the area in which the optimal solution can be found—is easily identified as a plane bounded by lines representing such constraints as driver availability and the speed at which the trucks can travel. In problems with more than two variables, the feasible region is represented not as a mere plane but as a multidimensional contour. Sam Savage, a consulting professor in Stanford's Department of Management Science and Engineering, uses the metaphor of a ball bearing being dropped into a tilted cardboard box to describe this mathematical process. The ball, going downhill, represents the algorithm, solving systems of equations, adding and removing solutions as it rolls along the planes of the enclosure. And the corner—where the ball always stops—is a point that represents the simultaneous solutions of the remaining equations. It could be the point, for example, indicating where the smallest number of trucks would be needed to make the required deliveries.

The underlying mathematics for creating much of logistics software is called the simplex method of optimization, a theory that was invented by former Stanford professor George Dantzig in 1947, when, as a Pentagon statistician, he was experimenting with mathematics to improve flight scheduling for the U.S. Air Force. The simplex method has become the basis for generations of advances used for solving linear programming problems—that is, any problem where there is an objective to be achieved and constraints to deal with. Simplex is widely applied to everything from optimizing financial portfolios and cash flow management to determining the proper mix of octane in gasoline. Dantzig's big innovation was determining that optimization solutions always lie on the boundary of the geometrical feasible region, so there's no point in even exploring the interior.

Here's Dantzig's own view of the beauty of simplex: "You have a bunch of people and a bunch of jobs and you want to assign 100 people to 100 jobs. There's a value attached to assigning the Kth guy to the Lth job, and you want to maximize that value, the sum of the values attached to assigning those 100 people to 100 jobs," he explains. "The number of possible combinations turns out to be 100 factorial [$100 \times 99 \times 98 \times 97 \ldots$], which happens to be more than the number of atoms in the universe. If you tried to go through every combination and put a value to the combination of the sum, you could never do it in a million lifetimes. Yet the simplex method is so powerful it solves this problem in a blink of an eye."

When combined with advances in CPU speed and satellite communications, simplex set the stage for Sheffi and others to build algorithms informed by their growing expertise in commercial transport. Rick Murphy, for example, now president of Integrated Decision Support, which sells software to carriers, was the first to use network models for truckload (as opposed to less-than-truckload) transport. Later, Warren Powell, who teaches operations research and financial engineering at Princeton and founded Transport Dynamics, developed algorithms for assigning one driver to multiple loads.

"The trucks running throughout America," says Sheffi, "are doing so based on the work of lots of academics who contributed to the theory and practice of logistics."

And their use of the simplex method isn't limited to solving for a single best scenario. While profitability is typically the first criterion considered in truck routing, when others are added— say, the need to get the truck in the Santa Fe vicinity for the trucker's daughter's wedding—*relative* profitability can change. Sheffi explains the process of setting up a problem with a variety of goals: "If I have many factors, I can create a balancing function between the factors," he says. "I may give 40 percent of the weight to profitability and 60 percent to driver consideration. So I look at every solution, and in some sense combine them into one number."

Contrast this high-level mathematics with how your typical trucking company tackled the scheduling problem 20 years ago. Relying not on simplex but on gut feel, dispatchers eyeballed a job, looked at a few options for each truck, and made a decision. "They didn't know if it was the right decision or the wrong decision, they just made a decision," says Sheffi. "And they made it in isolation, without considering its impact on the network."

A soft rain is falling on I-95 in dark eastern Connecticut. Mitchell sips the remains of the morning's Mountain Dew. He talks about how his savings have grown since he started living in the truck, how he's beginning to pay down his credit card debt, and how he wants to buy a high-definition television or a Dell PC, not that he has a house in which to put either. He explains that he owns neither a cell phone nor a computer. How do outsiders reach him? "If my mother wants me to call her, she can contact the company, and they can send a message to me on my Qualcomm," he says.

We talk prostitutes. Turn on the CB radio, Mitchell warns me, and you're just as likely to hear a trucker asking about the prospects for prostitutes in a particular city as you are to hear about road conditions. "It's always, 'Where are the girls?' " he reports. In the lingo of truckers young and old, prostitutes are referred to as Lot Lizards, and they typically market themselves by simply knocking on doors of parked trucks. "If you see a truck with a 'No Lot Lizards' sticker in its window—a lizard with a red line through it," Mitchell says, "that means they don't want any bothering them."

Yossi Sheffi is a serial entrepreneur trapped in the body of an academic. Since joining the MIT faculty as a professor in 1978, he has lived in two worlds: one in which he has taught thousands of students, and one in which he starts companies, builds them into flourishing businesses, then cashes out.

As a young man and a captain in the Israeli air force, Sheffi served in both the Six-Day War and the Yom Kippur War, shuttling cargo on a Hercules C-130. His Austrian-born engineer father fought with the British in North Africa and later joined the Hagganah. His Kiev-born mathematician mother worked for Israel's Mossad as a "librarian." Yossi raises his eyebrows when he uses the word. "She never talked about her work, so maybe she was a librarian, but with her mathematical background she probably had something to do with deciphering codes," he says half-jokingly. He's animated and confident.

In the late 1970s, as a student in MIT's graduate civil engineering program, Sheffi took an interest in network systems—representing them on computers, modeling and optimizing flows. That's when he got a taste of the beauty of transportation logistics. A company called IU International, which owned various truck lines, gave MIT several hundred thousand dollars to study how to improve the flow of trucks over its network—to lower costs and better serve customers. The company operated an array of fixed routes that it changed on an annual basis. Using the simplex method, Sheffi and his colleagues spent two years developing the algorithms for making IU's network far more dynamic, setting up a framework that could be changed on a weekly basis in response to the demands of customers. "Actually," Sheffi says, "our system meant they could change their networks on a daily or an hourly basis; they were constrained not by the calculations involved or the computing capabilities but by the ability of workers on the docks to absorb change."

Then in 1988, with Warren Powell, of Princeton's Castle Laboratory, and David Cape, who was Powell's student, Sheffi cofounded Princeton Transportation Consulting Group (PTCG) to sell decision support systems to the transportation industry. In the same year, Sheffi cofounded LogiCorp, one of the first pure logistics companies in the U.S.—with no trucks and no products—which he sold six years later to Ryder Systems, where it now is known as Ryder Integrated Logistics and generates $1.5 billion in annual revenue. In 1997, Sheffi cofounded e-Chemicals, an electronic commerce company for the chemicals industry, which he sold three years later to AspenTech. And in 1999, he cofounded Syncra, which develops online collaborative planning, forecasting, and replenishment software.

Perhaps Sheffi's biggest coup so far occurred in the early weeks of 2000, when, based on some sketches on a whiteboard, he was able to obtain $30 million from Internet Capital Group to buy back PTCG, which he had sold in 1996 to American Airlines Sabre Group. This operation, renamed Logistics.com, is now a

121-employee company and, despite recent layoffs, remains one of a handful of investments made by ICG—an incubator famous for squandering money in the B2B sector—to survive and show promise. Today, Logistics.com counts Wal-Mart and Procter & Gamble among the customers for its network bidding services, which are provided over the Internet in ASP mode. Sheffi estimates the company has saved shippers more than $400 million in logistics costs. An illustration: Because carriers can bid in advance on shipments that will fill up their unused capacity (the deadhead from Dallas), they can afford to charge less; one shipper, The Limited, says it saved $1.24 million in a single year using Logistics.com's automated service for negotiating annual contracts.

And it's this company, offering software based on the simplex method, that organizes the lives of truckers like Mitchell. Companies such as Marten Transport access the software on the Web and type in the factors—volume, destination, and so on—they're considering in scheduling a route. The input is crunched and sent back as a series of instructions. These are the directions that ultimately get spit out on Mitchell's Qualcomm, as he rumbles along America's interstates.

It is 7 A.M. in Providence, Rhode Island, and Mitchell's 18-wheeler grinds through the rush hour on I-95. Soon it is grinding through the rush hour on Route 128 in Boston's western suburbs. An on-again, off-again rain keeps the roads slick and slows traffic to an annoying crawl. We pass the big highway signs for Walden Pond State Reservation and Minute Man National Park. Mitchell spots a Honda Civic cutting off another vehicle. "Look at that four-wheeler," he yelps, using the trucker's term for a car. "That guy shouldn't be driving." Mitchell is a careful driver, but the truck helps him: It can't exceed 65 mph. He repeatedly pulls out a map to calculate how far we are from the Route 128/I-95 split. The rain intensifies.

Mitchell tells me that trucking gets in your blood, that it's hard to take a sedentary job once you've become hooked on the highway. He has his favorite spots (I-5 just north of the California-

Oregon border) and his favorite time-killers (spotting eagles in Washington State). But mostly, he is motivated by the same thing that motivated those other cultural heroes, the dotcommers: money.

Trouble is, a typical trucker's current salary of $41,000 doesn't go nearly as far today as the average $35,000 did during the CB madness of the Ford and Carter years. To some degree, truckers were romanticized then because many were making good money for folks without a college education. Many were able to own a house and a car and a cabin on the lake, and they had time to enjoy it.

Not Mitchell, the modern trucker. "I miss my TV," he says.

Finally he veers toward the highway that will be our last leg. "This is Gloucester," he says, as we cross the town line, and soon he is negotiating two rotaries and an old harbor road that leads us to the Americold Logistics storage facility, next to the Gorton's of Gloucester headquarters on the waterfront, right where his Qualcomm sent him. Birds circle the harbor and rain pounds white clapboard houses as Mitchell backs the trailer into a loading dock. It is 9:58 A.M. He's two minutes early.

Telecom has been deadly for investors. Gretchen Morgenson, 2002 Pulitzer Prize winner for *The New York Times,* believes overhyped, conflicted Wall Street analysts such as Jack Grubman were largely to blame. Her logical case pulls no punches. Grubman later resigned. Morgenson criticized the overpricing of weak-fundamental stocks long before that sentiment was fashionable.

Gretchen Morgenson

Telecom's Pied Piper: Whose Side Was He On?

Covad Communications: January 2, 1999–August 15, 2001
ICG Communications: October 18, 1994–November 14, 2000
Northpoint Communications: May 6, 1999–January 16, 2001
PSINet Inc.: May 1, 1995–May 31, 2001
Rhythms Netconnections: April 6, 1999–August 1, 2001

TAKEN SEPARATELY, the rise and fall of five once-highflying telecommunications concerns, all in bankruptcy, is hardly remarkable. But together, along with other recent telecom failures and those still likely to occur, they represent one of the most spectacular investment debacles ever. Bigger than the South Sea bubble. Bigger than tulipmania. Bigger than the dot-bomb. The flameout of the telecommunications sector, when it is over, will wind up costing investors hundreds of billions of dollars.

The telecommunications mess stands out for another reason: One man is at its center—Jack Benjamin Grubman.

No single person can be responsible for the entire debacle, of course, and investors must take responsibility for some of their losses. But as resident guru on telecommunications at Salomon Smith Barney and one of Wall Street's highest-paid analysts, Mr. Grubman, 48, was surely the sector's pied piper. During the height of the mania, in 1999 and 2000, he had buy recommendations on 30 companies, considerably more than most analysts. Mr. Grubman lured more investors into securities of nascent and risky telecom companies than perhaps any other individual.

Anyone can make mistakes, but Mr. Grubman's cheerleading epitomizes the conflict-of-interest questions that have dogged Wall Street for two years: Even as he rallied clients of Salomon Smith Barney, a unit of Citigroup, to buy shares of untested telecommunications companies and to hold on to the shares as they lost almost all their value, he was aggressively helping his firm win lucrative stock and bond deals from these same companies.

Since 1997, Salomon has taken in more investment banking fees from telecom companies than any other firm on the Street. Because of Mr. Grubman's power and prominence, and because his compensation is based in part on fees the company generated with his help, a part of those fees went to him. The firm declined to discuss Mr. Grubman's compensation on the record.

But one critic was blunt about the star analyst. "Jack Grubman is the king of conflicted analysts," said Jacob H. Zamansky, a securities lawyer who represents investors against Wall Street firms. "A strong case can be made that he used his picks to generate investment banking business for his firm and abused investor trust in his picks. He personifies the blurring of lines between investment banking and objective analysis." Mr. Zamansky recently won a settlement in an arbitration case against another star analyst, Henry Blodget, the Internet analyst at Merrill Lynch who decided to leave the firm last week.

It is impossible to tell how many investors profited from Mr. Grubman's advice on the way up. But those who stuck with him until the end, heeding his advice and holding on to the stocks,

have fared dismally. In one telecom arena that Mr. Grubman dominated, among the so-called competitive local exchange carriers,
some $140 billion in stock market value has vanished—95 per-
cent of the cash raised.

The money raised for telecom companies through the sale of
debt—notes, bonds and convertible issues—was even larger, with
bigger losses. From 1997 to 2000, according to Lehman Brothers,
telecom companies borrowed close to a half-trillion dollars. This
year alone, telecom companies that issued high-yield debt have
defaulted on $21.4 billion of it, according to Bear, Stearns & Com-
pany. That amount accounts for 56 percent of all defaults, across
all industries, in 2001. More defaults in the industry are expected.

Wall Street's role as enabler in the telecom binge, and
Salomon Smith Barney's part in particular, is undeniable. Since
1997, the firm has collected $809 million underwriting telecom
stocks and bonds and $178 million providing merger advice,
according to Thomson Financial—43 percent more than the fees
made by Merrill Lynch, its closest rival in the sector.

Despite repeated requests for an interview, Mr. Grubman
declined to comment for this article. Maryellen Hillery, a spokes-
woman for Citigroup, said: "We stand behind the quality and
integrity of our research department and management, and believe
the overwhelming recognition from objective third-party surveys
speaks for itself. The firm strictly adheres to or surpasses industry
and regulatory requirements designed to foster and preserve the
integrity of research. Suggestions to the contrary made by anonymous sources are baseless and without integrity."

THE BEGINNINGS OF A CRAZE

To some degree, the telecommunications crash is a case study in
how Wall Street goes overboard in a bull market, raising capital
for start-ups that never should have left the gate.

The craze had its roots in the Telecommunications Act of

1996, which deregulated the industry and swept out rules limiting competition. Soon, entrepreneurs saw a chance to build huge networks crisscrossing the globe to serve the big jumps in demand for data transmission.

Hundreds of new and established companies thronged Wall Street looking for capital. Some, like Metromedia Fiber Network, hoped to build high-capacity transmission systems in American cities. Others, like McLeodUSA, sought money to compete with the entrenched regional Bell companies. Still others, like Global Crossing, planned to wrap the globe in fiber optic networks.

All that stood between the hope of these networks and the glory of their completion was money—lots of it, because laying fiber networks, unlike starting Internet companies, required big purchases and laborious installation of costly equipment.

Some companies raised cash by issuing stock. But most network operations loaded up on what they thought would be a cheaper source of capital: debt. From 1996 to 2000, telecom companies raised $240 billion in the high-yield, or junk, bond market. When bank debt, money raised in convertible bonds and loans from vendors eager to sell equipment is added, the total raised by the sector climbs to $500 billion.

"A great number of these companies should never have been funded," said Alexi Coscoros, a high-yield analyst at Bear, Stearns. "As long as the market was prepared to buy them, Wall Street was quite happy to bring these companies to market. But high-yield investors were buying paper for companies that were not fully funded and that carried much higher risk than anyone understood."

Wall Street, of course, is not known for scaring off investors with too much talk of risk. But Mr. Grubman clung to his rosy view long after it became obvious to his counterparts that the telecom financing binge was going to end badly. On April 4, a year after most telecom stocks had begun steep descents, Mr. Grubman wrote a report titled "Don't Panic—Emerging Telecom Model Is Still Valid" and recommended seven stocks: Allegiance Telecom, Broadwing, Global Crossing, Level 3 Communications, McLeod-

USA, Metromedia Fiber Network and XO Communications. Since then, the stocks have fallen 58 percent, on average.

It wasn't until a few weeks ago that Mr. Grubman threw in the towel on three of his favorites. On November 2, he downgraded to neutral, from buy, the shares of McLeod—then selling at 60 cents each, down from a peak of $34.83 last year. He did the same for XO Communications, whose shares were trading at 85 cents, down from $66, and expressed caution on Williams Communications Group, whose shares were valued at $1.39, down from a high last year of $59.

Since then, the shares of all three companies are up by an average of 48 percent.

Mr. Grubman went pessimistic on McLeodUSA, a company that Salomon helped to expand through an initial stock offering in June 1996 and later with several other debt and equity issues, because he expected its third-quarter revenue to fall 4 percent from the previous quarter. "It will no longer be considered a growth stock," Mr. Grubman wrote, "and with free cash flow not expected until '06, it is still far from a value stock label, so investor interest is expected to be low."

Emmett Ryan, a former fund manager in Southport, Connecticut, who specialized in telecommunications investments, said that for Mr. Grubman, "everything was based on a model."

"They would project revenues, expenses and net cash flow out into the distant future and come up with a price target," Mr. Ryan said. "But when these things started going down, they would not adjust their projections until the thing was at zero."

What pushed these promising companies into the abyss? In short, the enormous demand for data transmission networks predicted by Mr. Grubman and others never materialized. Nor did the cash flows on which these companies depended to pay their interest costs. At least four companies recommended by Mr. Grubman have filed for Chapter 11 bankruptcy protection. More than half of the companies that he tracks are the equivalent of penny stocks, trading at less than $5 a share.

But back in the heady days of 1999 and 2000, analysts were

saying the sky was the limit on telecommunications and were telling investors to climb aboard for the ride of their lives. Nobody pounded the table quite as assiduously, or as effectively, as Mr. Grubman.

FROM AT&T TO WALL STREET

Mr. Grubman, an only child, grew up in a family of modest means, living in a Philadelphia row house. His father was a carpenter for the city; his mother worked in a dress shop. He received a bachelor of science degree in mathematics from Boston University in 1975 and a master's in probability theory from Columbia in 1977. Then he went to work for AT&T.

At first, he analyzed the demand for long-distance services, using computer models. He later worked in corporate planning for the company's breakup in 1984. In January 1985, he left for Wall Street, joining Paine Webber as a telecommunications analyst.

His Wall Street beginnings were inauspicious. In May 1986, according to regulatory filings, Mr. Grubman failed the exam, called the Series 7, that anyone who wants to be an investment professional must pass.

He subsequently passed. But even more important, he figured out how to stand out from the crowd of analysts covering telecommunications, which in those days meant analyzing AT&T and its recently freed regional Bell offspring. Mr. Grubman's knowledge of the company's internal operations gave him an edge. According to an analyst who is no longer in the business, Mr. Grubman regularly beat out competitors with information on AT&T that nobody else had.

"Jack had information that was never made public," said this person, who, like most others interviewed about Mr. Grubman, asked for anonymity for fear of ruining relationships on Wall Street. "I covered the company like a rug, and it was extremely concerned about leaks at the time."

Mr. Grubman gained attention from investors by being cautious about AT&T in a crowd that was mostly positive. He may also have recognized that the advent of competition after the AT&T breakup meant that there would be many more stocks to take public and bonds to issue than there were in the one-company era.

"By being negative on AT&T, Jack was able to gain the ear of other telco C.E.O.'s," the former analyst said. In 1988, for example, Mr. Grubman met Bernard J. Ebbers, the entrepreneur who eventually built WorldCom into a telecom colossus. Mr. Grubman parlayed the information he gleaned from small players in the business to become an expert in the sector.

FINDING FAME AND FORTUNE

In 1994, Mr. Grubman, well on his way to becoming a star analyst, left Paine Webber for Salomon Brothers. By the time the firm was taken over by Smith Barney in 1998, Mr. Grubman had toppled rivals and gained the top ranking in his industry on the All-American Research Team, as listed by *Institutional Investor* magazine.

Fortune followed fame. In 1998, Goldman Sachs tried to woo Mr. Grubman from Salomon Smith Barney, but he stayed put. Telecom deals were pouring in, and Mr. Grubman became the go-to guy. He ended up earning an estimated $20 million from the firm in 1999.

In January of that year, he and his wife, Luann, bought a town house on the Upper East Side of Manhattan for $6.2 million in cash. Soon, they were renovating the entire house.

As the number of telecom deals ballooned, and as Mr. Grubman's picks ascended, his hegemony in the industry and the firm took hold. That attracted still more business from executives who knew both how positive he was on the sector and how powerful his buy recommendations could be. In March 2000, for instance, when he raised his price target for Metromedia Fiber Network, the stock jumped 16 percent in one day. Companies deluged Salomon Smith Barney for their capital needs, and Mr. Grubman churned out glowing research reports, annually collecting a multimillion-dollar pay package.

Increasingly, that was the way Wall Street worked. "Equity research is a loss leader in most firms," said Philip K. Meyer, a money manager in Rowayton, Connecticut, who worked as an analyst on Wall Street for 18 years. "What it does is oil the pipeline so you have a good relationship with clients, so when you do deals you have a good distribution channel. Because the money you make on I.P.O.s is so much greater, the increased pressure from investment banking makes research dysfunctional."

Clearly, Mr. Grubman was very good at oiling the pipeline. Besides issuing securities, many telecom companies—primed for growth—were eager for advice on takeovers or mergers.

DAYS OF TELECOM MANIA

McLeodUSA's rise, and crashing fall, is typical of the stocks Mr. Grubman favored. Based in Cedar Rapids, Iowa, McLeodUSA began as a provider of local and long-distance telephone service to small markets in the upper Midwest. Advised by Salomon Smith Barney from the outset, McLeodUSA bought and resold local service from regional Bells and long-distance service from World-Com. The company was run by Clark E. McLeod, who in the 1980's built a long-distance business called Teleconnect that he later sold to MCI.

Salomon led the offering that brought the company public on June 11, 1996, raising $240 million. The firm made $10 million in fees on the deal, which priced the stock at $20 a share, not adjusted for subsequent splits. (Adjusting for splits, the deal came at $3.33 a share.)

Five weeks later, with the stock at $24.25, Mr. Grubman began covering McLeod with a buy recommendation and a 12-month

price target of $40. "McLeod represents one of the truly great
business models that will be executed in the new era of telecom,"
Mr. Grubman wrote, predicting that it would be "one of the best
return vehicles in what will be a high-return segment of the telecom industry."

Almost immediately, McLeod began buying other companies,
like Telecom USA Publishing, a phone book publisher, at $74
million, and, in 1997, Consolidated Communications at $420
million. But McLeod also needed hefty amounts of cash to build a
network. Since November 1996, when the stock traded at $28,
the company has gone to the stock or debt markets eight times,
raising $3.5 billion. Salomon led all the offerings, pulling in
almost $100 million in fees over the period, according to Thom-
son Financial. It also collected advisory fees for the acquisitions,
normally about 1 percent of each deal's price for transactions
worth more than $1 billion. The total is unclear, but Salomon
pocketed $7 million for advice on McLeod's acquisition, in Janu-
ary 2000, of Splitrock Services, a small telecom company in Texas.

According to a former analyst at the firm, Mr. Grubman's pay
was tied specifically to the deals that the firm did in telecommunications. "I remember meeting with these guys and they would
have a list of deals and they would say, 'Here's how much we're
paying you deal by deal,'" this person said. "There was a formula."

Salomon Smith Barney also generated fees in other ways from
the deals Mr. Grubman helped foster. Often, it executed stock
trades for the executives of the companies, for which it was paid
commissions. At McLeod, for example, Mary E. McLeod, the chairman's wife, sold $50 million in stock through Salomon on Febru-
ary 8, 2000. Some companies, like WorldCom, hired Salomon to
run their corporate stock-option plans for company employees,
generating fees and luring new brokerage customers in general.
Finally, Mr. Grubman's ability to move markets meant that
Salomon's trading desk probably made a good deal of money executing buy and sell orders for its customers.

In all, Salomon's earnings from McLeod over the years far outpaced McLeod's profits. As the company's revenue rose to $1.4 billion in 2000 from $267 million in 1997, it lost almost $1 billion over that period. So far this year, it has lost an additional $2.6 billion.

The losses, however, did not keep McLeod's stock from soaring. Every few months, Mr. Grubman would reiterate his enthusiasm for the company, coming out with a higher price target or another reason to own the stock. In January 1998, for example, just days after the company raised $225 million in bonds for McLeod, he increased his price target on the stock to $53 from $50.

By March 2000, McLeod shares reached a split-adjusted peak of $34.83, up almost tenfold from the initial offering price.

And Mr. Grubman, at the top of his game, was scoffing at anyone who questioned the propriety of having an analyst, whose job is to provide investors with objective investment advice, work closely with the firm's investment bankers. "What used to be a conflict is now a synergy," he told *BusinessWeek* in May 2000. "Objective? The other word for it is uninformed."

Soon, however, the bottom fell out of McLeod and the telecom sector.

It was not until August, with McLeod's stock at $2.44, down 93 percent from its 2000 peak, that Mr. Grubman allowed in a report that the company "had some missteps in the last year and a half, most notably the ill-advised acquisition of Splitrock." He made no mention that Salomon Smith Barney had advised McLeod that the acquisition was worth the $2.1 billion it paid. Nor did he acknowledge that in both January and April 2000, he wrote reports praising the Splitrock purchase as a "smart strategic merger" that dramatically enhanced McLeod's "position on the national stage."

McLeodUSA, to the chagrin of its investors, no longer finds itself on the national stage. Its stock sells for 73 cents a share, and its market capitalization, $455 million, represents 13 percent of the money it raised from investors. On Thursday, McLeod wrote off $2.9 billion, most of it related to the Splitrock acquisition.

AN UNFLINCHING OPTIMIST

In the months since the telecom mania began to dissolve, it has become clear that Mr. Grubman remained too optimistic far too long. Many companies he favored are defunct or are trading for pennies a share or have been delisted from the Nasdaq market.

Many other highly paid analysts also made the mistake of staying too long at the technology stock party that ended abruptly last year. But Mr. Grubman's reports show a particular disregard for the dangers of heavy debt piled on unproven companies. Debt, though not a big factor in the Internet debacle, was the 800-pound gorilla in telecommunications.

Nevertheless, Mr. Grubman continually swatted away speculation that debt might become a problem for his companies—talk that began creeping into the market a year ago when Ravi Suria, then a convertible-bond analyst at Lehman Brothers, warned of looming debt problems in telecommunications. One money manager said Mr. Grubman often played down risk. "If a company comes out and doubles its debt-to-equity ratio, you would say the risk is greater," the manager said. "But he was always writing positive reports around times when his companies were raising debt."

Reality may be catching up with Mr. Grubman. Last month, he dropped to third place from first on the *Institutional Investor* rankings for the wireless services sector. (He still ranks no. 1 in the competitive local exchange carriers sector.) His 2001 paycheck will undoubtedly reflect the desert in telecom deals. And according to regulatory filings, he has been named in two arbitration cases and one lawsuit brought by customers of Salomon Smith Barney, who claim breach of fiduciary duty or misrepresentation in his stock picks.

Mr. Grubman's reputation has also been tarnished inside Salomon Smith Barney, where the sales force used to treat him with deference. In the old days, on the morning call to brokers, listeners would hang on the analyst's every utterance, according to several witnesses. He would speak expansively about his favorite companies, taking 20 minutes to get through all his points.

Today, brokers say, Mr. Grubman is more often than not cut short by others on the call. One longtime salesman at the firm said recently: "Jack Grubman? His name is mud around here."

CEOs have no shame. While their shareholders take big hits, many at the top simply take the money and run. Roger Lowenstein scolds them in *SmartMoney* for accepting huge bonuses, stock awards and options that have no correlation to actual performance. He backs up his point with noteworthy examples.

Roger Lowenstein

License to Steal

IT'S SPRING proxy season, so here's my candidate for most overpaid chief executive of 2001: William Harrison of J.P. Morgan Chase. It was tough to pass up Jeffrey Immelt, the new CEO of General Electric, who proved he is fully up to standing in the shoes of Jack Welch, one of the most shamefully greedy chief executives ever ($244 million in his last three years). In fact, it was a banner year for performance-challenged replacements all around. Coca-Cola's Douglas Daft, in only his sophomore season at the top, snatched personal lucre in the midst of shareholder woe with the confident gluttony of a veteran. And in his rookie year at American Express, despite a performance that was distinctly double-A, Kenneth Chenault outearned his longtime, high-achieving (and also overpaid) predecessor. Excuse me, he didn't *earn* it. He took it.

Why the overheated prose? Because, face it, the American system of compensation is a license to steal, and—notwithstanding consultants' pap about salaries having fallen last year—CEOs have never used that license so shamelessly.

The heart of the problem is the stock option. In theory, it gives executives an incentive to perform. And if executives got only *one* set of options over their career, the system might have some merit.

Instead, executives get bundles of options every year or so, and they get them in obscene amounts. That makes cashing in on them easy. Some years the stock will be up, some years down, but over time—even if in the long haul the stock merely treads water—the options awarded at the bottom of the cycle will be worth a fortune.

Thus, a down year like 2001 becomes an excuse to hand over a piece of the shareholders' company to management on the cheap. It would be wrong to say the system is indifferent to performance— it encourages occasional down years, which provide for lower strike (buying) prices. But the system is truly indifferent to performance in the sense that mediocre and worse chief executives are both immensely rewarded and vastly overpaid.

Consider Immelt. He got options for 800,000 shares at $43.75 each in July. Then, in September, after markets plunged, he received 400,000 more options at $35.48 a share. Think about that. You get options as an incentive to raise the share price. But the stock falls. So you get more options at a lower price. A spokesman said Immelt needed "additional incentive." Gee, he's going to net $55 million from the first bundle—if he can raise the stock a so-so 10 percent a year. If that doesn't get him out of bed in the morning, he's in the wrong line of work. That second bundle is no incentive—it's a freebie.

Coca-Cola's board, including Warren Buffett, also subscribed to the flexible (change it as you go) theory of CEO pay. Flash back to when Daft took over as CEO. This column warned that setting a growth target was foolish and unrealistic. The company did it anyway, sticking Daft with a minimum five-year growth rate in order to claim a million-share award. Last year Daft realized growth would be slower than he reckoned. No problem—Coke canceled the old award and gave him a new one with a lower hurdle. For *starters*. Then it gave him 1 million options—a huge award—at a severely depressed stock price. And it's no wonder Daft got his options cheap—can anyone remember the last time Coke stock actually rose? (It ended last year below the close for 1996.)

The board cited Daft's "highly effective leadership and vision in a uniquely complex marketplace." Uniquely complex? Doesn't Coke sell soda concentrate? Orwellian truth-twisting aside, CEOs aren't paid for vision or even for mastery of complexity—they are paid for results.

AmEx at least admitted it "did not meet its long-term financial targets." And in a show of principle, it reduced Chenault's bonus and canceled a special retention award. So much for the show. Then AmEx handed Chenault a huge stock award, bringing compensation to $14.5 million, virtually double the previous year's. To top it off, Chenault grabbed options on 900,000 shares—at depressed prices, of course. This is standard compensation-committee double-talk—"punish" the underperforming CEO from one pocket, and lay it on thick from the other.

Okay, so now we get to Harrison. Last year Morgan Chase's net fell 70 percent. Its stockholders lost 20 percent on their shares, which fell to levels prevailing in 1998. And—the worst news—Morgan Chase got caught holding the bag in both of the recent lollapalooza bankruptcies—Enron and Global Crossing. Its exposure on Enron, after having written off $500 million, stands at $2.1 billion more.

You might think Harrison would be working for free after a year like that. You should live so long. The chief took a giant extra bonus totaling $10 million, for total pay of $17.5 million, up 80 percent. The special bonus was for arranging the merger between Chase and Morgan. And he did that. But guess what? Big deal.

CEOs aren't hired to make mergers; they are hired to earn and increase profits in a sustained way over time. If they do it via merger, that's fine. If not, that's fine too.

A bank CEO, who is the guardian of capital, is in particular paid to be a watchful steward. Harrison was so watchful he presided over a merged entity that gave capital away. Any CEO can arrange a merger—the board might have had the grace to see how this one would work out for the shareholders before paying Harrison all that loot.

Oh, yes, Harrison also got 423,000 options last year—at depressed prices, of course—though the amount was down from the 1.8 million options he was given in 2000. Maybe the reduction was supposed to be some kind of cruel and unusual punishment. But if you give a CEO a boatload of options in one year, giving him a smaller boat the next year doesn't make him Mother Teresa—it makes him yet another CEO who is chasing his stock down until it reaches a strike price—that is, a hurdle on his options—that even he will be able to surpass.

Bottom line? If a Marxist critic of capitalism were writing about executive compensation in the U.S., he'd say the bosses hire some consultant and director flunkies to justify whatever outrageous amount they want to pinch from the shareholders. And you know what? He'd be right.

Investors suffer through a company's bankruptcy while consultants and lawyers make lots of money from it. Rob Kaiser of the *Chicago Tribune* writes about the millions of dollars in fees that eroded shareholder wealth at bankrupt Comdisco Inc. Investors are usually unaware of this costly process until it takes place at a company whose shares they own.

Rob Kaiser

Turning Red Ink into Gold

FOR TOM MCGUIRE and other owners of Comdisco Inc. stock, the view from the bottom of the bankruptcy court pecking order is bleak indeed.

A steady stream of fees flow to lawyers, consultants and investment bankers, taking an ever-widening bite out of the company's already depleted cash supply. Arguments for preserving some wealth for investors like McGuire receive scant attention, making the likelihood of any significant shareholder recovery more and more remote.

"I'm not too optimistic," said McGuire, a retired Minneapolis stockbroker who put his four children through college and retired nearly nine years ago at age 47, largely on the strength of previous Comdisco gains. "Time is working against them at this point with all the money being spent."

Like Comdisco, many companies enter bankruptcy court protection with more assets than debts. Yet in the end, creditors typically recover healthy portions of their investments, while shareholders often get nothing.

The bankruptcy process has been especially frustrating for shareholders of Rosemont-based Comdisco, the equipment-leasing and disaster-recovery company that stumbled in the dot-com bust after three decades of enviable growth. While at times Comdisco investors have seemed tantalizingly close to recovering part of their losses, as the case drags on they appear increasingly likely to lose everything.

McGuire, a Comdisco shareholder since the late 1970s who diversified some of his holdings in recent years, still lost "an awful lot of money," he said. "I held a lot of hope a little too long."

As often occurs in corporate bankruptcies, Comdisco shareholders formed a committee to represent their interests—but got together two months after a similar group was formed for creditors, whose claims have a higher priority.

Since the influence of a shareholders committee is limited, its main role in bankruptcy cases is twofold: First, it creates enough courtroom conflict so that creditors share some wealth to mollify the shareholders group. And, second, it serves as a watchdog that barks from the sideline as more influential players take the lead.

In Comdisco's case, much of the growling has focused on the cost of professional advisers brought in after the July 16 filing to guide the company through its asset sales and eventual re-emergence as a significantly smaller entity.

Consultants from the blue-chip firm McKinsey & Co., for instance, get a $550,000 monthly fee for strategic advice. Comdisco's top-drawer investment banker, Goldman Sachs, gets $250,000 per month, plus "success fees" for completed deals.

Comdisco's lead attorneys in the case, Skadden, Arps, Slate, Meagher & Flom, charge hourly rates between $445 and $670 for partners' services. Already, the firm has billed Comdisco for $7.1 million in work done during the 3½ months before the company filed for bankruptcy.

Additionally, the company pays real estate advisers, financial auditors and others.

FEES ADD UP QUICKLY

In its last financial report, covering the quarter ending June 30, Comdisco revealed its spending on outside professional services leapt to $29 million from $2 million a year earlier.

Assuming every professional billed at $500 an hour, that means 58,000 hours were spent working on the case, said Mark Jordan, analyst at A. G. Edwards. "Ridiculous," said Jordan, who tracks Comdisco and has held the stock since the early 1990s.

The company's board also has drawn fire for its efforts to retain turnaround artist Norm Blake as chief executive. Blake took over in February after the departure of Nicholas Pontikes, the son of Comdisco's late founder, who presided over the company's disastrous fall. Since then, the board has revised Blake's contract three times, in part to make up for stock options that became worthless.

Originally slated to receive a $700,000 salary, annual bonuses between $700,000 and $1.4 million, and options on 2 million shares, Blake netted an instant $2 million bonus plus a combined incentive and severance package worth up to $9.6 million thanks to the revisions.

The sweeteners came even though Blake had told the board when he was hired that the company's chances of survival were 50-50, and so presumably was willing to accept the risk that his options would never pay off.

"BIGGEST TROUGH IN TOWN"

Even Blake concedes the Comdisco case has become a magnet for outside bankruptcy specialists squabbling for fees.

"We're the biggest trough in town, and every beast known to man is trying to wiggle their way into the trough," the veteran executive said. "It's a submarket that I didn't really know existed until now. I was really taken aback by it."

The equity committee has tried to preserve some money for shareholders by intervening in the bidding process for Comdisco's disaster recovery business, which was ultimately sold to SunGard Data Systems Inc. for $825 million.

The committee filed court papers opposing the payment of a $25 million breakup fee to Hewlett-Packard Co., which initially bid on the disaster recovery unit and later went outside the court-mandated bidding process to try to buy the unit.

It also unsuccessfully sought to block Goldman Sachs's $8.25 million fee from that transaction, arguing the investment bank had a conflict of interest because of other business it has with Hewlett-Packard.

One success the equity committee can point to is getting Sun-Gard to boost its bid from $800 million to $825 million by threatening to withhold support and extend the legal wrangling, according to sources familiar with the events.

At the beginning of the bankruptcy process, analyst Jordan estimated that, based on the book value of Comdisco's assets, shareholders would still see a return of $5 or $6 per share.

Yet on Friday, Comdisco's stock, which soared above $50 in March 2000, closed at 49 cents.

For his part, McGuire no longer closely tracks the bankruptcy case, which had more than 1,300 filings as of last week.

"As time has worn on, I'm becoming less and less confident," said McGuire. "I've certainly lost a lot of confidence in the last few months that I'll recover anything. I've given up trying to guess."

Fabrication of résumé information captured the public's attention when Notre Dame football coach George Leary was fired after lying about his degrees. Floyd Norris, respected columnist for *The New York Times,* is a sleuth on the paper trail of infamous corporate cost-cutter "Chainsaw" Al Dunlap. Norris documents the mix of fiction and fact in Dunlap's résumé.

Floyd Norris

The Incomplete Résumé

FOR THE YOUNG EXECUTIVE, it must have appeared that his world was falling apart. He had landed a job running a company despite being fired by his previous employer. But then he was fired again, with the company's board accusing him of overseeing a huge accounting fraud.

Twenty years later, that executive, Albert J. Dunlap, was famous. As the chief executive of a major consumer products company, Sunbeam, he was firing thousands of workers and wowing Wall Street. His memoir became a bestseller.

Along the way, Mr. Dunlap erased both jobs from his employment history. No one who checked his background discovered the omissions.

But his soaring career soon crashed. He was fired by Sunbeam in 1998 and confronted with fraud allegations—accusations remarkably similar to the ones he had faced two decades before. In both cases, amazingly high profits were reported and used to justify big payouts to Mr. Dunlap, only to have auditors later conclude the profits were fictitious.

Neither Sunbeam nor the Securities and Exchange Commission, both of which claimed he acted fraudulently, knew until now that Mr. Dunlap had faced similar allegations a quarter century ago. Those allegations are detailed in court records that *The New York Times* obtained from the National Archives, where they had been stored for years.

Mr. Dunlap declined to comment on whether he had misled employers about his employment history, said his lawyer, Frank Rizzano. The first fraud accusations, which Mr. Dunlap denied when they were made, were never proved, and Mr. Rizzano described them as "old and stale" and of no interest now.

Jerry Levin, who succeeded Mr. Dunlap at Sunbeam, disagreed. "We were shocked when we heard about this," he said. "I find it most unusual that anyone could be hired as a chief executive of a major company without having their background thoroughly checked," he added. "This seems to have escaped everyone's attention."

Mr. Dunlap has denied doing anything wrong at Sunbeam and has taken the company to arbitration to force it to honor the contract he was given in early 1998, months before he was fired. He is also preparing to defend himself in two court cases, one filed by Sunbeam shareholders and one by the S.E.C. Now 63 and living in Boca Raton, Florida, he has not taken a job since leaving Sunbeam.

The similarities between Mr. Dunlap's early troubles and those he faces today are striking. At both the Nitec Paper Corporation, a paper mill he ran during the 1970's, and at Sunbeam, high reported profits led to lucrative deals for Mr. Dunlap. At Nitec, his bosses agreed to pay him $1.2 million. At Sunbeam, they agreed to double his base pay to $2 million a year.

"It is remarkably analogous to our situation," Mr. Levin said.

Like virtually all major companies seeking a senior executive, Sunbeam relied on an executive search firm to find the best person for the job. Daniel Margolis, a spokesman for Korn/Ferry International, said his firm "conducted an exhaustive search that resulted in the Sunbeam board selecting Dunlap." When asked how the firm had missed the holes in Mr. Dunlap's employment history, he said, "It is our policy not to comment on our clients' business issues."

Sunbeam has filed a bankruptcy reorganization plan that would hand the company over to its bank creditors, leaving nothing for shareholders or bondholders.

THE NITEC YEARS

REPORTED PROFITS TURN INTO LOSSES

Mr. Dunlap was 36 years old in May 1974 when he became president of Nitec, which operated a paper mill in Niagara Falls, New York. Six months earlier, he had been fired by Max Phillips & Son of Eau Claire, Wisconsin, after just seven weeks. Phillips said Mr. Dunlap had neglected his duties and spoken so disparagingly of his boss that he hurt the company's business, court papers show.

At first, all went well at Nitec. Not only did the company report small profits in 1974 and 1975, but Mr. Dunlap shared Christmas dinner in both years at the home of Nitec's chief executive, George S. Petty. "Petty and Dunlap appeared to be pretty good friends," recalled Richard Cutting, who audited Nitec's books as a partner at Arthur Young.

Profits surged in 1976, and Mr. Dunlap was given credit. But his management style was grating, and on August 30, 1976, he was fired by Mr. Petty, the principal owner of the company.

Although he was fired, Mr. Dunlap left Nitec on excellent terms. The fiscal year that was to end a month later was expected to produce profits of almost $5 million. Mr. Petty agreed to have another company he controlled pay $1.2 million for Mr. Dunlap's stake in Nitec, a stake that had cost him only a nominal sum. The money was to be paid in 1979.

But weeks after Mr. Dunlap departed, the audit team from Arthur Young concluded that there were no profits. Instead, a loss of $5.5 million was posted.

The auditors found evidence of expenses that were left off the books, of overstated inventory and nonexistent sales. Nitec's books had overstated its cash by $201,700. Mr. Petty canceled the agreement to buy Mr. Dunlap's stock, and Mr. Dunlap responded by suing in federal court in New York. Nitec countersued, alleging fraud.

That case dragged on for years, as did a related case in which Nitec sought to force an insurance company to pay $2 million on policies it had issued, for $1 million each, to protect the company from misconduct by Mr. Dunlap and Nitec's former financial vice president, Albert J. Edwards.

Mr. Edwards at first denied wrongdoing, but later became the chief witness against his former boss.

Mr. Edwards, who moved to the United States from his native Britain in his 20's, retained both his accent and "some of the British mannerisms," recalled George Fraas, another of Nitec's outside auditors.

He was, said Mr. Cutting, the Arthur Young partner, "a nice, good straight guy and a competent accountant."

Mr. Edwards testified that the books had been falsified on orders from Mr. Dunlap, who sometimes would tell him what false entries to make and sometimes would simply tell him how much profits had to increase in a month and leave Mr. Edwards to accomplish it.

"He would say, in substance, he wanted X dollars in profit, and go get it," Mr. Edwards testified in an account that strongly resembles the S.E.C. allegations that Mr. Dunlap and his chief financial officer at Sunbeam falsified profits to meet Wall Street expectations.

Nitec was a private company, unknown to Wall Street. But Mr. Dunlap needed to satisfy Mr. Petty, who spent much time at other companies he controlled.

"Did he tell you why it was necessary to show more profit than you were showing?" Mr. Edwards was asked in his deposition.

"Because we were not reflecting what we had forecast we would show," Mr. Edwards replied.

By Mr. Edwards's account, Mr. Dunlap always assured him that the exaggerated profits could be made up, and the falsifications thereby concealed, when results improved later.

"I asked Mr. Dunlap how he felt that you could improve sales one month on the financial statements and hope to have it covered by the end of the year," he testified.

"His response in the case of sales was always, 'We are improving our sales department,' that we will gain the extra sales back by the months to come and by year-end we will have it nicely straightened out," he said. Mr. Dunlap advised him, "Don't worry about it," he added.

Mr. Dunlap testified he had never told Mr. Edwards to do anything but report accurate numbers. The only time he asked that a number be changed, he said, was when he saw a profit figure that seemed to be too large and suggested it be checked. An error was discovered, Mr. Dunlap said, and the number was reduced.

Nitec management also claimed in court that the accounting fraud had masked serious operating problems. It claimed that a new production process, purchased from a company that had paid for a trip to Las Vegas for Mr. Dunlap, was responsible for a sharp decline in the quality of an important product, the toilet paper that Nitec made for the A & P grocery chain. A & P had canceled its purchases after complaining of poor quality.

Mr. Dunlap denied that process had lowered quality, and said the Las Vegas trip had not influenced him.

Mr. Cutting, then Nitec's outside auditor, recalled examining the toilet paper on a visit to the Nitec plant. "I told him this was like telephone-book toilet paper," Mr. Cutting said in a recent interview. "He did not take well to that," he said, adding, "He was assertive about how wonderful he was."

Nitec said Mr. Dunlap's firing reflected conflicts with colleagues. "There were growing and increasing personal difficulties between Dunlap and the other senior members of Nitec's management," Mr. Petty said in papers filed in court. "These difficulties had become so serious that virtually all of Nitec's senior management below Dunlap threatened to resign en masse if Dunlap remained at Nitec."

Mr. Dunlap, in his deposition, said he had done nothing wrong. He never conceded that the profit numbers he had reported were incorrect, and disclaimed any responsibility if they were. "I did not have a strong financial background," he said, adding that he received financial reports from Mr. Edwards and passed them on to Mr. Petty, sometimes without even reading them. How many did he read? "Maybe half, maybe a third," he said.

He dismissed Mr. Edwards's testimony as "outrageously false" and said he thought Mr. Petty was simply trying to depress earnings so he could buy Mr. Dunlap's stock for very little. "If they could make it look bad, Mr. Petty could come in and buy a bigger share," he testified. Mr. Dunlap's lawyers suggested that the company had just taken an "accounting bath" by choosing to use different accounting methods.

The case dragged on for years, with Mr. Dunlap enduring 38 days of depositions. In 1982, Nitec filed for bankruptcy. The mill was seized by the city of Niagara Falls for nonpayment of taxes and remained closed for years. It was eventually reopened by Cascades Inc., a Canadian paper company, and now employs 140 people, a fraction of the 700 who worked there when Nitec ran the plant. When the bankruptcy was finally settled in 1994, creditors collected pennies on the dollar.

Nitec's legal battles with Mr. Dunlap ended inconclusively. In July 1983, Nitec told the bankruptcy court that it would cost $600,000 to bring the case to trial, money that the company did not have. The case was settled with Mr. Dunlap being paid $50,000, an amount that was far less than his lawyer's bills. The case seeking recovery from the insurance company was dropped.

Had the case gone to trial, Nitec would have faced some obstacles. Mr. Edwards testified that all the orders to alter the books had been oral, and did not mention any documents directing alterations. Moreover, in an earlier deposition in a suit between Nitec and a supplier, Mr. Edwards had denied any role in rigging the books. Under cross-examination by Mr. Dunlap's lawyers, he stuck to his testimony that the books had been falsified on Mr. Dunlap's orders, but did not explain the discrepancy with his earlier testimony.

Mr. Dunlap had sued Max Phillips after he was fired, and that suit was more successful than his later one against Nitec. Phillips eventually agreed to pay him $55,000, which included $10,000 for breach of Mr. Dunlap's three-year contract, $30,000 for unspecified personal injuries and $15,000 for "all damages to Mr. Dunlap's reputation and goodwill in the industry." Officials of Max Phillips did not return phone calls seeking comment.

GROWING REPUTATION

A MEMOIR OMITS UNPLEASANT FACTS

By the time Nitec's bankruptcy case was closed in 1994, Mr. Dunlap had become chief executive of Scott Paper, where he fired thousands of workers and gained a reputation as a determined cost-cutter.

After leaving Scott, he wrote his autobiography, *Mean Business,* which became a bestseller after he joined Sunbeam. "Most C.E.O.'s are ridiculously overpaid," he wrote in the book, "but I deserved the $100 million I took away when Scott merged with Kimberly-Clark."

The book discussed his time at Sterling Pulp and Paper, where he worked before Max Phillips, and at American Can, which he joined after being fired from Nitec. But it did not mention Max Phillips or Nitec. Nor did it mention the Manville Corporation, which he joined in 1982 and left the same year. But that job, from which former associates say he was fired, was known to later employees.

Scott retained Spencer Stuart, an executive search firm, when it was looking for a new chief executive. Like Korn/Ferry two years later, Spencer Stuart did not discover the omissions in Mr. Dunlap's employment history.

Asked about its work, Spencer Stuart issued a statement. "Mr. Dunlap made no reference to holding any jobs between working for Sterling Pulp and Paper and American Can," it said. "If, in fact, he was employed by others during that period, he concealed that information from us."

The firm added that it had talked to many people who had worked with Mr. Dunlap at previous jobs, but "did not believe that his record prior to American Can was relevant to the Scott Paper assignment." The firm continued, "We are confident that the portrait we developed and presented to Scott Paper reflected his pertinent experience and executive talents."

It would have been possible to learn that Mr. Dunlap's résumé was inaccurate. American Can knew he had worked at Nitec, and included it in a 1981 news release, still available on electronic retrieval services, announcing a promotion. And Mr. Dunlap was quoted in a number of publications while he was at Nitec. (One of Nitec's allegations, in fact, was that Mr. Dunlap had used company funds "to conduct a personal publicity and self-glorification campaign.")

DIFFERENT PATHS

WITNESS IN CASE IS LESS FORTUNATE

While Mr. Dunlap prospered in the years after Nitec accused him of fraud, the chief witness against him was not so fortunate.

After being fired from Nitec, Mr. Edwards moved to Dallas, leaving his family in Buffalo. In Dallas, he moved from apartment to apartment and, when Nitec sued him, chose to represent himself because, he said, he could not afford a lawyer.

"He appeared to be a very nice guy, a smart man," said Thomas P. Earls, a Dallas lawyer who accompanied Mr. Edwards to some of his deposition sessions but did not represent him. "If he had not been so likable, I would not have tried to help him."

An extensive effort to locate Mr. Edwards, who would now be in his mid-60's, was unsuccessful.

"I last saw him nine years ago," said Annette Cohen of Avon, Connecticut, a daughter. At that time, she said, he was back in the Buffalo area. Two years ago, Ms. Cohen said, she and her mother tried to locate him after the death of his brother, but were unable to find him.

Others who had dealt with Mr. Dunlap at Nitec noted his rise to celebrity but did not speak up about his past.

"I sort of wondered why Nitec never came up," said Mr. Cutting, now retired from Arthur Young, which has merged to become Ernst & Young. "But it would have been inappropriate of me to bring it up."

Mr. Petty said he was just too busy with his companies to discuss Mr. Dunlap during those years. But his wife, Ginger, said her husband was afraid that Mr. Dunlap would sue them again.

The closest she came to speaking out publicly was three years ago, Mrs. Petty recalled. "I was taking my daughter to a private school in New Jersey," she said, and decided to visit West Point on the way. At the visitors' center, she recalled, they saw a film that praised two great graduates of the United States Military Academy, Gen. Douglas MacArthur and Mr. Dunlap.

"I had a fit," she said, and complained to the staff at the visitors' center. She was told to write to the commandant if she thought the film was wrong, but did not do so for fear that Mr. Dunlap would learn of her complaint and perhaps file suit.

Now she is taking pleasure in Mr. Dunlap's problems. "What goes around," she said, "eventually does come around."

Did the 1990s really exist? The economic and market bust that followed has everyone wondering which of the decade's gains were real and which were not. Michael J. Mandel assesses the legacy of that era for the wealth, productivity, and living standards of Americans. *BusinessWeek* excels in such thought-provoking overviews.

Michael J. Mandel

Restating the '90s

CONJURE UP the economic gains of the 1990s, and what comes to mind? Perhaps it was how the stock market ruled: All those initial public offerings that raked in unprecedented billions for venture capitalists. Or the dramatic rise in 401(k)s and mutual funds. Or the growing ranks of the Investor Class who cashed in big-time as the Standard & Poor's 500-stock index quadrupled.

And wasn't it a great time to be a top manager, with productivity gains boosting the bottom line and igniting executive pay? While it was going on, venture capitalist L. John Doerr called the boom the "largest single legal creation of wealth in history." For both investors and managers, it seemed like nirvana.

Well, yes and no. With the recession apparently over, it's now possible to make a more realistic assessment of the entire business cycle of the 1990s: The sluggish recovery that started in March, 1991, the extraordinary boom, the tech bust, and the downturn of

2001. And guess what? A lot of things happened that defy the conventional beliefs about the decade.

For starters, over this 10-year period, productivity rose at a 2.2% annual rate, roughly half a percentage point faster than in the 1980s—a significant gain. But the real stunner is this: The biggest winners from the faster productivity growth of the 1990s were workers, not investors. In the end, workers reaped most of the gains from the added output generated by the New Economy productivity speedup. This revelation helps explain why consumer spending stayed so strong in the recession—and why businesses may struggle in the months ahead.

The key is that wage growth accelerated dramatically for most American workers in the 1990s business cycle. Real wage gains for private-sector workers averaged 1.3% a year, from the beginning of the expansion in March, 1991, to the apparent end of the recession in December, 2001. That's far better than the 0.2% annual wage gain in the 1980s business cycle, from November, 1982, to March, 1991. The gains were also better distributed than in the previous decade. Falling unemployment put many more people to work and swelled salaries across the board: Everyone from top managers to factory workers to hairdressers benefited. Indeed, the past few years have been "the best period of wage growth at the bottom in the last 30 years," says Lawrence F. Katz, a labor economist at Harvard University.

By contrast, the return on the stock market in the 1990s business cycle was actually lower than it was in the business cycle of the '80s. Adjusted for inflation and including dividends, average annual returns on the S&P-500 index from March, 1991, to the end of 2001 were 11.1%, compared with 12.8% in the previous business cycle. Bondholders and small savers saw their returns drop even more in the '90s. The real return on six-month certificates of deposit, for example, was only 3.1% over the past decade, compared with 4.7% in the '80s.

Overall, *BusinessWeek* calculates that workers received 99% of the gains from faster productivity growth in the 1990s at non-financial corporations. Corporate profits did rise sharply, but much of that gain was fueled by lower interest rates rather than increased productivity.

Why did workers fare so well in the 1990s? The education level of many Americans made an impressive leap in the '90s, putting them in a better position to qualify for the sorts of jobs that the New Economy created. Low unemployment rates drove up wages. And a torrent of foreign money coming into the U.S. created new jobs and financed productivity-enhancing equipment investment.

Meanwhile, U.S. corporations were hit by a one-two punch: an economic slowdown overseas following the 1997 Asia financial crisis and the tech bust at home in 2000. To the dismay of tech investors, the hundreds of billions poured into Internet ventures and new telecom equipment ended up lowering prices for users, not raising profits for corporations. "We convinced ourselves we had discovered some magic elixir of productivity that would elevate corporate profits far above historical standards," says Gary Hamel, head of consulting firm Strategos and author of the 1994 best-seller *Competing for the Future.* "But most of the productivity gains that are made possible by e-business will never go to the bottom line. They will all go to customers."

The fact that workers reaped the bulk of the benefits of New Economy productivity gains helps explain why consumer spending and the housing market stayed strong during the 2001 recession. Heftier wages have "sustained consumption at levels higher than we would have expected," says Barry Bluestone, an economist at Northeastern University.

Moreover, it is now easier to understand why corporate executives remain relatively bleak about the future despite the apparent recovery. Labor costs now absorb almost 87% of the output of non-financial corporations, the highest level ever, and way above what companies were paying out at the end of the last recession. When the economy improves, companies are likely to face a lethal combination of rising interest rates and rising wages. "If the recovery is taking hold, workers will be in a position to bargain for wage gains," says George Magnus, chief economist at UBS Warburg. "The benefits of productivity growth are being drained away by labor."

There are two possible outcomes for this kind of profit squeeze. In the positive scenario, companies can increase productivity fast enough to fund both higher wages and decent profits for shareholders. The darker possibility is a double-dip recession, with rising wages depressing corporate profits even as the economy recovers. That would mean lower levels of business investment and slower growth rates. Eventually, companies would resort to wholesale layoffs to try to eke out profits—leading to another downturn.

Whatever the outcome, there's little doubt that the productivity gains of the 1990s are real and sustainable. They have been tested during this recession and have remained strong, breaking the historic pattern of sagging during downturns. "You can look at Enron and the dot-com bust and wring your hands," says Martin N. Baily, who served as chairman of the Council of Economic Advisers under President Bill Clinton. "But I wouldn't be surprised to see 2.5%" annual productivity growth in the coming years.

The real issue is determining who benefits most. When the productivity revolution started in 1995, it seemed that corporations, not workers, were going to be the big winners. As late as mid-1997, real wages were still growing slowly, while profits soared.

But historically, wage gains have trailed productivity increases by a year or two, and that's exactly what happened this time. As productivity continued to stay strong and unemployment fell below 5%, wage gains took off. From mid-1997 to 2001, real wages accelerated at a 2.1% clip. Real compensation per hour—which includes benefits—in the nonfarm business sector rose at an incredible 3.1% rate. The last time compensation rose that fast for a four-year stretch was in the 1950s.

The wage gains in the past few years were so momentous that they made up for the slow growth in the early part of the 1990s. All told, real wages for the average private-sector worker rose by about 14% in the 1990s business cycle, measured by the Labor Department's employment cost index. That's compared with a slim 1.4% gain in the previous decade.

What's more, workers with a wide range of skills and occupations thrived over the past decade. In the '80s business cycle, real wages of blue-collar and service workers fell substantially. Blue-collar wages, for example, declined by 3.5% from 1982 to 1991. But in the '90s, real wages for these less-skilled jobs rose by 12%. Full-time cashiers saw their median weekly earnings jump by 11% (adjusted for inflation), while auto mechanics' pay went up by 14%, after falling sharply in the 1980s. Hairdressers got an almost 18% boost. That's despite Clinton-era welfare reform and a huge influx of immigrants, both of which were expected to hold down wages at the bottom.

That said, the income gap between rich and poor did continue to widen, but not as fast as it did in the 1980s. One reason: The 20% increase in the minimum wage in the mid-1990s, which immediately benefited people at the bottom. Equally important, low unemployment rates forced employers to reach deeper into the pool of low-skill workers, hiring and training people who would otherwise have been left out in the cold. "Tight labor markets for a long-lasting period do more good at the bottom than we would have predicted," says Katz.

In many ways, the most tangible sign of worker gains in the 1990s was the home-buying boom. Home ownership has always been a critical part of the American dream. During the 1980s, that dream seemed elusive, as the percentage of households owning their homes fell slightly from 1982 to 1991. By contrast, home ownership rates over the past decade rose from 64% in 1991 to 68% in 2001, the highest level ever.

Even the economic slowdown of 2001 and the events of September 11 have failed to put much of a dent in wage growth. When William M. Mercer Co., a human-resources consulting firm, surveyed corporations in January, projected pay increases in 2002 had come down a bit since last summer. Nevertheless, expected wage increases are still running well ahead of inflation. The reason? Fear of being caught without enough workers in the recovery, says Steven Gross, principal at Mercer. "Corporations worry [that] if they disenfranchise core workers too much, they'll leave."

A key reason many Americans could take advantage of the New Economy is that they absorbed the big lesson of the 1980s: Education pays, especially in an information-based economy. The latest numbers show that 51% of the adult population now has at least some college education, up sharply from 40% in 1991 and 33% in 1982. Among the critical 25- to 34-year-old age group, the percentage with some college education has risen from 45% in 1991 to 58% in 2000.

Particularly encouraging was the rising participation of minorities in higher education, especially among blacks and Hispanics in their 20s, groups that traditionally had lagged behind. For blacks age 22 to 24, the percentage enrolled in school rose from 19.7% in 1990 to 24% in 2000, nearing the 24.9% level for non-Hispanic whites. The improvement among Hispanics age 22 to 24 was even more dramatic, almost doubling from only 10% school enrollment in 1990 to 18% by 2000.

And contrary to the conventional wisdom, U.S. workers were the big beneficiaries of globalization. Many expected that globalization meant U.S. corporations would shift their capital spending abroad, building factories and back-office operations in low-wage countries and shifting jobs overseas. Competition from low-wage foreign workers would then drive down U.S. pay—what economists call factor-price equalization.

Guess what? The jobs went the other way. True, U.S. companies did boost their direct foreign investment abroad in the 1990s, with $1.2 trillion flowing out of the country between 1991 and the end of 2001. But foreign companies invested even more—$1.3 trillion—in U.S. factories and businesses, creating new jobs and raising demand for labor.

More important, the foreign money that flooded the U.S.

stock and bond markets during the 1990s financed a big chunk of the New Economy productivity gains. From 1991 to 2001, total foreign investment in U.S. financial markets reached $2.3 trillion more than U.S. investment abroad. This inflow provided the resources for much of the $3.4 trillion spent by businesses on information-technology equipment and software over the decade. Without that foreign money, it would have been a lot more expensive for companies to make the investments that boosted productivity—and wages—in the 1990s.

Despite fears that U.S. incomes would be dragged down by foreign competition, the wage gap between U.S. manufacturing jobs and those in the rest of the world actually widened in the 1990s, according to government data. In 1991, the hourly compensation for U.S. factory workers was 17% higher than the average for foreign workers, measured in U.S. dollars. By 2000, the difference had increased to 31%, as high-tech, high-wage manufacturing industries expanded and low-wage industries shrank. "Factor-price equalization is out the window," says Donald R. Davis, a trade expert who is chairman of the Columbia University economics department. "It isn't happening, in any form."

It's not just the impact of trade that needs to be restated. Technology, too, had a very different effect on wages than most people anticipated. The common belief was that technology eliminated many low-skill jobs and depressed wages for the rest. That's certainly what happened in the 1980s. But new research suggests that technology has a much more selective impact. Jobs that can be boiled down to a set routine—such as making a loan, assembling an engine, or processing a bill—are prime targets for computerization, whether they are done by low-education or high-education workers. Computers are good at "rules-based" tasks, argues Frank Levy, an economist at Massachusetts Institute of Technology. Indeed, the amount of work using routine skills, both manual and cognitive, plunged in the 1990s, according to a new paper by Levy and two other economists, David H. Autor of MIT and Richard J. Murnane of Harvard.

But there are plenty of nonroutine tasks that cannot be easily replaced by technology—and those were the ones that boomed in the 1990s. They span a wide range of skill and education levels and include such jobs as sales, truck driving, and network installation.

But this litany of good news raises a question: If workers prospered in the 1990s, why didn't investors get their fair share of the gains? After all, corporate profits did rise substantially in the 1990s. Over the entire business cycle, inflation-adjusted earnings per share for S&P 500 companies averaged $36, measured in 2001 dollars. That's 40% above the '80s average. And this gain is not the result of squirrelly accounting: An even bigger increase shows up in the government's numbers for operating profits, which, unlike S&P earnings, deduct the cost of exercised stock options.

The bad news for investors is that much of these corporate gains were a result of companies paying lower interest rates for debt. At several points in the 1990s, long-term corporate interest rates plunged below 7%, enabling companies to borrow at low cost, helping the bottom line. At Gillette, for example, interest expenses have gone up less than 25% since 1991, even though debt has more than tripled. Indeed, adjusted for inflation, interest expenses have been roughly flat.

And remember that the average investor has a portfolio not only of stocks but also of bonds and money-market funds. These funds invest in corporate bonds and commercial paper. So when companies cut their interest costs, it shows up as lower interest payments to investors. Building up profits by cutting interest costs is like robbing Peter to pay Paul: It all comes out of the same investor pocket in the end.

It's important to step back and quantify how the productivity gains of the 1990s were distributed. Consider nonfinancial corporations, where annual productivity growth accelerated from less than 1.8% in the 1980s to 2.2% in the 1990s. Over the course of the 1990s business cycle, this increase in added productivity translated into $812 billion in additional output, measured in

2001 dollars. Out of that sum, an astounding $806 billion—or 99%—went to workers in the form of more jobs and higher compensation, including exercised stock options. In effect, not only did the economy speed up in the 1990s but the workers got a bigger share of the pie.

At the same time, faster productivity was not propelling corporate profits with the same intensity. Corporate profits went up by an extra $559 billion, a truly striking performance. But that was mainly because companies paid lower interest rates on debt.

Look beyond nonfinancial corporations to the economy as a whole, and the results are similar. Faster productivity growth created $1.9 trillion in additional output in the 1990s business cycle, measured in 2001 dollars, and almost all of that gain went to workers and small-business owners. The combined gains for corporate profits, interest, and returns on real estate amounted to only about $50 billion.

To understand why investors failed to cash in from the productivity gains, it's important to recall the devastating impact of the tech bust. Enormous sums of money were thrown away in the dot-com mania and the telecom meltdown. Furthermore, globalization compounded investors' headaches. Increased trade and higher levels of investment abroad were supposed to pay off by getting U.S. companies access to fast-growing foreign markets. The result was expected to be a big shot of profits from abroad.

But that didn't materialize. Export growth over the decade fell short of expectations, and net profits from overseas actually grew only slightly faster than domestic profits. The reason: Foreign markets did not boom as expected, especially after the 1997 Asian financial crisis. Many countries, both industrialized and developing, actually posted slower growth in the 1990s business cycle than they did in the '80s. The one big exception was China—but even with that country included, global growth slowed from 3.6% in the 1980s to 3.3% in the 1990s business cycle.

Of course, there's no reason why the factors that depressed profits in the 1990s should be repeated in the coming decade. It's possible that as the U.S. moves into a new expansion, profits could bounce back quickly. Germany and France show signs of escaping the doldrums, while key exporters like Korea and Taiwan are picking up speed. Certainly a synchronized global recovery could help profits, just as the worldwide slowdown of the late '90s hurt them.

Moreover, technology investments by companies could produce even bigger productivity payoffs than in the 1990s. Productivity surged in the fourth quarter of 2001 at an amazing 5.2% rate. That level of productivity growth is not sustainable. Still, big enough productivity gains could enable companies to boost profits while paying high wages. That could start a new virtuous cycle, as it did in the 1990s when high levels of investment produced faster productivity gains, fueling growth and investment.

But it won't be as easy as the 1990s, because workers are starting with a bigger share of output and faster wage growth. To satisfy workers and build profits at the same time, companies are going to have to do better than the 2.2% productivity growth of the 1990s. And that will likely take place in an environment of rising interest rates, putting more pressure on profits.

As it turns out, our original perceptions of who benefited most from the productivity gains of the 1990s was flipped on its head. Looking ahead, the economic pie is growing bigger all the time, but it's still up for grabs who will get the largest piece in the future. "At a national level we may get substantial productivity gains, but the real question is how are they shared," says management consultant Hamel. And in the end, that's the real lesson of the 1990s.

This joyous send-up of the (shrinking) disposable diaper by Malcolm Gladwell in *The New Yorker* showcases his attention to detail and his appreciation of inventions, history, and the simpler things in life. Warning: Expect to encounter trouble putting down a beautifully crafted Gladwell article once you've started.

Malcolm Gladwell

Smaller

THE BEST WAY to explore the mystery of the Huggies Ultratrim disposable diaper is to unfold it and then cut it in half, widthwise, across what is known as the diaper's chassis. At Kimberly-Clark's Lakeview plant, in Neenah, Wisconsin, where virtually all the Huggies in the Midwest are made, there is a quality-control specialist who does this all day long, culling diapers from the production line, pinning them up against a lightboard, and carefully dismembering them with a pair of scissors. There is someone else who does a "visual cull," randomly picking out Huggies and turning them over to check for flaws. But a surface examination tells you little. A diaper is not like a computer that makes satisfying burbling noises from time to time, hinting at great inner complexity. It feels like papery underwear wrapped around a thin roll of Cottonelle. But peel away the soft fabric on the top side of the diaper, the liner, which receives what those in the trade delicately refer to as the "insult." You'll find a layer of what's called polyfilm, which is thinner than a strip of Scotch tape. This layer is one of the reasons the garment stays dry: it has pores that are large enough to let air flow in, so the diaper can breathe, but small enough to keep water from flowing out, so the diaper doesn't leak.

Or run your hands along that liner. It feels like cloth. In fact, the people at Kimberly-Clark make the liner out of a special form of plastic, a polyresin. But they don't melt the plastic into a sheet, as one would for a plastic bag. They spin the resin into individual fibres, and then use the fibres to create a kind of microscopic funnel, channelling the insult toward the long, thick rectangular pad that runs down the center of the chassis, known as the absorbent core. A typical insult arrives at a rate of seven millilitres a second, and might total seventy millilitres of fluid. The liner can clear that insult in less than twenty seconds. The core can hold three or more of those insults, with a chance of leakage in the single digits. The baby's skin will remain almost perfectly dry, and that is critical, because prolonged contact between the baby and the insult (in particular, ammonium hydroxide, a breakdown product of urine) is what causes diaper rash. And all this will be accomplished by a throwaway garment measuring, in the newborn size, just seven by thirteen inches. This is the mystery of the modern disposable diaper: how does something so small do so much?

Thirty-seven years ago, the Silicon Valley pioneer Gordon Moore made a famous prediction. The number of transistors that engineers could fit onto a microchip, he said, would double every two years. It seemed like a foolhardy claim: it was not clear that you could keep making transistors smaller and smaller indefinitely. It also wasn't clear that it would make sense to do so. Most of the time when we make things smaller, after all, we pay a price. A smaller car is cheaper and more fuel-efficient, and easier to park and maneuver, but it will never be as safe as a larger car. In the nineteen-fifties and sixties, the transistor radio was all the rage; it could fit inside your pocket and run on a handful of batteries. But, because it was so small, the sound was terrible, and virtually all the other mini-electronics turn out to be similarly imperfect. Tiny cell phones are hard to dial. Tiny televisions are hard to watch. In making an object smaller, we typically compromise its performance. The remarkable thing about chips, though, was that there was no drawback: if you could fit more and more transistors onto a microchip, then instead of using ten or twenty or a hundred microchips for a task you could use just one. This meant, in turn, that you could fit microchips in all kinds of places (such as cellular phones and laptops) that you couldn't before, and, because you were using one chip and not a hundred, computer power could be had at a fraction of the price, and because chips were now everywhere and in such demand they became even cheaper to make— and so on and so on. Moore's Law, as it came to be called, describes that rare case in which there is no trade-off between size and performance. Microchips are what might be termed a perfect innovation.

In the past twenty years, diapers have gotten smaller and smaller, too. In the early eighties, they were three times bulkier than they are now, thicker and substantially wider in the crotch. But in the mid-eighties Huggies and Procter & Gamble's Pampers were reduced in bulk by fifty per cent; in the mid-nineties they shrank by a third or so; and in the next few years they may shrink still more. It seems reasonable that there should have been a downside to this, just as there was to the shrinking of cars and radios: how could you reduce the amount of padding in a diaper and not, in some way, compromise its ability to handle an insult? Yet, as diapers got smaller, they got better, and that fact elevates the diaper above nearly all the thousands of other products on the supermarket shelf.

Kimberly-Clark's Lakeview plant is a huge facility, just down the freeway from Green Bay. Inside, it is as immaculate as a hospital operating room. The walls and floors have been scrubbed white. The stainless-steel machinery gleams. The employees are dressed in dark-blue pants, starched light-blue button-down shirts, and tissue-paper caps. There are rows of machines in the plant, each costing more than fifteen million dollars—a dizzying combination of conveyor belts and whirling gears and chutes stretching as long as a city block and creating such a din that everyone on the factory floor wears headsets and communicates by radio. Computers monitor a million data points along the way, ensuring that each of those components is precisely cut and attached according to principles and processes and materials protected, on the Huggies Ultratrim alone, by hundreds of patents. At the end of the line, the Huggies come gliding out of the machine, stacked upright, one after another in an endless row, looking like exquisitely formed slices of white bread in a toast rack. For years, because of Moore's Law, we have considered the microchip the embodiment of the technological age. But if the diaper is also a perfect innovation, doesn't it deserve a place beside the chip?

The modern disposable diaper was invented twice, first by Victor Mills and then by Carlyle Harmon and Billy Gene Harper. Mills worked for Procter & Gamble, and he was a legend. Ivory soap used to be made in an expensive and time-consuming batch-by-batch method. Mills figured out a simpler, continuous process. Duncan Hines cake mixes used to have a problem blending flour, sugar, and shortening in a consistent mixture. Mills introduced the machines used for milling soap, which ground the ingredients much more finely than before, and the result was New, Improved Duncan Hines cake mix. Ever wonder why Pringles, unlike other potato chips, are all exactly the same shape? Because they are made like soap: the potato is ground into a slurry, then pressed, baked, and wrapped—and that was Victor Mills's idea, too.

In 1957, Procter & Gamble bought the Charmin Paper Company, of Green Bay, Wisconsin, and Mills was told to think of new products for the paper business. Since he was a grandfather—and had always hated washing diapers—he thought of a disposable diaper. "One of the early researchers told me that among the first things they did was go out to a toy store and buy one of those

Betsy Wetsy-type dolls, where you put water in the mouth and it comes out the other end," Ed Rider, the head of the archives department at Procter & Gamble, says. "They brought it back to the lab, hooked up its legs on a treadmill to make it walk, and tested diapers on it." The end result was Pampers, which were launched in Peoria in 1961. The diaper had a simple rectangular shape. Its liner, which lay against the baby's skin, was made of rayon. The outside material was plastic. In between were multiple layers of crêped tissue. The diaper was attached with pins and featured what was known as a Z fold, meaning that the edges of the inner side were pleated, to provide a better fit around the legs.

In 1968, Kimberly-Clark brought out Kimbies, which took the rectangular diaper and shaped it to more closely fit a baby's body. In 1976, Procter & Gamble brought out Luvs, which elasticized the leg openings to prevent leakage. But diapers still adhered to the basic Millsian notion of an absorbent core made out of paper—and that was a problem. When paper gets wet, the fluid soaks right through, which makes diaper rash worse. And if you put any kind of pressure on paper—if you squeeze it, or sit on it—it will surrender some of the water it has absorbed, which creates further difficulties, because a baby, in the usual course of squirming and crawling and walking, might place as much as five kilopascals of pressure on the absorbent core of a diaper. Diapermakers tried to address this shortcoming by moving from crêped tissue to what they called fluff, which was basically finely shredded cellulose. Then they began to compensate for paper's failing by adding more and more of it, until diapers became huge. But they now had Moore's Law in reverse: in order to get better, they had to get bigger—and bigger still wasn't very good.

Carlyle Harmon worked for Johnson & Johnson and Billy Gene Harper worked for Dow Chemical, and they had a solution. In 1966, each filed separate but virtually identical patent applications, proposing that the best way to solve the diaper puzzle was with a peculiar polymer that came in the form of little pepperlike flakes and had the remarkable ability to absorb up to three hundred times its weight in water.

In the Dow patent, Harper and his team described how they sprinkled two grams of the superabsorbent polymer between two twenty-inch-square sheets of nylon broadcloth, and then quilted the nylon layers together. The makeshift diaper was "thereafter put into use in personal management of a baby of approximately 6 months age." After four hours, the diaper was removed. It now weighed a hundred and twenty grams, meaning the flakes had soaked up sixty times their weight in urine.

Harper and Harmon argued that it was quite unnecessary to solve the paper problem by stuffing the core of the diaper with thicker and thicker rolls of shredded pulp. Just a handful of super-absorbent polymer would do the job. Thus was the modern diaper born. Since the mid-eighties, Kimberly-Clark and Procter & Gamble have made diapers the Harper and Harmon way, pulling out paper and replacing it with superabsorbent polymer. The old, paper-filled diaper could hold, at most, two hundred and seventy-five millilitres of fluid, or a little more than a cup. Today, a diaper full of superabsorbent polymer can handle as much as five hundred millilitres, almost twice that. The chief characteristic of the Mills diaper was its simplicity: the insult fell directly into the core. But the presence of the polymer has made the diaper far more complex. It takes longer for the polymer than it does paper to fully absorb an insult, for instance. So another component was added, the acquisition layer, between the liner and the core. The acquisition layer acts like blotting paper, holding the insult while the core slowly does its work, and distributing the fluid over its full length.

Diaper researchers sometimes perform what is called a re-wet test, where they pour a hundred millilitres of fluid onto the surface of a diaper and then apply a piece of filter paper to the diaper liner with five kilopascals of pressure—the average load a baby would apply to a diaper during ordinary use. In a contemporary super-absorbent diaper, like a Huggies or a Pampers, the filter paper will come away untouched after one insult. After two insults, there might be 0.1 millilitres of fluid on the paper. After three insults, the diaper will surrender, at most, only two millilitres of moisture—which is to say that, with the aid of superabsorbents, a pair of Huggies or Pampers can effortlessly hold, even under pressure, a baby's entire night's work.

The heir to the legacy of Billy Gene Harper at Dow Chemical is Fredric Buchholz, who works in Midland, Michigan, a small town two hours northwest of Detroit, where Dow has its headquarters. His laboratory is in the middle of the sprawling chemical works, a mile or two away from corporate headquarters, in a low, unassuming brick building. "We still don't understand perfectly how these polymers work," Buchholz said on a recent fall afternoon. What we do know, he said, is that superabsorbent polymers appear, on a microscopic level, to be like a tightly bundled fisherman's net. In the presence of water, that net doesn't break apart into thousands of pieces and dissolve, like sugar. Rather, it just unravels, the way a net would open up if you shook it out, and as it does the water gets stuck in the webbing. That ability to hold huge amounts of water, he said, could make superabsorbent polymers useful in fire fighting or irrigation, because slightly gelled water is more likely to stay where it's needed. There are superabsorbents mixed in with the sealant on the walls of the Chunnel between England and France, so if water leaks in, the polymer will absorb the water and plug the hole.

Right now, one of the major challenges facing diaper technology, Buchholz said, is that urine is salty, and salt impairs the unravelling of the netting: superabsorbents can handle only a tenth as much salt water as fresh water. "One idea is to remove the salt from urine. Maybe you could have a purifying screen," he said. If the molecular structure of the superabsorbent were optimized, he went on, its absorptive capacity could increase by another five hundred per cent. "Superabsorbents could go from absorbing three hundred times their weight to absorbing fifteen hundred times their weight. We could have just one perfect particle of superabsorbent in a diaper. If you are going to dream, why not make the diaper as thin as a pair of underwear?"

Buchholz was in his laboratory, and he held up a small plastic cup filled with a few tablespoons of superabsorbent flakes, each not much larger than a grain of salt. "It's just a granular material, totally nontoxic," he said. "This is about two grams." He walked over to the sink and filled a large beaker with tap water, and poured the contents of the beaker into the jar of superabsorbent. At first, nothing happened. The amounts were so disproportionate that it looked as if the water would simply engulf the flakes. But, slowly and steadily, the water began to thicken. "Look," Buchholz said. "It's becoming soupy." Sure enough, little beads of gel were forming. Nothing else was happening: there was no gas given off, no burbling or sizzling as the chemical process took place. The superabsorbent polymer was simply swallowing up the water, and within minutes the contents of the cap had thickened into what looked like slightly lumpy, spongy pudding. Buchholz picked up the jar and tilted it, to show that nothing at all was coming out. He pushed and prodded the mass with his finger. The water had disappeared. To soak up that much liquid, the Victor Mills diaper would have needed a thick bundle of paper towelling. Buchholz had used a few tablespoons of superabsorbent flakes. Superabsorbent was not merely better; it was *smaller.*

Why does it matter that the diaper got so small? It seems a trivial thing, chiefly a matter of convenience to the parent taking a bag of diapers home from the supermarket. But it turns out that size matters a great deal. There's a reason that there are now "new, improved concentrated" versions of laundry detergent, and that some cereals now come in smaller boxes. Smallness is one of those changes that send ripples through the whole economy. The old disposable diapers, for example, created a transportation problem. Tractor-trailers are prohibited by law from weighing more than eighty thousand pounds when loaded. That's why a truck carrying something heavy and compact like bottled water or Campbell's soup is "full," when the truck itself is still half empty. But the diaper of the eighties was what is known as a "high cube" item. It was bulky and not very heavy, meaning that a diaper truck was full before it reached its weight limit. By cutting the size of a diaper in half, companies could fit twice as many diapers on a truck, and cut transportation expenses in half. They could also cut the amount of warehouse space and labor they needed in half. And companies could begin to rethink their manufacturing operations. "Distribution costs used to force you to have plants in lots of places," Dudley Lehman, who heads the Kimberly-Clark diaper business, says. "As that becomes less and less of an issue, you say, 'Do I really need all my plants?' In the United States, it used to take eight. Now it takes five." (Kimberly-Clark didn't close any plants. But other manufacturers did, and here, perhaps, is a partial explanation for the great wave of corporate restructuring that swept across America in the late eighties and early nineties: firms could downsize their workforce because they had downsized their products.) And, because using five plants to make diapers is more efficient than using eight, it became possible to improve diapers without raising diaper prices—which is important, because the sheer number of diapers parents have to buy makes them a price-sensitive product. Until recently, diapers were fastened with little pieces of tape, and if the person changing the diapers got lotion or powder on her fingers the tape wouldn't work. A hook-and-loop, Velcro-like fastener doesn't have this problem. But it was years before the hook-and-loop fastener was incorporated into the diaper chassis: until overall manufacturing costs were reduced, it was just too expensive.

Most important, though, is how size affects the way diapers are sold. The shelves along the aisles of a supermarket are divided into increments of four feet, and the space devoted to a given product category is almost always a multiple of that. Diapers, for example, might be presented as a twenty-foot set. But when diapers were at their bulkiest, the space reserved for them was never enough. "You could only get a limited number on the shelf," says Sue Klug, the president of Catalina Marketing Solutions and a former executive for Albertson's and Safeway. "Say you only had six bags. Someone comes in and buys a few, and then someone else comes in and buys a few more. Now you're out of stock until someone reworks the shelf, which in some supermarkets might be a day or two." Out-of-stock rates are already a huge problem in the retail business. At any given time, only about ninety-two per cent of the products that a store is supposed to be carrying are actually on the shelf—which, if you consider that the average supermarket has thirty-five thousand items, works out to twenty-eight hundred products that are simply not there. (For a highly efficient retailer like Wal-Mart, in-stock rates might be as high as ninety-nine per cent; for a struggling firm, they might be in the low eighties.) But, for a fast-moving, bulky item like diapers, the problem restocking was much worse. Supermarkets could have allocated more shelf space to diapers, of course, but diapers aren't a particularly profitable category for retailers—profit margins are about half what they are for the grocery department. So retailers would much rather give more shelf space to a growing and lucrative category like bottled water. "It's all a trade-off," Klug says. "If you expand diapers four feet, you've got to give up four feet of something else." The only way diaper-makers could ensure that their products would actually be on the shelves was to make the products smaller, so they could fit twelve bags into the space of six. And if you can fit twelve bags on a shelf, you can introduce different kinds of diapers. You can add pull-ups and premium diapers and low-cost private-label diapers, all of which give parents more options.

"We cut the cost of trucking in half," says Ralph Drayer, who was in charge of logistics for Procter & Gamble for many years and now runs his own supply-chain consultancy in Cincinnati. "We cut the cost of storage in half. We cut handling in half, and we cut the cost of the store shelf in half, which is probably the most expensive space in the whole chain." Everything in the diaper world, from plant closings and trucking routes to product improvements and consumer choice and convenience, turns, in the end, on the fact that Harmon and Harper's absorbent core was smaller than Victor Mills's.

The shame of it, though, is that Harmon and Harper have never been properly celebrated for their accomplishment. Victor Mills is the famous one. When he died, he was given a *Times* obituary, in which he was called "the father of disposable diapers." When Carlyle Harmon died, seven months earlier, he got four hundred words in Utah's *Deseret News,* stressing his contributions to the Mormon Church. We tend to credit those who create an idea, not those who perfect it, forgetting that it is often only in the perfection of an idea that true progress occurs. Putting sixty-four transistors on a chip allowed people to dream of the future. Putting four million transistors on a chip actually gave them the future. The diaper is no different. The paper diaper changed parenting. But a diaper that could hold four insults without leakage, keep a baby's skin dry, clear an insult in twenty seconds flat, and would nearly always be in stock, even if you arrived at the supermarket at eight o'clock in the evening—and that would keep getting better at all those things, year in and year out—was another thing altogether. This was more than a good idea. This was something like perfection.

Perhaps you saw its 60-second Super Bowl commerical with small-business owners singing Queen's "We Are the Champions." This glitzy Texas-based Web company managed to burn through $65,900 a day before it imploded. Lori Hawkins of the *Austin American-Statesman* examines why high-profile investors can fall so hard for a pitch.

Lori Hawkins

Agillion's Brief, Fast Life

IN FEBRUARY 2000, Steve Papermaster stepped to the front of an Agillion Inc. staff meeting wearing a sombrero, margarita in hand. Taking a sip, Agillion's co-founder told the 90 employees that every one of them, and a guest, would be going to Cabo San Lucas, Baja California Sur, for an all-expense-paid trip in mid-May.

Papermaster's announcement seemed in sync with the zeitgeist of the moment. The cost of the trip—about $500,000—was a small price to pay for team building and the buzz it would generate about the software start-up.

Besides, money wasn't an obstacle. Just two months earlier, the company announced it had raised $45 million from big-name investors including Morgan Stanley and Goldman Sachs.

The investors were betting as much on Agillion's leaders as they were on its product—software to help small businesses manage their Web operations. Papermaster and co-founder Frank Moss, former chief executive of Tivoli Systems Inc., had track records as successful entrepreneurs and rock star status in the tech world.

One and a half years later, the money was gone, and so was the company. Agillion filed for bankruptcy in July. It owes $22 million to 400 creditors, most of whom will be lucky to receive a few pennies on the dollar.

Besides a few truckloads of furniture and equipment, the company's only hard asset was its software technology, which sold at auction to a lone bidder for just $100,000. According to a lawsuit filed by Comdisco Ventures, an Agillion investor, Papermaster's venture group, Powershift Ventures LLC, was the buyer.

The rise and fall of Agillion is emblematic of a time when anything seemed possible. Thousands of people, from entrepreneurs with ideas to high-tech workers with a hunger for excitement, got swept up in the euphoria over the commercial possibilities of the Internet and the chance to get rich. Venture capitalists poured money into companies with shaky strategies.

With the Internet bubble burst, start-ups are having to grovel for venture capital. This time around, burned investors are demanding sound business plans and frugality from the companies they back. The story of Agillion is unlikely to be repeated.

"They were a classic case of a company that was born in an era when money was free and died in an era when money was extinct," says Gene Lowenthal, a venture capitalist with Sanchez Capital Partners in Austin, which did not invest in Agillion.

In its short 33-month life, Agillion ate through $67 million. That means the company spent at the rate of approximately $65,900 a day. But its sales totaled only $146,947, according to the bankruptcy filing, which works out to $144 a day.

The investors aren't talking about Agillion. Privately, several concede that in hindsight, it was a foolish investment made in the heat of the Internet boom.

Neither Papermaster nor Moss will discuss Agillion. Papermaster runs a venture investment firm, Powershift Group, and says he is spending much of his time on technology issues in

Washington, D.C. In December, he was appointed, along with
Dell Computer Corp. chief executive Michael Dell, to the President's Council of Advisors on Science and Technology. He asserts
that his government role "precludes me from commenting on
pretty much anything."

Moss did not return phone calls. A receptionist at Boston software company Bowstreet Software Inc., where Moss is chairman,
said, "He prefers not to talk about Agillion anymore."

EASY SELL TO INVESTORS

Unlike the scrappy dot-coms cobbled together by 20-somethings
with no track records, Agillion came with a first-rate pedigree.

Frank Moss had led Austin's Tivoli Systems through a sizzling
initial public offering in 1995 and its sale to IBM Corp. for $743
million in 1996. The deal made Tivoli Austin's first software
blockbuster, creating millions of dollars in wealth and eventually
spinning off dozens of other companies.

As a result, Moss developed an iconic prominence in Austin's
tech community. Young entrepreneurs wanted to be Frank Moss.

Papermaster's high-tech home run was BSG Corp., a software
services firm he founded in Houston at age 28. He made millions
in 1991 by selling a big piece of his ownership to Novell Corp.
founder Ray Noorda. Five years later, Medaphis Corp. of Atlanta
bought BSG for $350 million in stock.

When the two teamed up to start Agillion in October 1998,
it was an easy sell for investors.

"It was a no-brainer—Frank and Steve had done it before, and
of course they'd do it again," says Sheryl Kingstone, an industry
analyst with the consulting firm The Yankee Group in Boston who
followed Agillion. "Venture capitalists were flush with money,
and they wanted in on the action."

Agillion took advantage of the late-1990s style of investing:
Many venture firms and wealthy individuals were putting money

in dozens of companies, hoping just one would hit—sell stock to the public or be acquired—which would repay them many times their original investment.

High-profile investors such as Austin Ventures wrote checks, as did many of the region's high-tech movers and shakers, including former Dell Computer Corp. Chief Financial Officer Tom Meredith and America Online co-founder Marc Seriff.

The investors put in relatively small amounts, in most cases less than $2 million. No investor sat on the board of directors—a sign, analysts say, that they weren't engaged in decision making or oversight.

In fact, the board consisted of just three people: Papermaster, Moss and a former Federal Express executive named Dennis Jones.

"There was little accountability," Kingstone says. "They spend a lot of money very foolishly. They acted as though they were an established company, rather than a start-up that had to prove itself."

The company spent millions of its investors' money to create an image and stand out from the scores of other start-ups that were sprouting at the time.

In January 2000, the company spent $3 million to run an ad during the Super Bowl. The 60-second spot featured assorted small-business owners singing Queen's "We Are the Champions," the idea being that Agillion's software helped small businesses manage their Web functions.

A few months later, it hired the Porter Novelli public relations firm to raise its profile with the trade press and industry analysts, for $65,000 a month.

In September 2000, Agillion moved into lavish new offices on Duval Road in North Austin. The 77,000-square-foot space was designed to accommodate 500 workers. At the time, Agillion had about 150 employees.

The company furnished its new headquarters with the best of everything: dozens of ergonomic Herman Miller Aeron chairs, a granite-topped conference table, three kitchens with bins for gourmet coffees, an exercise room.

The rent came to more than $1.5 million a year.

Some of the investor money also went to raise Agillion's civic profile. The company sponsored Lance Armstrong's Ride for the Roses charity bicycle event and the 360 Summit, a tech community event that Papermaster helped launch. It contributed $10,000 to help the city of Austin's hosting of a *Fortune* 500 CEO conference, and it was a national underwriter for *Austin City Limits* on KLRU-TV.

"It was a huge experiment," says Dave Skillem, Agillion's former vice president of product operations. "Some people have come back and said, 'How could you have spent so much money?' People think we were doing it for sport, but we were doing it for competition. It was the way things were being done, and you didn't exist unless you spent this kind of money to get attention."

SMALL-BUSINESS MISTAKE

Agillion wasn't just building a name for itself. Its software drew rave reviews from industry analysts and Agillion's small-business customers, who used it to connect with their clients.

A typical customer was tiny Concierge Services International, an eight-person business in Miami, which used Agillion's software to offer customers personalized Web pages. Rather than wait on hold to speak with a Concierge staffer, a customer could request a service, such as dry-cleaning pickup, by typing it onto her Web page. The software would send an e-mail page to alert the concierge of the request. Customers could later go back to the Web page to see if their clothes had been delivered.

But Agillion was charging the company only $29.95 a month for its software. At that low price, Agillion would need hundreds of thousands of customers to make money.

Targeting the small-business market, analysts say, was Agillion's biggest mistake, because small companies come and go quickly and rarely spend money on cutting-edge technology.

"Just about every company that tried to tackle the small-business market has died the big death," says Laurie Orlov, an industry analyst who followed Agillion for Forrester Research in Boston. "Trying to sell to them is a nightmare—they don't need the latest, greatest stuff. They're functioning pretty well on shrink-wrapped software."

Kingstone, the Yankee Group analyst, was a fan of the technology and believed the company had some promise, but was skeptical of Agillion's projection for how many customers it would be able to get.

"They would throw out these huge small-business numbers and I'd look at them and say, 'You guys are out of control,'" she says. "I agreed that what they had was great, but they weren't taking into account that the majority of small businesses wouldn't buy it. I'd run my own numbers, and it always blew me away because I couldn't possibly see how they would make money."

But making money wasn't the immediate goal anyway.

In 1999, it was all about branding—getting your company's name out there and signing up customers faster than your competitors. Whether you lost money on those customers was irrelevant.

"WORK THAT MATTERED"

Inside Agillion, the excitement was contagious, former employees say. Yes, there was the anticipation of an eventual public stock offering, which would turn their stock options into big money. But the real motivator, they say, was the satisfaction of creating something big.

"You felt like you were doing work that really mattered, and that made you want to get up in the morning and put everything you had into it," says Jay Barnes, 36, a former Agillion production graphic artist, one of scores of employees who have little chance of collecting their severance pay in the bankruptcy. "It was the job of a lifetime, and that made it all the much harder when it all blew up."

The excitement and camaraderie took the edge off the long hours.

"It wasn't uncommon to work until 10 at night, go home and be on Yahoo instant messenger with each other for another couple hours. They you'd get some sleep and go do it again," Barnes says. "We weren't doing it because some manager said we had to. We did it because everyone was having too much fun."

Maybe that's why few suspected the company was headed for trouble.

By the spring of 2000, the Internet mania was fizzling, and many start-ups had begun cutting back on their free-spending ways. Agillion continued to operate as if the boom times would never end.

But the experiment was failing. Several thousand small businesses had signed up for a free test of Agillion's software, but that was a far cry from the hundreds of thousands needed to generate adequate revenues. And money was running out fast.

In June, the company's vice president of marketing, Mary Oliver, quit after only six months on the job. According to court filings, Agillion paid her $407,633 in severance, but she later sued, saying she had been promised $590,000 more.

In November, Papermaster left the chief executive post but stayed on as chairman. A new chief executive, Jim Travers, desperately tried to line up more money.

In a last-ditch effort to save the company, executives decided to scrap the small-business strategy and pitch Agillion to deep-pocketed corporations. But the shift would cost millions, and Agillion already owed millions. Investors declined to step in and save it.

On January 11, 2001, as Papermaster played emcee at the Austin 360 Summit, the annual gathering of Austin business executives, Agillion was in the process of firing half its staff.

According to court filings, Papermaster's venture investment firm, Powershift Ventures, pumped $3 million into Agillion between February and May 2001, apparently in an attempt to keep it afloat.

It was too late. On July 24, Agillion filed for bankruptcy.

For many employees, the biggest disappointment was not Agillion's failure. After all, dozens of other Austin companies had self-destructed, and more were sure to follow.

"All I wanted was for [Papermaster] or [Travers] to pull us into a conference room and say, 'Hey, we gave it our best shot and it didn't work,'" says Barnes. "But instead we were told there would be layoffs by e-mail, and we never heard another word from the company's leaders. It was like everyone just wanted to pretend the whole thing had never happened."

BANKRUPTCY DOMINOES

Agillion's list of creditors runs 23 pages and contains more than 400 names.

Many are large companies: Porter Novelli, the PR firm, is owed $220,000. GSD&M, the Austin-based ad agency that produced the Super Bowl ad, is owed $1.3 million. Vignette Corp., which provided software to manage Agillion's business, is out $362,000.

The $71,000 that Agillion owes Michael Quirl will put his company out of business, he said.

Austin Dataline Services had done work for other Papermaster companies in the past, and Quirl had not hesitated when Agillion called.

"We turned down a lot of work for dot-coms because I didn't want anything to do with companies that said outright they were going to lose money for years," Quirl says. "But I had a lot of confidence in Steve because I knew his track record and knew he was a good businessman. It never crossed my mind we would get stiffed."

Now, he says, his company will go out of business.

"I'm going to have to file for bankruptcy, which means I'll be doing the same thing to other businesses," Quirl says.

In November, KLRU-TV, Austin's public television station, laid off eight employees as part of a reorganization brought on in part by the closure of Agillion. The company owes KLRU $75,000, according to the bankruptcy filing.

The final humiliation came on July 19, when Agillion's doors were thrown open and its treasures—from still-in-the-box Herman Miller chairs to mahogany tables, next-to-new computers and cell phones—sold in an auction.

The event drew 1,000 people—some to buy, others to snoop around the skeleton that once was Agillion.

"It's the end of an era," Charlotte Hair, Agillion's facility manager, said as she watched the crowd pick its way through the company's scraps. "The champagne bubbles have stopped flowing. We all fed into the frenzy. It was too good to be true."

The Standard & Poor's 500 is considered the ultimate market measure. However, Jason Zweig of *Money* pops that balloon by demonstrating that its composition is constantly being changed—often in order to load up on volatile tech and growth stocks. That turns historical comparisons into a basket of apples and oranges.

Jason Zweig

Is the S&P 500 Rigged?

MANY INVESTORS THINK that Standard & Poor's 500-stock index, the most popular benchmark for measuring market performance, is a stable list of the country's 500 biggest companies. Not so. The S&P 500 is, in fact, made up of the 500 stocks that most appeal to seven people who meet once a month on the 44th floor of 55 Water Street in downtown New York City. Like the admissions committee of an elite country club dropping white or black balls into a wooden box, the Index Committee of Standard & Poor's meets in secret; its proceedings are at least as private as those of the Federal Reserve Board, with no minutes released or memorandums issued. But it's become clear that the index keepers are changing the S&P in a radically new and potentially disruptive way. They are systematically tearing out sluggish Old Economy value stocks and replacing them with trendy New Economy names. The implications for investors are huge. One example: The switches made last year hurt the performance of the index by an estimated total of $100 billion.

Vast sums of money ride on the S&P index committee's deliberations. The S&P 500 makes up about 70% of the value of all U.S. stocks; roughly $1 trillion is invested in index funds that seek to track its performance precisely, with trillions more in other funds that shadow it. To sophisticated investors, the S&P 500 *is* the market.

When the S&P committee replaces one stock and adds another, it issues a terse press release at 5:15 P.M. New York time, after the stock market closes. Only then does an S&P official contact the companies that have been added and deleted. The announcement sets off a huge chain reaction, as the index funds swing into action, buying the new stock in massive volumes. By the end of the first day a stock is included in the S&P 500, roughly 8% of its shares disappear into the portfolios of index funds, where they remain indefinitely. Nonindex funds load up on a newly minted member as well, betting that the stock's price will rise now that it has joined the ultimate honor roll for American companies. Meanwhile, the shares that the committee deletes from the index drop that day like ducks shot out of the sky.

"The idea in running the index," explains index committee chairman David Blitzer, "has always been that it should reflect the stock market and, through the market, the U.S. economy as a whole." Blitzer, an affable and refreshingly forthright fellow who looks like a blend of an Amish farmer and a rabbi, is S&P's chief investment strategist and the author of a solid new book on index funds, *Outpacing the Pros.*

Beneath the surface, however, the S&P 500 is in tectonic turmoil. The index always contains 500 stocks, no more and no less, so a new company can enter the list only by dislodging one that's already there. Historically, new stocks have joined the list through attrition, as existing members have been acquired, merged or gone bankrupt—what S&P calls nonvoluntary changes. To be sure, the index committee used to make the occasional judgment call, kicking out a stock whose value had shriveled to almost nothing. But from 1990 through 1994, S&P booted off only 10 stocks for "lack

of representation"—code for "we don't want you in our club anymore."

Over the past few years, however, S&P's committee has been
increasingly twitchy. Staring in 1995, it has evicted old stocks
from the S&P 500 and stuffed in new ones at an unprecedented
pace. And last year, the committee threw out 18 companies—
more than one of every 30 stocks in the entire index—for the
dreaded "lack of representation" and fallen market value. That's
the highest annual total in the index's 75-year history.

Of the 18 companies added, more than half were technology
stocks. What's more, even in its nonvoluntary changes triggered
by mergers and the like, S&P has been using its discretion to plug
in New Economy replacements. By the time tech stocks peaked in
March 2000 at 33.47% of the S&P 500's entire capitalization, just
under two-thirds of that tech total came from stocks added since
January 1, 1991, including such lesser-known outfits as Mercury
Interactive and Xilinx.

Largely as a result of this rejiggering, historical comparisons
using the S&P 500 have become an exercise in juggling apples and
oranges. True, the index now trades at roughly 24 times earnings,
far above its historical average of 15. But the old average reflects a
period when the index committee wasn't packing the 500 with
high-priced stocks. How can we tell if the market is overpriced
when "the market" is different?

Then there's the impact these changes have on the managers
of mutual funds and hedge funds, whose reputations—and
bonuses—are often tied to beating the index. If they want to be
rewarded by their bosses, and by investors, they need to respond to
the S&P committee's adjustments by juicing up their own portfolios. It's a lesson that fund manager Bill Miller of Legg Mason
Value learned well during the '90s, as he shifted his portfolio
toward growthier and growthier stocks, making a name for himself by repeatedly beating the index. Other, less flexible value
managers found themselves out of favor and, sometimes, out of
work. Meanwhile, we investors have continued to apply the S&P

500 as a universal benchmark rather than the growth-stock index it has become. In the process we may well have distorted the shapes of our own portfolios.

THE LAST SHALL BE FIRST

In many ways the changes to the index have been backfiring on all of us whose investment results are tied to the health of the market as the S&P 500 measures it. First of all, the companies that S&P has added to the 500 index often perform worse than the ones it has thrown out. I asked Aronson & Partners, a Philadelphia-based investment firm that manages $5.2 billion, to analyze the performance of the voluntary substitutions S&P has made in the index since 1997. Looking at the 12-month periods before the committee made its changes, Aronson found that the average stock that was added (and is still trackable) had gone up 65.75%, while the average stock that was deleted had fallen 11.9%. Over the next 12 months, the typical newcomer went on to lose 47.66%, while the average exile gained 16.71%. These numbers are not adjusted for the market's overall return, but if you view the addition of a stock to the index as a "buy" and a deletion as a "sell," the S&P committee has lately been buying high and selling low.

The voluntary changes made to the S&P 500 in the year 2000 alone, reckons Aronson & Partners, reduced the index's return by 0.84%. That may sound like chicken feed, but for a $12 trillion market, it amounts to $100 billion.

A big chunk of that immense loss can be traced back to last July, when the S&P committee threw out Rite Aid Corp., one of the nation's largest drugstore chains, and replaced it with JDS Uniphase, the fiber-optics giant. JDSU soared 27.3% on the news, to $126.6 billion—the biggest stock ever added to the S&P 500. Poor Rite Aid, meanwhile, lost 10.1% on the news of its departure and left the index with a value of just $1.1 billion. In one fell swoop, JDSU raised the total value of the S&P 500 by more than

$125 billion and diluted the influence of every other stock in the index. The aftermath was ugly. JDSU has tumbled 84.4%—and Rite Aid is up 104.2%.

Probably the most ironic substitution of all occurred last June, when Agilent Technologies, the equipment maker spun off from Hewlett-Packard, elbowed into the S&P 500, knocking aside Nacco Industries, an Old Economy grab bag of coal mining, forklift trucks and Hamilton Beach and Proctor-Silex kitchen appliances. In market value, Nacco was then dead last in the index at just $300 million. "When you rank near the bottom of the S&P by market cap," says Nacco investor-relations manager Ira Gamm, "you just know you're on their hit list." (Blitzer doesn't deny this; as he puts it, "Stocks no. 497 or 498 or 499 are generally the ones our analysts are nervous about.") Agilent shot up 18.9% as it went into the index, while Nacco dropped 15.4%. It just so happens that Nacco's chairman and CEO Alfred Rankin serves on the board of directors of Vanguard's Index 500 fund; he had no choice but to sit by while the fund replaced his own stock with Agilent. The ironies don't end there: Agilent has since fallen by 53.9%, while Nacco is up nearly 103.1%.

A SUBJECTIVE PURGE

Blitzer denies that S&P has a master plan to pack the index with technology and growth stocks. "I don't really think we're liable to that charge," he says. "We just followed the show." As tech stocks boomed in the late 1990s, S&P's mandate to reflect the total market gave the committee no choice but to add more tech; otherwise, investors would have cried, "Dinosaur!" Blitzer insists that "outperformance is *not at all* one of our criteria. We don't say, 'This is a hot stock.' We say, 'This is a leading company in a leading industry.'"

And S&P does have quantitative criteria: A stock should be valued at a minimum of $3 billion to $5 billion, at least 50% of its stock should be public, no less than a third of its shares should trade regularly and its industry's weight in the index should be similar to its weight in the total stock market.

Yet Blitzer makes no bones about how subjective S&P's decisions can be. He admits that the committee used last year's crash as a pretext to purge some of the most sluggish Old Economy stocks (like Bethlehem Steel, Owens-Illinois and Polaroid). "There are a lot of stocks in the 500 that if they weren't in already, wouldn't go in," says Blitzer. "There's a reluctance to do a big housecleaning, though every once in a while there's a little of that." For example? "If a company's very, very small and nobody [on the committee] thinks it's going anyplace, or if, like steel, a whole industry seems to be getting left behind." In the end, despite Blitzer's assertions to the contrary, it's hard not to feel that S&P's moves are driven at least partly by desire to make room for what's hot.

WHAT'S THE MANDATE?

So how do the folks at Standard & Poor's feel about the carnage among the stocks they've added to the index—and about the stellar returns among the stocks they've removed? "It's a disappointment," says Blitzer, laughing at the sound of his own understatement, "but I don't think that it impugns what we're doing." After a pause, he adds, "There's not an excessive amount of Monday-morning quarterbacking here. I can't think of anything where the index committee sat down a month later and said, 'We really shouldn't have done that.'"

Blitzer says that in 1999, "especially with Amazon," S&P hotly debated relaxing its rule that companies must have positive earnings (or have had them recently) to be eligible for the index. The rule remains, at least for now. But insisting on earnings is one thing; insisting on reasonable stock prices in relation to earnings is another. "We get accused of being crazy on [price/earnings ratios]," says Blitzer, "but we don't pass judgment on valuations. P/E is not one of our criteria." It's an intriguing comment for the keeper of an index that for most of us is all about investing.

To be fair, Standard & Poor's is mainly trying to ensure that the 500 index lives up to its mandates of reflecting the overall stock market and providing a benchmark of leading companies in leading industries. But at the same time, S&P has altered the index so aggressively that, as I see it, chasing higher performance seems to be part of the mandate as well.

So what should you make of all this? One thing that's clear is that you have to think about the S&P 500 differently. You shouldn't abandon index funds; they remain the cheapest and most reliable way to capture the maximum return on stocks in the long run. But you need to realize that the S&P 500 is no longer a good yardstick for value stocks and funds, and that it's rapidly becoming useless as a tool to compare today's market valuations with those of the past. Finally, it's far from clear whether Standard & Poor's remarkable reconstruction of the 500 index will turn out to be a good idea or a disaster. Like it or not, we're all stuck going along for the ride.

Additional reporting by Andrea Bennett

Excitement over a dramatic Huntsville, Alabama, landmark that is a tribute to the U.S. space program turned to consternation when final expenses were tallied. Brian Lawson of *The Huntsville Times* analyzes how even the best of intentions can be jettisoned by haste, no-bid construction, and alterations in plans.

Brian Lawson

The Rocket's Red Ink

IT IS THE ROCKET City's perfect symbol, a three-story replica of the Saturn V rocket built here to propel man to the moon.

It doesn't dominate the Huntsville skyline; it is the Huntsville skyline.

But as state auditors have found, the U.S. Space & Rocket Center's construction project was "highly unusual." The auditors' report, a two-month-long *Times* review of project records and interviews with key figures, show violation of securities regulations and of the state bidding law, a price tag far in excess of the cost of the replica and healthy profits for the companies involved in the deal.

Among the specifics that emerged during *The Times*'s review of the project:

- A rocket replica that cost $8.6 million to build will end up costing the Space & Rocket Center more than $18 million even with a recent refinancing.

- The project's only potentials for revenue—an accompanying restaurant and a Space Camp dormitory—were cut out of the plan as too expensive.
- Space & Rocket Center staff first said the project was viable only if the center could use someone else's capital, but the center itself ended up borrowing $11.9 million to foot the bill.
- No bids were taken on the construction or financing package, and the lawyer who advised center leadership was paid to work on the refinancing.
- The race to complete the project in time for the 30th anniversary celebration of the first moon landing, two years ago this week, raised construction costs and dictated unconventional financing.
- Members of the center's state-appointed governing commission approved the rocket plan, but now say details were lacking; as questions mounted, they were told it was too late to stop the project without paying $7 million in damages to the construction company involved.
- The Space & Rocket Center violated federal rules for financial disclosure during the financing process, and questions continue about whether investors were intentionally misled.

In the end, Huntsville got its rocket model, but the Space & Rocket Center still pays between $30,000 and $35,000 a month in interest alone. The cost goes to $50,000 monthly when payments on the principal begin in 2003.

Meanwhile, the center is struggling financially. Attendance is down in the museum and flat at Space Camp. And the rocket won't ever make money.

"I can see it out my office window," said Gene Pospicil, a Huntsville financial planner who was a commission member when the Saturn V was constructed. "I love it. It's a great landmark for the city.

"It just wasn't done right."

MIKE WING'S INFLUENCE

The project was led by Mike Wing, former CEO of the U.S. Space & Rocket Center. Wing started at the center in September 1998 and resigned under pressure in August 1999. Over that time, according to state auditors, his creation of a free Space Camp program for fifth-graders cost the center $7.5 million.

Wing did not return calls seeking comment for this article, but he has said that the fifth-grade program debt is not his to repay.

In an interview that followed the release of the audit, he characterized his tenure at the Space & Rocket Center this way: "My management philosophy in all [my] companies, ever, ever, has always been open-door and everything's aboveboard. I did nothing different there."

The rocket project was part of a visitor's center in a Space & Rocket master plan that predated Wing. By the time Wing pitched it to commissioners, it was part of an $80 million plan that included a major expansion of Space Camp facilities to support the fifth-grade program.

The drive to erect the Saturn V replica in time for the Apollo anniversary was pushed by Wing and supported by most of Wing's ultimate bosses, the commissioners on the Alabama Space Science Exhibit Commission, which governs the center.

"It was gonna be the be-all, end-all," said Mike Gillespie, who served as commission chairman in 1999. "We had to have the rocket up for the celebration. The whole community embraced it."

But as the project progressed, that support was tempered by repeated challenges from commission members on the need for more details about the project, the importance of limiting costs, and other safeguards. Tom Noojin, who headed the commission's finance committee, was a frequent opposition voice.

"I was astounded the bonds were ever sold, given the financial condition of the center," Noojin said recently.

The commission hired Wing following a consultant's recommendation that the center needed a professional manager who would have the freedom to run daily operations. In Wing, the center got a persuasive, charismatic figure. That strength of personality and the board's efforts to have a reduced operational role seem to have set the stage for the whirlwind Saturn V project.

In recalling the events of 1999, commission members said they had tremendous difficulty in securing details about Wing's fifth-grade program, and some acknowledge that distracted attention from the rocket project.

The record shows Wing neatly deflected commission objections and promised to manage the project carefully. Here's a typical exchange as recorded in commission meeting minutes from March 26, 1999:

> Commission Vice Chairman Taze Shepard commented that the commission members need more information concerning the proposed camp facility. Mr. Wing responded that the Saturn V drawing was the first item on the timeline. . . . Shepard asked if there is an increase in costs because of the fast track to have the Saturn V in place by July 1999. Mr. Wing responded that there may be but he will have to determine the numbers.

By the time that meeting ended, Shepard had seconded the motion to go forward with the plan.

OTHER PEOPLE'S MONEY

To examine the rocket deal, *The Times* sought and reviewed financial records, studied minutes of commission meetings and interviewed former commission members, state and federal regulators, financial experts and officials who worked on the project.

On March 19, 1999, Wing went into a meeting of the Alabama Space Science Exhibit Commission's executive committee with a plan to build a rocket. He emphasized two things:

- The need for an outside company to help finance it;
- The importance of making the rocket part of a larger, $80 million project—the replica, a gantry that would include moneymakers such as a restaurant and meeting rooms, and improvements to Space Camp facilities that would help the Space Camp program grow and generate needed cash.

Wing projected dramatic gains in Space Camp and museum attendance over 10 years. Though some committee members expressed skepticism about the projections, the executive committee gave Wing the go-ahead to work out a deal with Turner Universal Construction Co.

Within a month, one of Wing's two main ingredients had changed dramatically. Instead of an outside party—in this case Turner's Universal/BP Leasing Corporation—paying to build the rocket, then leasing it back to the Space & Rocket Center, the commission borrowed money for the project.

By the time the rocket construction was finished in July 1999, the other key aspect of the overall project outlined by Wing had also changed. The commission realized it could not afford the Space Camp improvements. And by the end of that summer, the gantry had been put on hold, leaving an $8.6 million rocket without any revenue potential.

FAST TRACK

The rocket project was complicated by the commission's self-imposed deadline.

"The anniversary rationale didn't make sense to me," said Noojin, "but there were several people on the commission who spent their entire lives with NASA. They were very excited about it. I said, 'We're going to have a 31st anniversary, too.'

"It added a lot to the cost."

Work began in early April 1999, before the commission had

formally approved the project and before any financing was secured. At a committee meeting on April 14, Wing said as many as 15 contractors were already working on the project.

On April 15, the commission heard a plan to pay for the work already under way. Stan Gregory, a Montgomery-based attorney who had worked with commissioners on financing other projects, told commissioners their need for a "fast track" approach would require a contractor willing to put money up front until financing was secured.

That was Turner Universal.

Turner got the job without a bid; no other construction companies were given a chance to compete. It remained Turner's construction project even though Turner wasn't going to finance it as Wing had suggested less than a month earlier.

Gregory also told the commission's finance committee that the only practical way to get the project done in time was to work with a Montgomery investment banking firm, Blount Parrish and Co., to sell uninsured "certificates of participation" to raise construction money. Gregory warned of possible pitfalls: publicity risks because the history of certificates of participation had not always been good, and financial risks because their interest rates might become less attractive.

The fast-track schedule caused another problem for the commission. Because Turner was buying materials and putting people to work before the commission had its financing arranged, Turner wanted to know its costs would be covered even if the project was canceled.

The longer Turner worked, the higher a guarantee it demanded—eventually $7 million.

Construction projects usually include protection for the contractor in the event of a cancellation, but in this case, it created a slippery slope for the commission. By June, the Space Center was already losing money on Wing's fifth-grade Space Camp program. Yet under the agreement with Turner, either the rocket would be finished, or the commission would lose millions and have nothing to show for it.

At Wing's urging, the commission approved a 24-hour-a-day construction schedule, with an expected higher cost, to meet the July celebration deadline.

NO COMPETITIVE BIDS

State auditors, reviewing the rocket center's 1999 activities, found that the failure to solicit bids on the rocket project violated state law.

It is Gregory's opinion that the commission was protected by its chosen method of financing.

It worked this way: The commission created a private corporation, Alabama Space Leasing Corp., to pay for the rocket project. Space Leasing sold the certificates of participation, which are similar to bonds, and paid the contractor. To retire the debt, the commission made lease payments to Space Leasing, which passed the money to a bank, which repaid the people who bought the certificates.

Since Alabama Space Leasing was a private corporation, the state law requiring bids on major public projects did not apply, Gregory argues.

The Alabama attorney general's office recently said the auditor's finding of bid law violation is not likely to be prosecuted because the commission acted on legal advice, and it's too late anyway for another contractor to bid on the job.

Richard Allen, deputy state attorney general, said the only way the commission and its lawyer would be in trouble for acting as they did would be if there were collusion where the legal advice was somehow tainted by the attorney's financial interest.

In this case, though Gregory did not serve as bond counsel on the initial financing deal, he was paid $35,000 when the project was refinanced earlier this year.

When asked if Gregory's role constituted a financial interest, Allen replied that he knows Gregory well and doubts Gregory would have done anything inappropriate.

RISKY BUSINESS

Phil Dotts, Huntsville managing partner and principal at Blount Parrish, said the rocket deal wasn't an easy sell.

The project was not something a bank would lend money for, he said. The certificates, unlike more common municipal securities, did not have a rating that would help investors evaluate their risk, and they were uninsured.

Even doing business with the Space & Rocket Center was more risky for investors, Dotts said, because repayment would have to come from the center's ongoing operations. The Space & Rocket Center has no taxing power to raise money.

Although the deal-makers used the idea that Space Leasing was a private corporation when deciding to ignore bid laws, they issued the certificates as tax-free because of Space Leasing's connection to the Space & Rocket Center, a state agency that gets some state money.

Gregory said the project was "imbued with public interest" and likened it to the use of public money to help the private construction of the Mercedes-Benz and Toyota plants in Alabama.

Bond experts said the tax-free provision adds roughly 3 percentage points to the effective interest rate of the bonds, making them more attractive for buyers.

Blount Parrish set up Space Leasing with Dotts, company founder Bill Blount and a company employee as officers. The corporation's board of directors was made up solely of other Blount Parrish employees. State auditors noted the makeup of Space Leasing, but did not criticize.

Then Blount Parrish lined up buyers, and Space Leasing issued the certificates.

In choosing that approach, the commission bypassed its own finance authority, which was the established process for issuing bonds to pay for capital improvements. When a new commission refinanced the rocket debt earlier this year, the finance authority issued the bonds.

Using the finance authority in 1999 would have taken longer but would have given the commission direct oversight of the deal and might have saved money. Instead, minutes show commissioners were requesting the specifics of the financing arrangement when the certificates had already been sold.

Space Leasing sold $11.9 million in certificates for a rocket with a $10 million price estimate. The money went to build the rocket, create reserve accounts for debt repayment and construction costs, and pay Blount Parrish and others for the costs of issuing the certificates.

All told, the rocket would have cost $25 million, including nearly $14 million in interest to investors.

Analysts who reviewed the deal for *The Times* said Blount Parrish's underwriting charge of $540,325, 4.5 percent of the total cost, is high but not unreasonable. That figure includes costs for an attorney to review the transaction and banking fees.

Although underwriters' fees for municipal issues tend to hover around 1 percent, the unrated nature of the certificates made them a tougher sell, according to a local securities dealer.

"What they did was find some of their customers, large insurance companies or mutual funds who have thousands of customers, and got them to buy it," the analyst said. "Tax-free makes it a sweet deal."

MONEY CRUNCH

The same analyst, however, faulted the commissioners who approved the deal: "The problem I have is what the commissioners were thinking, with the debt service."

The repayments started in October 1999 with monthly interest payments of $66,074. Beginning in October 2000, principal payments of $17,500 per month were added for a monthly bill of $83,574—in an operation that was quickly becoming strapped for cash.

Fifth-graders from across the country had been coming to

Space Camp for free, based on Wing's assurances that corporate donors would cover the costs. That money didn't materialize, and the rocket center wound up having to cover more than $6 million in related costs.

Noojin told fellow commissioners on August 12, 1999, that center finances were in "serious jeopardy" and laid out a plan to cut costs. Layoffs at the Space & Rocket Center soon followed. The center had to more than double its line of credit from a local bank and used $3.9 million of that line by September 1999. Interest charges alone that year were nearly $720,000. Wing resigned in August and in November, Gov. Don Siegelman fired all but two board members, Huntsville Mayor Loretta Spencer and Roy Nichols, who serves as the board's chairman today.

But none of that information was ever formally passed on to investors in the rocket project.

Rules set by the U.S. Securities and Exchange Commission require disclosure of serious financial problems that might affect a borrower's ability to repay debt. The center never missed a payment, but Mary Simpkins, a municipal securities specialist for the SEC, said that doesn't mean there wasn't a violation.

"The issue is whether the information provided to investors was materially misleading," Simpkins said. "It's hard to know in hindsight, without an investigation."

AUDIT SEASON

Rocket project investors were also entitled to an annual financial update. But it wasn't until after it refinanced the rocket in January 2001 that the new commission filed any kind of financial disclosure. That failure is not uncommon but violates SEC rules.

Center officials blame the violation on a fired audit firm's failure to deliver its work.

But that aborted audit by Dudley, Hopton-Jones, Sims & Freeman also included a more serious allegation: The rocket center submitted misleading financial information to Space Leasing in connection with the sale of the certificates of participation.

The official statement describing Space & Rocket Center finances given to investors that June described an uncharacteristic 25 percent increase in projected revenue for 1999. Most of the gains were expected to come from pledges for the fifth-grade program.

Dotts and others involved in the project say Wing prepared the financial projections, and they were unaware that the estimates were so far off target.

In replying to the auditors, the center said the "unsubstantiated nature" of fifth-grade program pledges was not shared with Space Leasing. Nor was a second issue involving $1 million in checks Wing wrote to the center.

The checks were recorded by center financial staff as received payments for the fifth-grade program, though Wing had asked that the checks not be cashed.

It is standard practice for an auditor to provide its client a letter outlining the audit's findings. That letter often has many drafts as the two sides negotiate its content.

In this case, the two sides could not agree on the significance of the center's conduct in sharing information with Space Leasing.

The commission's revised draft doesn't use the word "misleading." And while the audit firm's draft urged the commission to state flatly that there had been no fraud by commissioners or center officials, the commission's wording hedged "to the best of our knowledge and belief, there has been no fraud involving management or employees. . . ."

Larry Capps, now the Space & Rocket Center's chief executive officer, has since said that because current center leadership was not involved in the 1999 project, less definitive wording was appropriate.

The new commission leadership would not accept the audit conducted by the Dudley firm, which is based in Birmingham with a Huntsville office. The firm was fired in August 2000.

Capps said it was because the firm failed to deliver its audit in a timely manner and its fees were beyond the scope of the contract.

The commission's minutes from early 2000, however, indicate the firm was authorized to expand the scope of its work with an expected increase in fees. The firm would not comment for the story, citing client confidentiality and unresolved billing issues.

The commission subsequently hired another audit firm; its report did not reflect the same concerns. The state audit, made public in April 2001, found numerous problems with the fifth-grade program and seeks almost $7.6 million in repayments from Wing.

It is that audit that says the commission violated bid law and calls the rocket construction project "highly unusual."

GENTLER TERMS

The rocket was refinanced in January with AmSouth Bank serving as a credit enhancer. That means if the commission can't make a payment, the bank will. The terms of the new deal are much gentler, with the Space & Rocket Center's interest payments averaging $30,000 to $35,000 per month, according to Capps. Beginning in 2003, with principal added, the costs will be about $50,000 per month and the total cost of the project will be about $7 million less—$18 million for the $8.6 million rocket.

Capps said the commission shopped around for a better financing deal, and falling interest rates will help reduce costs.

Blount Parrish served also as the underwriter on the refinance, which cost $310,000 in fees to it and others, including Gregory, who assisted in the deal.

The last payment on the rocket is scheduled to be made in 2022.

The three men standing at the top of AOL Time Warner, American Express, and Merrill Lynch happen to be black. *Newsweek's* Johnnie L. Roberts describes the path each took to reach the pinnacle, the implications of race, and the challenges each must face to keep his giant corporate ship on course.

Johnnie L. Roberts

A Race to the Top

SUN-SPLASHED AND BLANKETED with golf courses, Boca Grande, Florida, is a natural habitat for that most elite breed of American capitalism: members of the old boys' network. On a single day last spring, you could spot an intimate gathering of these Masters of the Universe flown down from the north: honchos from American Express and AOL Time Warner and Merrill Lynch. The scene was as you'd expect: lots of backslapping, nostalgic talk about Harvard M.B.A. days and the requisite ribbing about the precision (or lack thereof) of their golf games.

There was also something about this elite gathering that may warrant a footnote in the nation's history of racial progress. Everyone in the group was African-American. In fact, the pairings in this particular golf match included a Who's Who of Black America: Kenneth I. Chenault, elevated to chief executive of American Express in January 2001; E. Stanley O'Neal, poised to occupy the corner office at Merrill Lynch after a bitter succession battle;

and Richard D. Parsons, taking the reins at AOL Time Warner come May. At each company—all of which are multibillion-dollar behemoths with brands recognizable worldwide—these men were handpicked by the CEOs they are succeeding, all of them white: AOL Time Warner's Gerald Levin, American Express's Harvey Golub and Merrill Lynch's David Komansky. And to a man, all three departing executives are unanimous about one point: race wasn't a factor. "Having been the person who made the recommendation to the board, I can tell you race didn't enter my mind once during the whole process," says Komansky. But if the rise of these three executives owes nothing to their skin color, each has succeeded in part thanks to skills—conciliation, bluntness and boldness—that owe something to their unique personal perspectives. And it clearly says something about a new level of opportunity that is now open to talented and dedicated people of color. As Vernon Jordan, the famed Washington insider and professional board member, puts it, it shows that "hard work, sacrifice and working within the system has its benefits."

Neither Parsons nor Chenault nor O'Neal is comfortable with having his enormous professional accomplishments viewed through the prism of race. "I think that's a narrow definition of a person because it's only one element of who they are," says O'Neal. So how should we view these men—as black CEOs, or CEOs who happen to be black? All three realize that their appointments come with heightened expectations, especially from other African-Americans who see in them the opportunity for social progress. But they are understandably ambivalent about what their proper roles should be when it comes to questions of race, and they calibrate their answers carefully. Take the issue of workplace diversity. Parsons says "all CEOs have the duty" to foster diversity. "The difference is, we might bring a different sensibility and personal commitment to bear." Chenault notes that a CEO's primary obligation is to enrich shareholders—but that looking for the best talent from the widest possible pool is one sure route to that end.

Throughout their careers, all three men have shown a capacity for answering such Solomonic questions. What has changed—because of their rise to the highest reaches of corporate America—is the number of people who are listening carefully to them. So what significance do they see in their triumphs? Are they a noteworthy shift or a fleeting aberration? The answer from all three is characteristically measured and philosophical. "It is a good trend, but an early one," says Chenault. "When there is an open playing field, people from different groups can succeed."

How did these exceptional men get their start? For AOL Time Warner's Dick Parsons, it was working for the storied Rockefeller family. After serving eight years as a trusted aide and lawyer to former vice president and New York governor Nelson Rockefeller, Parsons was called on in 1977 to help settle a family feud over leadership, finances and ideology. At first, many in the family suspiciously viewed Parsons as Nelson's flunky. But Parsons plunged into this cauldron of rich egos. Through quiet, persistent coaxing, he finally prevailed, pressing the family to form a corporation to handle their affairs and put an end to the intergenerational tensions, says a Rockefeller associate.

Call him the Great Mediator. Parsons ascended to the helm of America's biggest media company—a cable giant, owner of Warner Bros. studio and the AOL Internet empire—precisely because he understands the critical role of the go-between. "Richard Parsons is a player in this country," says Gerald Levin, who with unanimous board approval picked Parsons last month to succeed him as AOL Time Warner's CEO. "People in the organization like him even when he's dealing with some harsh realities," says Fay Vincent, an AOL Time Warner director. Ever self-effacing, Parsons offers this success formula: "Ten percent who you know, 10 percent what you know and 80 percent luck."

Many point to Parson's ties to the old-moneyed Rockefellers as a big reason for his steady rise. Even Parsons says that "falling under the protective aegis of Nelson Rockefeller was a major stepping-stone in my life." Yet this powerful connection—a rare one for an African-American when it was forged in the early

1970s—is widely misperceived as a one-way street. "It's his personal capacities rather than his personal associations which have contributed to his success," says patriarch David Rockefeller, now 86, who over the years has tapped Parsons to serve on numerous boards and family enterprises.

As a Rockefeller emissary, Parsons only rarely encountered issues involving his race. On one occasion in the late 1970s, Nelson Rockefeller dispatched Parsons to the Metropolitan Museum in Manhattan to negotiate a dispute. The loyal deputy arrived and presented himself to the museum's lawyers. The group ignored him, and for several minutes they kept looking at the door, apparently expecting a team of Rockefeller attorneys. "Finally, I said, 'What are we waiting for, guys?'" Parsons recalls. They quickly looked for a way out of the awkward moment. "Someone looked at me and said, 'Oh, but you are so young.' It was such a hoot." He adds: "Frequently, people who haven't met me are surprised to discover I'm black."

It's hard to miss Dick Parsons. Bearded and the size of a lumberjack, the 53-year-old says he's getting even bigger these days, thanks to the tins of cookies still arriving from well-wishers, now several weeks after the news of his appointment as CEO. A Brooklyn native, Parsons grew up with his parents and four sisters in a solidly middle-class household. After high school he ventured off to college in Hawaii, where he relished the climate more than the classes. It wasn't until he returned to New York and Albany Law School that his talents blossomed. He snared an internship at the state legislature and caught the attention of aides to Governor Rockefeller, who went on to hire him after Parsons garnered the top score on the state bar exam in 1971.

When Rockefeller became Gerald Ford's vice president, Parsons went with him to Washington, ultimately helping run the domestic-policy council. Rockefeller had big plans for his protégé: a long political career, maybe even a seat someday on the Supreme Court. But Ford lost the White House, and Rockefeller and Parsons returned to New York in 1977—just in time for the family blowup, which was precipitated in part by Nelson's return. Parsons's deft handling of Rockefeller family business led to a job as managing partner of Patterson, Belnap, a Rockefeller-connected law firm. After several years, he abruptly changed course, accepting the CEO post at troubled Dime Savings Bank in New York in 1988, even though he had no banking experience. Parsons managed to stave off regulators, raising $300 million in new capital and ultimately merging Dime with another thrift in 1994. The following year, Levin tapped him as president of Time Warner.

That move stunned Wall Street—and everybody else. Although he was an influential member of Time Warner's board, Parsons had no experience to speak of in media and entertainment. "Nobody could figure it out, because half the people thought the board had imposed this on Jerry," says Parsons. Yet almost everything at that time on Gerald Levin's corporate agenda—from acquisitions, to unburdening the balance sheet, to pressing regulatory issues—was a project that could benefit from Parsons's skills. Parsons also kept squabbling executives from each other's throats, helped negotiate the purchase of Ted Turner's company and settled nasty disputes between Levin and other moguls. Ultimately, it was Parsons who spearheaded the company's yearlong regulatory battle to win approval of AOL's purchase of Time Warner. When the deal closed, he became a co-chief operating officer, landing responsibility for the company's movie and music operations. Before long, the slumping music company started showing signs of life, and the studio caught fire with a string of hits including *Harry Potter, Lord of the Rings* and *Ocean's Eleven*.

Parsons still faces plenty of challenges. In his first address to Wall Street since the news of his promotion, Parsons had to explain the details of a $60 billion write-down of the company's value. The bumpy economy continues to rattle the media, publishing and Internet giant, and now that the honeymoon has passed, AOL and Time Warner have to deal with the pesky little details of wedding the two vast—and vastly different—companies.

One of "the biggest challenges I have is making the pieces work together, so we can shape our own destiny," Parsons says.

For American Express's Kenneth Chenault, the early challenges were far more concrete—and far more wrenching. Millions of TV viewers got their first glimpse of him on October 3, though most people didn't realize that it was the new AmEx CEO sitting next to President George W. Bush, who was in Manhattan to reassure some of America's corporate chieftains in the wake of the terrorist attacks. "I think the reason I was sitting next to him was that he had asked me to summarize the meeting" for the press following the gathering, Chenault recalled last week.

If not many Americans knew who Ken Chenault was last year, they certainly do now. Few companies suffered as much collateral devastation from the September 11 attacks as AmEx did. It has been Chenault's unenviable task to put the best face on what has clearly been an awful year for his company. "The role of a leader is to define reality and give hope," says Chenault, 50. "And this certainly was the year where it was important to constantly do both." The company's battered world headquarters, directly across the street from the World Trade Center, is still uninhabitable for Chenault and the 3,200 employees who worked there.

Even before September's tragedy, the view from Chenault's office on the Hudson River was gloomy. A big move by American Express into junk-bond investments years earlier was turning into a $1 billion blunder. The choppy stock market had cut into its money-management business. After the terrorist attacks, the company's core travel services and charge-card businesses were sputtering from the weakening economy. Last month Chenault had to lay off 6,500 employees, on top of 7,700 let go earlier in the year.

To say the Chenault's job is more than he bargained for is putting it mildly. Yet most observers believe he is up to the challenge. As a 20-year veteran of American Express, Chenault is the consummate insider. And yet he has an uncanny ability to take an outsider's view of his company that will prove crucial in rebuilding American Express. Time and again, Chenault has stuck by his guns, even when his suggestions were opposed by the AmEx old guard. "He was the only senior executive who had the courage to express issues we faced in the card business, and had ideas to help solve some," says Harvey Golub, who picked Chenault as heir.

Born into a middle-class family in Hempstead, on New York's Long Island, he attended private schools. As a youngster, he was a mediocre student—his early report cards were loaded with Cs and his parents, both of whom graduated at the top of their dentistry classes at Howard University, were hardly impressed. But by high school Ken had turned things around, and he graduated with honors as class president. He attended the tiny but prestigious Bowdoin College in Maine. It was there he first joined in heated debates within the small klatch of African-American students about whether blacks should work within the system. Though classmates recall Chenault encouraged discussion of both sides, to him the answer was clear: yes, they should. Chenault's next stop was Harvard, where he collected a law degree and an M.B.A. Then it was on to jobs in law and consulting.

American Express came calling in 1981, while Chenault was working at Bain, a top consulting firm in Boston. Chenault was among a small group of special recruits considered "high-potential candidates," recalls Lou Gerstner, the IBM chief who was then a top American Express executive. Hired to plan strategy, Chenault did well toeing the company line, and was attracting attention. At the time, recalls Amy Digeso, a former AmEx personnel executive, there was a lot of buzz around the company about the exceptional young newcomer. A straggler who'd heard about Chenault but had yet to meet him entered a room one day and was introduced. "'My God, you're black,'" Digeso recalls the man saying. "Ken said, 'Yes, I know.'" She adds: "That could have been very tense. Because Ken is so elegant and warm, it ended up being a light moment."

The outsider's perspective helped Chenault take chances that other fast-trackers might have avoided. He eventually sought a position—against the wishes of his superiors—in the AmEx division that peddles merchandise to cardholders. That wasn't a route to the top, they told him. But Chenault believed he could retool the business through aggressive marketing and upgrading of its products. The upshot: sales jumped from $100 million to $600 million in about two years. Chenault also bucked tradition when in the 1990s he moved over to the troubled American Express card business. Among other things, AmEx was facing heavy assaults from rivals Visa and MasterCard. Chenault found himself arguing against old-line managers who didn't want to introduce credit cards aimed at the mass market, fearing that such a move would dim the company's upscale luster. But Chenault prevailed, successfully launching cobranded credit cards with the likes of Delta and Costco, as well as signing up mass retailers like Kmart, which AmEx had previously snubbed, to accept The Card.

Chenault's strong convictions not only won him admiration at American Express. They also resulted in big gains for the company in terms of customer loyalty and, of course, the bottom line. "By the time I made the decision on succession, it was clear Ken had the full capacity to become CEO," says Golub. Adds Chenault's old boss Gerstner: "I'm really proud of what he's done."

If there's one shot that's gotten Stanley O'Neal to the top of his game, it's the swift, decisive stroke. Named president and chief operating officer of Merrill Lynch in July, O'Neal had emerged victoriously from a tumultuous two-way battle to succeed David Komansky when he retires in 2004. O'Neal wasted little time demoting his rivals, prompting two of them to resign.

As president of the brokerage division before his promotion to no. 2, O'Neal radically revamped the business. Profits jumped, apparently providing the final boost he needed to become the board of directors' top choice as the next CEO. Even as a youngster, O'Neal realized he'd likely get somewhere faster in life if he throttled his ambition to be a writer, an option he nixed at his father's urging. "His thought was that it's sort of an interesting ambition," recalls O'Neal. "But he had trouble thinking of people he knew who actually made a living from it. I had to admit he had a point."

Instead, O'Neal focused on ways to write his ticket to the top. Among the keys, he discovered, were speed, boldness and focus. Those qualities have become even more the essence of Stanley O'Neal in the months since he reached the stop below the summit. On Wall Street, dawdling never paid. And now that the charging bull market has run out of steam, slowness in reacting could mean going bust or winding up on the auction block. Predictably, O'Neal has moved with alacrity. Under his direction, the nation's largest brokerage is revamping at warp speed, pulling in its horns from Canada to South Africa to Japan. Since October, the company has cut its workforce by 9,000, for a 2001 total of 15,000 layoffs—fully one out of every five employees—a move that could result in extra profits of $700 million. When the market rebounds, Merrill expects to deliver turbocharged profits. "We have, I think, achieved a lot; I think there's a lot more to be done," says O'Neal as he gazes out his office window at a panoramic view of New York Harbor and the Statue of Liberty.

It's a view his grandfather, a former slave, could never have imagined. Born in tiny Wedowee, Alabama, O'Neal used to pick cotton as a child, and walked about a mile from his family's small farm to a one-room schoolhouse heated with a wood-burning stove. During his early teens, the family relocated to Atlanta in search of a better life, but ended up living in public housing for a while. O'Neal's father eventually landed a job at a nearby General Motors plant. "We never went hungry and somehow miraculously managed to be fully clothed and pretty happy," O'Neal says. GM proved a springboard for O'Neal, and he wound up attending the General Motors Institute, a cooperative college now renamed Kettering University. In 1978, he earned an M.B.A. from Harvard, then returned to GM in New York to work in the treasurer's office.

Eight years later Merrill came knocking. And what O'Neal saw and heard, he liked. "There was an openness to talent from many different backgrounds," O'Neal says. "That's a wonderful aspect of the culture." From the start, it was clear to O'Neal that he could have a bright future at Merrill. And, as he had guessed, it rapidly began unfolding for him. "He really excelled at all of the assignments," Komansky says. In 1991, O'Neal began running the junk-bond group, leading Merrill to dominance. Merrill's ranking sank after he was pulled away in 1996 to run other divisions. Komansky then made him chief financial officer in 1998. "One element of that assignment was to get him a broad view of the overall organizations," Komansky says. "Once again he did a terrific job."

Komansky then ended up throwing O'Neal in what initially must have seemed a lion's den, dispatching him to the Princeton, New Jersey-based brokerage division. O'Neal had never been a broker, and Merrill's 15,000-strong army wasn't exactly waiting with open arms to greet him. In fact, the brokers grew downright anxious when O'Neal announced he was implementing a dramatic new strategy to refocus the brokerage on luring only customers with at least $1 million in assets. "It was obvious to Stan and me that the business needed a lot of reconstruction," Komansky says. "When Stan set about doing that, it wasn't a popular task. What happened is he earned their respect."

And the respect of Merrill's directors. Now that O'Neal has taken charge with a vengeance, many on Wall Street are speculating that Komansky will step down well ahead of his scheduled exit in 2004. Does O'Neal believe his timetable, like much of everything else that has happened for him, will also be accelerated? "I spend almost no time thinking about that," he says.

Given their ages, Parsons, Chenault and O'Neal could have 15 years or more to make their mark on their companies. Or, thanks to the vagaries of corporate life, any one of them could get sacked tomorrow. What will remain, in either case, is the indelible mark they've made in the history books on racial progress.

"This is a powerful affirmation to young people that anything is possible," says Hugh Price, president of the National Urban

League. Or, as O'Neal puts it, "It gives people a chance to see someone who looks like themselves . . . and maybe creates some thoughts of success in a way that's different." To a generation of young black Americans who've been led to believe they have a better chance of landing in prison than in the executive suite, the rise of Parsons, Chenault and O'Neal is redefining what black power can—and should—ultimately be about.

A worrisome new study of female executives found that women are still frustrated in their attempts to mix careers and children. In a *Harvard Business Review* article adapted from her book *Creating a Life* (Talk Miramax Books), economist Sylvia Ann Hewlett paints a bleak picture of the situation but also calls upon business, government, and women themselves to work together toward meaningful work-life policies.

Sylvia Ann Hewlett

Executive Women and the Myth of Having It All

THERE IS A SECRET OUT THERE—a painful, well-kept secret: At midlife, between a third and a half of all successful career women in the United States do not have children. In fact, 33% of such women (business executives, doctors, lawyers, academics, and the like) in the 41-to-55 age bracket are childless—and that figure rises to 42% in corporate America. These women have not chosen to remain childless. The vast majority, in fact, yearn for children. Indeed, some have gone to extraordinary lengths to bring a baby into their lives. They subject themselves to complex medical procedures, shell out tens of thousands of dollars, and derail their careers—mostly to no avail, because these efforts come too late. In the words of one senior manager, the typical high-achieving woman childless at midlife has not made a choice but a "creeping nonchoice."

Why has the age-old business of having babies become so difficult for today's high-achieving women? In January 2001, in partnership with the market research company Harris Interactive and the National Parenting Association, I conducted a nationwide survey designed to explore the professional and private lives of highly educated, high-earning women. The survey results are featured in my new book, *Creating a Life: Professional Women and the Quest for Children*.

In this survey, I target the top 10% of women—measured in terms of earning power—and focus on two age groups: an older generation, ages 41 to 55, and their younger peers, ages 28 to 40, as defined for survey purposes. I distinguish between high achievers (those who are earning more than $55,000 in the younger group, $65,000 in the older one) and ultra-achievers (those who are earning more than $100,000). I include a sample of high-potential women—highly qualified women who have left their careers, mainly for family reasons. In addition, I include a small sample of men.

The findings are startling—and troubling. They make it clear that, for many women, the brutal demands of ambitious careers, the asymmetries of male-female relationships, and the difficulties of bearing children late in life conspire to crowd out the possibility of having children. In this article, I lay out the issues underlying this state of affairs, identify the heavy costs involved, and suggest some remedies, however preliminary and modest. The facts and figures I relate are bleak. But I think that they can also be liberating, if they spur action. My hope is that this information will generate workplace policies that recognize the huge costs to businesses of losing highly educated women when they start their families. I also hope that it will galvanize young women to make newly urgent demands of their partners, employers, and policy makers and thus create more generous life choices for themselves.

THE CONTINUING INEQUITY

When it comes to career and fatherhood, high-achieving men don't have to deal with difficult trade-offs: 79% of the men I

surveyed report wanting children—and 75% have them. The
research shows that, generally speaking, the more successful the
man, the more likely he will find a spouse and become a father.
The opposite holds true for women, and the disparity is particularly striking among corporate ultra-achievers. In fact, 49% of
these women are childless. But a mere 19% of their male colleagues are. These figures underscore the depth and scope of the
persisting, painful inequities between the sexes. Women face all
the challenges that men do in working long hours and withstand-
ing the up-or-out pressures of high-altitude careers. But they also
face challenges all their own.

Slim Pickings in Partners. Let's start with the fact that professional women find it challenging even to *be* married—for most,
a necessary precondition for childbearing. Only 60% of high-
achieving women in the older age group are married, and this
figure falls to 57% in corporate America. By contrast, 76% of
older men are married, and this figure rises to 83% among ultra-
achievers.

Consider Tamara Adler, 43, a former managing director of
Deutsche Bank in London. She gave her take on these disturbing
realities when I interviewed her for the study. Adler was the bank's
most senior woman, and her highly successful career had left no
room for family. She mentioned the obvious reasons—long hours
and travel—but she also spoke eloquently about how ambitious
careers discriminate against women: "In the rarified upper reaches
of high-altitude careers where the air is thin . . . men have a much
easier time finding oxygen. They find oxygen in the form of
younger, less driven women who will coddle their egos." She went
on to conclude, "The hard fact is that most successful men are not
interested in acquiring an ambitious peer as a partner."

It's a conclusion backed up by my data: Only 39% of high-
achieving men are married to women who are employed full-time,
and 40% of these spouses earn less than $35,000 a year. Meanwhile,
nine out of ten married women in the high-achieving category
have husbands who are employed full-time or self-employed, and

In January 2001, in partnership with Harris Interactive and the National Parenting Association, I conducted a nationwide survey targeting the top 10% of women—measured in terms of earning power—and a small sample of men for comparative purposes. Responding were 1,168 high-achieving career women ages 28 to 55; 479 high-achieving, noncareer women ages 28 to 55; and 472 high-achieving men ages 28 to 55. (The group of ultra-achieving men was not large enough to disaggregate.) The sample was drawn from the Harris Poll on-line database of cooperative respondents. Data were weighted for key demographic variables to reflect each sample's national population. My analysis delineated an older generation, 41 to 55, and that group's younger peers, 28 to 40. I also distinguished between high achievers (those earning more than $65,000 or $55,000, depending on age), ultra-achievers (those earning more than $100,000), and high-potential women—highly qualified women who have left their careers, mainly for family reasons. Corporate women were defined as working in companies with more than 5,000 employees. The two charts below contain some of the startling—and sobering—findings.

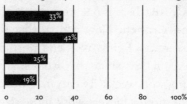

Percentage of professionals childless at ages 41 to 55

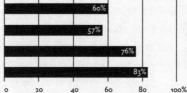

Percentage of married professionals at ages 41 to 55

The survey was carried out by Harris Interactive under the auspices of the National Parenting Association, a nonprofit research organization. Funding for the survey and the associated research was provided by Ernst & Young, Merck, the Annie E. Casey Foundation, and the David and Lucile Packard Foundation. For more about the methodology and findings, go to www.parentsunite.org.

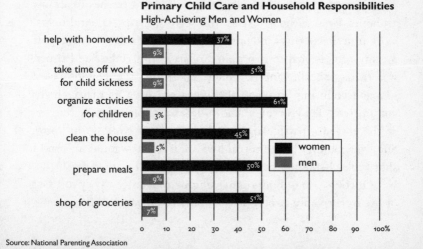

Primary Child Care and Household Responsibilities
High-Achieving Men and Women

Source: National Parenting Association

a quarter are married to men who earn more than $100,000 a year. Clearly, successful women professionals have slim pickings in the marriage department—particularly as they age. Professional men seeking to marry typically reach into a large pool of younger women, while professional women are limited to a shrinking pool of eligible peers. According to U.S. Census Bureau data, at age 28 there are four college-educated, single men for every three college-educated, single women. A decade later, the situation is radically changed. At age 38, there is one man for every three women.

The Time Crunch. Now add to that scarcity of marriage candidates a scarcity of time to spend nurturing those relationships. My survey results show that women are dealing with long and lengthening workweeks. Twenty-nine percent of high achievers and 34% of ultra-achievers work more than 50 hours a week, and a significant proportion of these women are on the job ten to 20 more hours a week than they were five years ago. Among ultra-achievers, a quarter are away on business at least five nights every three months. According to research by sociologists Jerry Jacobs and Kathleen Gerson, the percentage of women working at least 50 hours a week is now higher in the United States than in any other country.

Think of what a 55-hour week means in terms of work-life balance. If you assume an hour lunch and a 45-minute round-trip commute (the national average), the workday stretches to almost 13 hours. Even without "extras" (out-of-town trips, client dinners, work functions), this kind of schedule makes it extremely difficult for any professional to maintain a relationship. Take Sue Palmer, 49, managing director of Grant Thornton, the London-based global accounting firm, and the only woman on its management committee. "Ten years ago," she said, "an assistant of mine told me at the end of a particularly grueling 70-hour week, 'You know, Sue, you couldn't have a torrid love affair if you wanted to.' And I shot back, 'I couldn't have a *tepid* love affair if I wanted to.'"

Of course, long hours aren't unique to women. They're a fact of life in corporate America, where management is under intense pressure to use its professional workforce for as many hours a week as possible. The reasons for this go back to 1938, when Congress passed the Fair Labor Standards Act, which institutionalized the 40-hour workweek and required employers to pay overtime for additional hours worked. One provision, however, exempted managers and professionals and still does. For those workers, extra hours carry no marginal costs to employers. The temptation for companies to take advantage of that provision might not have been so problematic back in 1938 when only 15% of employees were exempt, and most of them were men with stay-at-home spouses. But it produces significant overload today when close to 30% of employees are in the exempt category, many of them women who rarely have the luxury of a spouse at home tending to domestic responsibilities.

An Unforgiving Decade. Women pay an even greater price for those long hours because the early years of career building overlap—almost perfectly—the prime years of childbearing. It's very hard to throttle back during that stage of a career and expect to catch up later. As policy analyst Nancy Rankin points out, the career highway has all kinds of off-ramps but few on-ramps.

In fact, the persistent wage gap between men and women is due mainly to the penalties women incur when they interrupt their careers to have children. In a recent study, economists Susan Harkness and Jane Waldfogel compared that wage gap across seven industrialized countries and found it was particularly wide in the United States. For example, in France, women earn 81% of the male wage, in Sweden 84%, and in Australia 88%, while in the United States, women continue to earn a mere 78% of the male wage. These days, only a small portion of this wage gap can be attributed to discrimination (getting paid less for doing the same job or being denied access to jobs, education, or capital based on sex). According to recent studies, an increasingly large part of the wage gap can now be explained by childbearing and child rearing, which interrupt women's—but not men's—careers, permanently depressing their earning power. If the gap between what men and women earn in this country is wider than elsewhere, it isn't because this country has done an inferior job combating discrimination. It is because it has failed to develop policies—in the workplace and in society as a whole—that support working mothers.

Ironically, this policy failure is to some extent the fault of the women's movement in the United States. Going back to the mid-nineteenth century, feminists in this country have channeled much of their energy into the struggle to win formal equality with men. More recently, the National Organization for Women has spent 35 years fighting for a wide array of equal rights, ranging from educational and job opportunities to equal pay and access to credit. The idea is that once all the legislation that discriminates against women is dismantled, the playing field becomes level and women can assume a free and equal place in society by simply cloning the male competitive model.

In Europe, various groups of social feminists have viewed the problem for women quite differently. For them, it is not woman's lack of legal rights that constitutes her main handicap, or even her lack of reproductive freedom. Rather, it is her dual burden—taking care of a home and family as well as holding down a job—that leads to her second-class status.

The Second Shift. The problem with the notion that American women should be able to successfully clone the male competitive model is that husbands have not picked up a significant share of women's traditional responsibilities on the home front. Even high-achieving women who are married continue to carry the lion's share of domestic responsibilities. (See the exhibit "Primary Child Care and Household Responsibilities.") Only 9% of their husbands assume primary responsibility for meal preparation, 10% for the laundry, and 5% for cleaning the house. When it comes to children, husbands don't do much better. Only 9% of them take time off from work when a child is sick, 9% take the lead in helping children with homework, and 3% organize activities such as play dates and summer camp.

Yes, these percentages have grown over the years—but not much. At the end of the day, the division of labor at home boils down to one startling fact: 43% of the older, high-achieving women and 37% of the younger, high-achieving women feel that their husbands actually create more household work for them than they contribute. (Thirty-nine percent of ultra-achieving women also feel this way, despite the fact that half of them are married to men who earn less than they do.)

Stubborn Biology. So this is the difficult position in which women find themselves. According to Lisa Benenson, former editor of *Working Woman* and *Working Mother* magazines, "The signals are very clear. Young women are told that a serious person needs to commit to her career in her 20s and devote all her energies to her job for at least ten years if she is to be successful." But the fact is, if you take this advice you might well be on the wrong side of 35 before you have time to draw breath and contemplate having a child, exactly the point in life when infertility can—and overwhelmingly does—become an issue.

Media hype about advances in reproductive science only exacerbates the problem, giving women the illusion that they can delay childbearing until their careers are well established. My survey tells us that 89% of young, high-achieving women believe that they will be able to get pregnant deep into their 40s. But sadly, new reproductive technologies have not solved fertility problems for older women. The research shows that only 3% to 5% of women who attempt in vitro fertilization in their 40s actually succeed in bearing a child. This kind of information is hard to come by because the infertility industry in this country likes to tout the good news—with dire consequences. Too many career women put their private lives on the back burner, assuming that children will eventually happen for them courtesy of high-tech reproduction—only to discover disappointment and failure.

A COSTLY IMBALANCE

I can't tell you how many times over the course of this research the women I interviewed apologized for "wanting it all." But it wasn't as though these women were looking for special treatment. They were quite prepared to shoulder more than their fair share of the work involved in having both career and family. So why on earth shouldn't they feel entitled to rich, multidimensional lives? At the end of the day, women simply want the choices in love and work that men take for granted.

Instead, they operate in a society where motherhood carries enormous economic penalties. Two recent studies lay out these penalties in very specific terms. In her study, economist Waldfogel finds that mothers earn less than other women do even when you control for marital status, experience, and education. In fact, according to her research, one child produces a "penalty" of 6% of earnings, while two children produce a wage penalty of 13%. In a more recent study, economists Michelle Budig and Paula England find that motherhood results in a penalty of 7% per child.

Given such a huge disincentive, why do women persist in trying to "have it all"? Because, as a large body of research demonstrates, women are happier when they have both career and family. In a series of books and articles that span more than a decade, University of Michigan sociologist Lois Hoffmann has examined the value of children to parents and finds that, across cultures, parents see children as enormously important in providing love and companionship and in warding off loneliness. Children also help parents deal with the questions of human existence: How do I find purpose beyond the self? How do I cope with mortality?

Thus, the fact that so many professional women are forced to sacrifice motherhood is patently unfair, and it also has immense implications for American business, since it causes women intent on motherhood to cut short their careers. This is, of course, the flip side of the same coin. For if a large proportion of women who stay on track in their careers are forced to give up family, an equally large proportion who opt for family are forced to give up their careers. According to my survey, 66% of high-potential women would like to return to full-time jobs.

The cost to corporations and to our economy becomes monumental in the aggregate. Our nation needs professional women to stay in the labor force; we can ill afford to have a quarter of the female talent pool forced out of their jobs when they have children. But in 2000, at the height of the labor church, Census Bureau data showed that fully 22% of all women with professional degrees (MBAs, MDs, PhDs, and so on) were not in the labor market at all. What an extraordinary waste of expensively educated talent!

At the same time, we need adults at all income levels to become committed, effective parents. When a parent devotes time, attention, and financial resources to help a child become a well-adjusted person—one who succeeds in school and graduates from college—not only do parents feel deeply fulfilled, but society, of course, is graced with productive workers who boost the GDP, obey the law, and pay their taxes. Thus, we are all stakeholders in parents' ability to come through for their children.

And when women come to understand the value of parenthood to the wider community, they can quit apologizing for wanting both a career and a family. A woman can hold her head high when she goes in to her boss and asks for a schedule that fits her needs.

THE CHALLENGE TO BUSINESS

The statistics I've laid out here would be bearable if they were purely historical—the painful but isolated experience of a pioneering generation—but they are not. My survey shows that younger women are facing even more difficult trade-offs. Can we reverse these pernicious trends and finally create the possibility of true work-life balance? I believe we can.

The first challenge is to employers, to craft more meaningful work-life policies. Professional women who want both family and career know that conventional benefit packages are insufficient. These women need reduced-hour jobs and careers that can be interrupted, neither of which is readily available yet. And more than anything, they need to be able to partake of such benefits without suffering long-term damage to their careers.

High-achieving women make it abundantly clear that what they want most are work-life policies that confer on them what one woman calls "the gift of time." Take Joanna, for example. At 39, Joanna had worked for five years as an account executive for a Chicago headhunter. She believed her company had great work-life policies—until she adopted a child. "My main problem," Joanna said, "is the number of hours I am expected to put in. I work 60 hours a week 50 weeks of the year, which leaves precious little time for anything else." Joanna asked for a reduced schedule, but it was a "no go. The firm didn't want to establish a precedent," she said. Joanna began looking for another job.

According to my survey, some employers take family needs into account: 12% offer paid parenting leave and 31% job sharing. Many more, however, provide only time flexibility: 69% allow staggered hours, and 48% have work-at-home options. These less ambitious policies seem to be of limited use to time-pressed, high-achieving women.

So, what do professionals want? The high-achieving career women who participated in my survey were asked to consider a list of policy options that would help them achieve balance in their lives over the long haul. They endorsed the following cluster of work-life policies that would make it much easier to get off conventional career ladders and eventually get back on:

A Time Bank of Paid Parenting Leave. This would allow for three months of paid leave, which could be taken as needed, until the child turned 18.

Restructured Retirement Plans. In particular, survey respondents want to see the elimination of penalties for career interruptions.

Career Breaks. Such a leave of absence might span three years—unpaid, of course, but with the assurance of a job when the time came to return to work.

Reduced-Hour Careers. High-level jobs should be created that permit reduced hours and workloads on an ongoing basis but still offer the possibility of promotion.

Alumni Status for Former Employees. Analogous to active retirement, alumni standing would help women who have left or are not active in their careers stay in the loop. They might be tapped for advice and guidance, and the company would continue to pay their dues and certification fees so they could maintain professional standing.

Policies like these are vital—though in themselves not enough to solve the problem. In particular, companies must guard against the perception that by taking advantage of such policies, a woman will tarnish her professional image. Outside the fiction of human resource policies, a widespread belief in business is that a woman who allows herself to be accommodated on the family front is no longer choosing to be a serious contender. Top management must work to banish this belief from the corporate culture.

The good news is that, where top management supports them, work-life policies like the ones I've listed do pay off. My survey data show that companies offering a rich array of work-life policies are much more likely to hang on to their professional women than companies that don't. High-achieving mothers who have been able to stay in their careers tend to work for companies that allow them access to generous benefits: flextime, telecommuting, paid parenting leave, and compressed workweeks. In contrast, high-achieving mothers who have been forced out of their careers tended to work for companies with inadequate work-life benefits.

I heard a wonderful example of the loyalty these kinds of policies engender when I spoke with Amy, 41, a marketing executive for IBM. Her son had just turned three, and Amy was newly back at work. "People don't believe me when I tell them that my company offers a three-year personal leave of absence," she said. As she described the policy, it applies not only to mothers; others have used it to care for elderly parents or to return to school. The leave is unpaid but provides continuation of benefits and a job-back guarantee. "IBM gave me this gift," she said, "and I will always be grateful." Clearly, in the aggregate, business leaders hold the power to make important and constructive change.

Because companies can't be expected to craft all the policies that will make a difference in women's lives, government should also take action. I have urged policy makers at the national level, for example, to extend the Family and Medical Leave Act to workers in small companies and turn it into paid leave. State and federal governments could also accomplish much by providing tax incentives to companies that offer employees flextime and various reduced-hour options. And we should promote legislation that eliminates perverse incentives for companies to subject their employees to long-hour weeks.

THE CHALLENGE TO WOMEN

My book focuses on what women themselves can do to expand their life choices. In a nutshell, if you're a young woman who wants both career and family, you should consider doing the following:

Figure out what you want your life to look like at 45. If you want children (and between 86% and 89% of high-achieving women do), you need to become highly intentional—and take action now.

Give urgent priority to finding a partner. My survey data suggest that high-achieving women have an easier time finding partners in their 20s and early 30s.

Have your first child before 35. The occasional miracle notwithstanding, late-in-life childbearing is fraught with risk and failure. Even if you manage to get one child "under the wire," you may fail to have a second. This, too, can trigger enormous regret.

Choose a career that will give you the gift of time. Certain careers provide more flexibility and are more forgiving of interruptions. Female entrepreneurs, for example, do better than female lawyers in combining career and family—and both do better than corporate women. The key is to avoid professions with rigid career trajectories.

Choose a company that will help you achieve work-life balance. Look for such policies as reduced-hour schedules and job-protected leave.

That's an easy list to compile, but I have no illusions that it will change the world, because identifying what each woman can do is only half the battle. The other half is convincing women that they are entitled to both a career and children. Somehow the perception persists that a woman isn't a woman unless her life is riddled with sacrifice.

AN END TO SELF-SACRIFICE

In February 2001, I conducted an informal focus group with young professionals at three consulting firms in Cambridge, Massachusetts. During that session, a young woman named Natalie commented, "This is the third consulting firm I've worked for, and I've yet to see an older, more senior woman whose life I would actually want."

Natalie's colleague Rachel was shocked and asked her to explain. She responded, "I know a few hard-driving women who are climbing the ladder at consulting firms, but they are single or divorced and seem pretty isolated. And I know a handful of working mothers who are trying to do the half-time thing or the two-thirds-time thing. They work reduced hours so they can see their kids, but they don't get the good projects, they don't get the bonuses, and they also get whispered about behind their backs. You know, comments like 'If she's not prepared to work the client's hours, she has no business being in the profession.'"

This is the harsh reality behind the myth of having it all. Even in organizations whose policies support women, prevailing attitudes and unrelenting job pressures undermine them. Women's lives have expanded. But the grudging attitudes of most corporate cultures weigh down and constrain what individual women feel is possible.

Are church and business compatible? Deborah O'Neil and Jeff Harrington of the *St. Petersburg Times* spent four months compiling this story about Digital Lightwave, a Florida company whose leadership had strong ties to the Church of Scientology. The plot twists read like a novel.

Deborah O'Neil and Jeff Harrington

The CEO and His Church

MONTHS OF INTERVIEWS and thousands of pages of court papers show the effect that influential church members had on a Clearwater company that was a darling of the dot-com boom. It was New Year's Eve 1997 when Digital Lightwave's chief, Bryan Zwan, made his biggest deal: a $9 million contract for his signature product, a 10-pound device that tests telephone lines.

At 5:30 P.M., Zwan phoned his production staff and gave them a tall order: Ship the 308 units right away. It would help prop up dismal sales numbers.

But his overtaxed workers—they had put in 100-hour weeks during the holidays—didn't have enough time or materials.

As the night wore on, the crew sent incomplete and unassembled units to a shipping warehouse, giving the impression the order was filled. Digital had done this before. The company even had shipped units to salesmen's homes for storage and booked them as sales.

A manufacturing manager named Chuck Anderson became fed up. Most company whistleblowers typically alert the Securities and Exchange Commission to possible wrongdoing. But Anderson reported the trouble to his own higher authority: the Church of Scientology.

He wrote a "knowledge report," addressed to church leaders, warning that the New Year's Eve shipments were the latest in a troubling pattern in Digital that could create a "huge potential flap" for Scientology.

"What happens if someone goes to the newspapers, the investors, the SEC?" Anderson, a Scientologist, wrote in his report. "Not to mention putting Scientology and Scientologists at risk."

Zwan, a longtime Scientologist who has given millions to the church, had moved his high-tech start-up company from Santa Monica, California, to downtown Clearwater two years earlier, locating it just two blocks from the church's international spiritual headquarters.

He has long insisted that Digital has no connection to the controversial church. Zwan said he never hired people because they are Scientologists and never sought church advice on company matters.

"We are a public company," Zwan said. "We have nothing to do with the Church of Scientology. It has no role in this company."

But a four-month review by the *St. Petersburg Times,* drawing on thousands of pages of court documents and dozens of interviews, makes it clear that the fortunes and the misfortunes of Digital Lightwave have been profoundly affected by influential Scientologists with close ties to the church.

Zwan's stewardship of Digital has been tumultuous, marked by wild success that made the Belleair physicist one of America's richest men, and by a debacle that badly wounded the company.

Other local companies are run by Scientologists with little scrutiny. But Digital's high profile as a publicly traded company subject to federal regulation yields a rare look at how Scientology factors into the workplace when the CEO is a church follower and major contributor.

Digital's inside story is one of Scientologists emerging at critical points to play key roles. A Scientologist helped Zwan develop Digital's fiber-optic technology. Scientology facilities, including the landmark Fort Harrison Hotel in Clearwater, were backdrops for important company negotiations. Zwan tapped Scientologists for his early management team. And fellow Scientologists were Zwan's early backers, many reaping riches from Digital's run on Wall Street.

To further understand Scientology's tie to Digital Lightwave, consider that Zwan hired as one of his top executives Denise Licciardi, the sister of Scientology's worldwide leader, David Miscavige.

Quickly promoted and given a six-figure salary, Licciardi was widely regarded as Zwan's right hand at Digital. She urged him to run day-to-day operations by following Scientology founder L. Ron Hubbard's business practices known as "LRH Tech."

Digital could "become a showcase of LRH Tech," Licciardi wrote in one memo to Zwan. "This was what you communicated to each of us was your dream."

But when federal regulators investigated Digital in the late 1990s for allegedly inflating its sales, Licciardi escaped blame. Her central role remained under wraps for years. The church was spared the "huge flap" feared in the knowledge report.

Scientology's leaders insist the church neither acted on the knowledge report nor protected Licciardi. They emphatically say they play no part in Digital Lightwave and never have.

"The church doesn't get involved in managing their business," said Marty Rathbun, a high-ranking church leader based in Los Angeles.

But Zwan's interest in and devotion to Scientology was front and center in his creation of Digital Lightwave. One of his earliest investors, onetime Scientologist Brian Haney, recalls Zwan's can't-miss pitch to join him in building the company.

"We were going to keep some for ourselves and live like kings, of course," Haney said. "The main amount of money was going to end up in Scientology's hands."

INSIDE THE LIGHT

As a boy in East Texas, Bryan Zwan surprised his parents by buying a secondhand 40-foot radio tower and erecting it in his backyard. In high school, the future physicist impressed his friends by hooking up a ham radio in his car to contact people halfway around the world.

Zwan, 54, earned his doctorate at Rice University in the same field of science that once interested Scientology founder L. Ron Hubbard. The Scientology patriarch used physics to design an experiment with sound waves that led to one of his first conclusions about the mind. Zwan used physics to design an instrument that led to one of the hottest light-wave products on the digital market.

Fiber optics—high-speed, hair-thin lines that use light waves to transmit data—were emerging as the technology of the future in 1990. Zwan and a co-developer came up with a portable, lightweight device for technicians in the field to test fiber-optic lines.

Phone companies, cable companies and Internet providers all soon would look to fiber-optic lines to handle burgeoning voice and data traffic.

Zwan coined the name "Digital Lightwave" and created a logo of multicolored rectangles seemingly in motion. "Pretty cool, huh? I came up with that," Zwan said with a dimpled grin.

Gushing about Digital's technology, Zwan goes from CEO to professor. It uses logic. Algebra is involved. And voltages and polarities.

It's "40 colors of light pulsing at 2½ billion times a second in one little fiber the size of a human hair," Zwan says, tugging on an arm hair.

Digital's technology can reach in, pick one of those colors and separate it out for inspection. Or as Zwan puts it, "This is technology to reach inside the light."

SUPER POWER—WORLDWIDE

In 1993, Zwan needed investors to take Digital Lightwave out of the incubator. He found a wealthy business partner while visiting Scientology's international spiritual retreat, the Fort Harrison Hotel in Clearwater.

One day over lunch in the hotel's Hibiscus room, a Scientology staff member introduced Zwan to Brain Haney, a fellow entrepreneur visiting from Columbus, Ohio. Haney had become a millionaire in his 20s selling toys through his Great American Fun Corp.

Digital Lightwave was no more than a start-up then, fueled by Zwan's enthusiasm and vision. He had yet to manufacture a product and had just a handful of employees. Haney was intrigued.

Days later, Zwan traveled to Columbus to discuss a deal, meeting Haney at the Scientology facility there. But there was a twist: Zwan had a Scientology staff member in tow. Haney had plenty of questions about Digital, but they would have to wait.

First on the agenda was Scientology. The church wanted $100,000 for its planned Super Power building in Clearwater, a massive, $50 million complex now under construction. Haney balked. He had already given the project $200,000. But Zwan and the church staffer kept asking. Eventually, Haney wrote the check.

The businessmen then turned to Digital Lightwave. The two Scientologists discussed using Hubbard's teachings to run the company.

They had an unspoken understanding, Haney said: No one would mention Scientology and Digital in the same breath. "It was known people would frown upon it," Haney said. Investors and potential customers might be leery of a company with ties to a controversial church.

As Digital grew, Haney said, they planned to donate millions back to the church.

"We were going to be two Scientologists who ran a Scientology company that would bring in a ton of money that would get donated to Scientology so Scientology could put up Super Power buildings all over the globe," said Haney, now 43.

Zwan refuses to talk about his early days with Haney. But he insists: "I did not start Digital Lightwave with the aspiration of it as a vehicle to invest in Scientology." Further, he says Scientology's business principles were never used at Digital.

The entrepreneurs made a pact. For $5 million, Haney said, he wound up with 49 percent of the company and left daily operations to Zwan.

MORE KNOWLEDGE REPORTS

With Haney's millions, Zwan moved his small company to Clearwater in 1995, renting space in the green glass Atrium Building on Cleveland Street near Scientology headquarters.

The move, Zwan said, had nothing to do with the church. The Tampa Bay area topped an 11-city survey because it was near water and in a state with no income tax.

Haney believes otherwise: "One of his reasons for moving the company to Florida was . . . he could hire Scientologists. It was a given that all Scientologist employees were superior to all non-Scientologist employees."

By late 1995, Digital was ready to debut its flagship optic tester: the ASA 312.

The relationship between Haney and Zwan had frayed, though. Haney and his wife, Linda, had grown disillusioned with Scientology and left the church. The church labeled Mrs. Haney a "suppressive person," a name given to people the church believes are working against it. Church members are not to associate with a suppressive person.

Haney said Zwan summoned him to a meeting at Fort Harrison with church staff member Mary Voegeding Shaw, now president of FLAG, Scientology's spiritual retreat in Clearwater. Haney recalled the conversation:

"Mary Voegeding says to me because my wife is a declared [suppressive] person I cannot be a partner in business with Bryan Zwan and that I only have two choices: I have to either divorce my wife or stop being Bryan Zwan's partner."

Haney looked at Zwan.

"That's right," Zwan said to Haney. "Those are the two choices."

Haney thought: "I'm in a room with crazy people."

Church officials bristle at Haney's account, describing it as "completely fabricated" and "out there." They say he has no credibility. His funding of anti-Scientology efforts in recent years is evidence he targets Scientology to "drag it through the mud," Rathbun said.

Haney says Zwan told him that the company's future was rocky and that he should get out while he could. Haney agreed.

Needing money to buy out Haney, Zwan turned to Scientologists Leon Meekcoms and Gerald Ellenburg, both real estate investors.

The two agreed to help raise the cash. But within a few months, they were complaining Zwan had not repaid investors and had not followed through on other promises.

Ellenburg and Meekcoms detailed their complaints in March 1996 in two knowledge reports addressed to high-ranking church officials.

Ellenburg requested an immediate review by the church. He warned that while he, Zwan and Meekcoms were "bound" to settle their disputes through "church channels," other investors were not. Those "not bound by the rules of our church" could go to court, he noted.

A church ethics officer told Ellenburg and Zwan to settle their dispute themselves.

TAKING IT TO THE STREET

Despite the friction among investors, Digital started selling its product, recording $6 million in sales in 1996. Zwan decided to sell stock to the public, a bold move to generate cash so his young company could grow faster.

To help navigate the expansion, Zwan recruited Seth Joseph, a 41-year-old securities lawyer from Miami, as his no. 2. One of the few non-Scientologists in Digital management, Joseph was given a $250,000 salary and up to 656,666 stock options, potentially worth millions.

Another executive came aboard then, too: Denise Licciardi, a 36-year-old Scientologist and sister of the church's leader, Miscavige.

While she had no formal education beyond high school, Licciardi was a go-getter with administrative experience at other companies, including a New Hampshire firm run by Scientologists who followed L. Ron Hubbard business principles.

Zwan soon promoted Licciardi to vice president of administration, paid her a $123,000 salary and gave her 60,000 stock options.

Her authority bothered Joseph, who questioned her qualifications. "She was very, very close to Bryan beyond what her skills would warrant," he said. "It was because of her relationship with Bryan in Scientology."

Zwan said he "didn't know her, [she] wasn't a friend." Licciardi applied for the job after hearing about it from her mother, who lives in Clearwater.

With Zwan's management team in place, the once-tiny private company had grown to 90 employees and was about to become a Wall Street player.

But first, a personnel matter needed tidying up before the company could go public. Digital's investment banker asked company brass if it was true that executive vice president Elizabeth

Weigand was, indeed, a felon. She was. In 1980, Weigand was convicted of trying to extort money from her uncle, former U.S. Sen. Thomas Eagleton, D-Mo., who said at the time that he believed his niece intended to give the money to Scientology. She resigned from Digital.

On February 6, 1997, Digital Lightwave staged a successful initial public offering, trading at $12 a share. For Zwan, that meant his 20 million shares were suddenly worth $240 million.

After Zwan, the biggest stakeholder was Norton Kamo, L. Ron Hubbard's former personal attorney, whose shares jumped to more than $7 million in value.

Also hitting the jackpot was Scientologist Doug Dohring, who served as Digital's president for just eight months. When he cashed out his stock options in late 1997, long after leaving the company, he made more than $1 million.

Left out of the millionaire's jubilee was Haney, the early investor who had left Scientology. Saying he had been tricked into selling back his shares, Haney later sued Zwan, claiming his stock would eventually have been worth $235 million.

Not visible to Wall Street were the atmospherics at Digital Lightwave.

Just months after coming aboard, a frustrated Licciardi wanted more of Hubbard's "Admin tech" in the workplace. She wrote Zwan a nine-page memo reminding him that in recruiting her and other Scientologists, he had promised to use the Scientology methods.

"We left our lives behind for a reasonable salary [and] a small . . . amount of stock to help you attain your goal," she wrote. "Here all we are trying to do is get to be a billion-dollar company in the telecom industry. Why don't we just apply the tech?"

Though Hubbard's practices were not formally adopted, the aura of Scientology was present at Digital. The company's organizational chart closely resembled Scientology's "org boards," where departments are referred to as divisions.

Former controller Mike Tinsley said he didn't understand the company's structure until he visited a Clearwater drugstore run by a Scientologist. "They had the exact same org chart on their wall as we had in our company," Tinsley said.

Gossiping and joking about Scientology even got workers in trouble. Tinsley said he was instructed to fire an accounting clerk who mentioned to a co-worker that she had seen credit card statements detailing how much some Scientologists had donated to the church.

Technical writer Sean Ward was fired as a contractor after e-mailing three Digital employees and saying about Scientology: "Can you believe people in your company really believe this?"

SCIENTOLOGY . . . AT RISK

In early 1997, the newly public Digital was being directed by Zwan from his Clearwater "war room." Employees said he set unrealistic goals: Double sales every quarter; quadruple sales by the end of the year.

The aggressive efforts came after first-quarter sales missed the targets and the stock tumbled as low as $3 a share.

In the following months, Digital reported overblown sales numbers. Salesmen loaned to clients demonstration units that were counted as sales. Units were stored at employees' homes but counted as sold goods.

Documents obtained by the *Times* detail another messy episode not revealed to investors. At the center: Zwan's fellow Scientologist Licciardi.

It was December 1997, and Digital was racing to fill orders before the year-end closing of the books.

Customers were returning Digital's product. Manufacturing employees were working late, filling orders that had already been booked as sales in the previous quarter. Without a big contract, the company might have to declare fourth-quarter "negative

sales"—a nearly unheard-of admission that more product was
returned than sold.

Then that big contract arrived, literally at the last moment:
New Year's Eve. Pac Pacific of California ordered $9 million worth
of Digital's testing units.

Zwan turned to Licciardi to get the shipment out ASAP.

Company records suggested all the units were assembled and
shipped New Year's Eve. In fact, only 71 of the 308 units were finished despite the scrambling.

Some workers labored until 3 A.M., then grudgingly came
back in later on New Year's Day. One was Chuck Anderson. His
wife was five months pregnant and fed up with his overtime.
Moreover, Anderson was tired of Licciardi's bossy ways. He just
had to tell somebody.

So days later, he did. He wrote an 11-page, single-spaced
knowledge report to Scientology leaders and Zwan, detailing all
he had seen the last few months.

Anderson wrote that Licciardi was out of control. She was
hurting morale by screaming, cursing and pushing people too far,
he said. She was bypassing the chain of command. It was Licciardi,
he wrote, who came up with the idea of putting half-built, half-
tested units into boxes to give the impression production was done.

Digital Lightwave was "vulnerable" because too many people
knew what was happening, he wrote, and bad publicity could put
"Scientology and Scientologists at risk given the local scene."

The "local scene" in January 1998 was the rancorous contro-
versy over the death of Scientologist Lisa McPherson. A month
before, police had taken the unprecedented step of recommending
criminal charges in connection with her death while in the care of
fellow Scientologists. The case was making headlines around the
world.

Anderson also reminded church officials of a Scientology-
related business scandal: "Look what happened with TradeNet."

A Dunedin company owned and run by Scientologists, Trade-
Net was investigated by state regulators as a possible pyramid

scheme. State records showed that Scientologists at TradeNet also were keeping the church in the loop. One communication said church officials were "s—— bricks" over the company's bad press.

Zwan said he relayed Anderson's report to Licciardi without reading it. Later, he ordered Anderson to shred it.

In a recent interview, Zwan said he has never written any knowledge reports to the church about company business and he found the fact Anderson did "extremely odd."

"It's never been done before, never done since," he said.

Church officials say there is no record they ever received Anderson's report. "We could spend hours and hours and hours going and checking this to say with absolute certainty that nobody ever got any copy of that," said Scientology official Mike Rinder. "We can't guarantee that there may not be a person out there that may have seen something."

As it turned out, all the commotion on that memorable New Year's Eve ended in a whimper. Digital's board of directors refused Zwan's plea to count the Pac Pacific sale as revenue.

But the overblown sales had caught up to Digital. Three weeks after the New Year's Eve episode, the company issued a "restatement" of its earnings to investors, publicly acknowledging earlier financial reports were not accurate.

Nearly half the sales Digital reported in the second quarter of 1997 involved deals that either never happened or were not closed. A stunning 79 percent of third-quarter sales were wiped off the books.

The restatement triggered SEC and Nasdaq investigations, and more than 20 shareholder lawsuits. And as the company was reeling from the bad publicity, it was facing another crisis internally.

Licciardi told higher-ups that on New Year's Eve she had shipped out a couple of dozen partly filled boxes to be counted as sales. And co-workers said she had done it before. The company's top brass was astounded.

"It was clear she had to go," said Joseph, the lawyer who served as Zwan's no. 2. "She had committed criminal conduct. She admitted to it. . . . It was devastating."

A FATEFUL MONDAY

Tensions came to a head on January 26, an overcast Monday just four days after the restatement.

Scientologists and non-Scientologists turned on each other as the company's top two financial officers, Joseph and Steve Grant, called for Zwan to fire Licciardi.

A group of Scientologists in the company went to Zwan to rally support for Licciardi.

That morning, some said they saw Scientologists in distinctive naval uniforms in the corridors. Others said it was hired security.

But the effect was the same, particularly on Grant, the company's chief financial officer. Grant, who is not a Scientologist, feared retribution if a prominent Scientologist like Licciardi was asked to leave. He removed photos of his family from his desk.

"There were some very, very angry shareholders [because of the restatement] and now there were some very, very angry Scientologists," Grant said.

The skittish financial officer even arranged for a security guard at his home. Grant wasn't the only one taking precautions. Zwan signed off on a $1,500 request for an electronic sweep for eavesdropping devices in Digital's offices.

Licciardi said she was shocked when Zwan started pointing fingers at her. She felt "like I'm in the f—— twilight zone," Licciardi would later tell SEC investigators. "Suddenly he was making it seem like I was running wild over the organization, unbeknownst to him."

But Licciardi saw Zwan soften, and by day's end she was helping him coordinate a legal strategy to combat the SEC investigation. For help, she contacted widely known broadcaster and fellow

Scientologist Greta Van Susteren, who recommended a former SEC attorney.

"She said we should say we are friends of Greta Van Susteren's," Licciardi wrote in an e-mail to Zwan.

Joseph said he received the unexpected news that Licciardi was still part of the team from Zwan himself. Zwan reminded him "whose sister she is" and said it would be "excruciating" to try to terminate her, Joseph said. Zwan won't discuss his conversations with Joseph and Licciardi.

Three days later, it was non-Scientologist Joseph who was forced out. Zwan said Joseph's firing was part of a companywide restructuring. Joseph cried foul, filing an arbitration complaint to recoup thousands of stock options. An arbitrator later sided with Joseph, ordering Digital to pay him $3.8 million.

Joseph's attorney accused Zwan of orchestrating a "cover-up" in which "the person who wouldn't go along with it was terminated and the people who went along get enriched."

But Licciardi didn't survive either. In two weeks, she was gone too. Yet her departure was largely on her own financial terms, which she spelled out in an e-mail to Zwan titled "Ending Cycle," a Scientology term. She told Zwan she was "without a doubt guilty of executing on orders without question."

Licciardi wrote she applied "Simon Bolivar to a 'T,'" a Scientology phrase referring to loyalty.

She promised Zwan she would not bail on him. "For you," she added, "I will take the fall."

Other than receiving one year's salary instead of three, Licciardi received the severance package she demanded: vesting of her 70,000 stock options, forgiveness of a $71,000 Digital loan, three cell phones, and a laptop computer.

She also successfully pleaded with Zwan not to publicly mention her departure or connect her with any wrongdoing. Her fear: "In the public eye, I will take the heat for the mistakes made at Digital Lightwave Inc. and due to my familial connections, will pay for this dearly on my road to spiritual freedom," she wrote.

With Joseph and Licciardi gone, Digital's board zeroed in on Zwan, worried the company was faltering under his stewardship.

Board member Bill Seifert, a Boston-area venture capitalist, said he urged Zwan to turn Digital over to a professional manager or "his baby would die."

Jeff Marshall, another director at the time, called Zwan "incompetent."

"He was a big shareholder and I wish we had had the guts to fire him right then and there," he said, "but we didn't."

NEW LEADER, BIG BUCKS

Digital's stock continued its slump through 1998. By year's end, the shares traded at $2.31 a share, an 83 percent annual decline. Sales were up, but so were losses. The board's dissatisfaction mounted.

That December, Zwan stepped aside as CEO, and the board found a replacement with no ties to Scientology.

Gerry Chastelet, CEO of Wandel & Goltermann Technologies in North Carolina, arrived on a self-described mission to build up Digital's reputation with customers and play down ties to Scientology.

With Digital's stock hovering around $2 a share, Chastelet believed he could pump up the stock tenfold.

Raised on a farm in Niagara Falls, Ontario, Chastelet wasn't averse to hard work. As a youth, he spent summers stacking 100-pound bags of flour in a mill and sweating inside a steaming-hot nickel refinery.

Digital was moving into new headquarters, a $19 million building at the south end of the Bayside Bridge. Yet, old ghosts lingered.

Tension between Scientologists and non-Scientologists was still palpable. Employees complained their e-mails were being read, although Chastelet never found proof.

"There was a general mistrust between certain factions about what other factions may be thinking, saying or doing," Chastelet recalled. "Some felt every action they did was being watched."

Seeking to defuse tension, he held a companywide briefing to declare any infringements on privacy would not be tolerated. He ordered an electronic sweep looking for bugs. Nothing was found, he said.

He told his human resources director to remove and destroy any Scientology-related documents in personnel files. The purge included some "statistics reports," a Scientology business tool used to track employee productivity.

Scientology-based organizational charts were used when he arrived, Chastelet said, but not for long. "Divisions" such as sales and manufacturing were renamed "departments." The treasury division under Zwan became the finance department under Chastelet.

Chastelet brought analysts and customers to Digital's new offices for PowerPoint briefings.

He thought: "If we do a good job . . . all of the chattering about Scientology will no longer absorb the Internet pages, and people will start to recognize the company for what it is."

In May 1999, Digital landed Lucent as a customer; a month later, Cisco placed its first order. Then came Nextel and Level 3.

By July, Digital showed signs of weathering the restatement fiasco, recording a profit amid the dot-com bull market.

Sales continued to surge, and by January 2000, Digital shares were trading at a lofty $62.75. The company was profiled as a poster child of overpriced tech stocks in a front-page article in *The Wall Street Journal.*

Two months later, Digital's stock reached $150 a share, giving it a remarkable value of $4 billion. The Clearwater enterprise, with about 200 workers and $50 million in annual sales, was valued more at the time than today's market value for Toys "R" Us, an international company with 60,000 employees and more than $11 billion in sales.

So impressive was Digital's growth, the company topped the

St. Petersburg Times list of the 50 best-performing public companies in the Tampa Bay area for its 2000 results.

Digital got more good news in March: The SEC settled its case against Digital and various company officers. But there was bad news for Zwan. The SEC sued him separately, singling him out as the one principally responsible for false filings in an "earnings management scheme" in 1997.

But while facing that action, Zwan, even from the sidelines, became a very rich man. He cashed out about $430 million in stock between 1999 and the fall of 2001 while still retaining majority ownership in the company. *Forbes* estimated Zwan's net worth at $600 million in elevating him to the magazine's 2001 list of the 400 wealthiest Americans.

The wealth creation spurred by Digital was hardly restricted to Scientologists. Several top executives with no connection to the church made millions, notably Chastelet, who cashed out more than $19 million in stock options in one year alone.

The party lasted longer than expected. Even when tech companies were retrenching in early 2001, Digital was hiring engineers and expanding overseas. To build morale, Chastelet arranged to give away three white 2001 Volkswagen Beetles to workers whose names were drawn at random.

But there were growing hints Chastelet wouldn't stay in the driver's seat for long.

Zwan still was the company's biggest shareholder and was exerting control behind the scenes, putting allies on the board.

"Bryan wants to control the board, control the company, control the CEO," Chastelet said, "and in a public company, that's pretty difficult to do."

Bill Seifert, an exiting board member, noted: "This was a founder who was not going to go anywhere and was accustomed to and insisted on calling certain shots."

On October 24, the SEC settled its lawsuit with Zwan, paving the way for his comeback. Two days later, he rejoined Digital's board of directors.

In January, frustrated by Zwan's growing involvement in day-to-day operations, Chastelet resigned.

"I don't think we ever anticipated it would work out in the long run," Chastelet said.

EPILOGUE

Today, Digital still is a big player in fiber-optic testing, with a 36 percent market share in the United States and specific strategies to push its international sales.

It has 110 employees, and this year contracted with Jabil Circuit of St. Petersburg to manufacture all its units. Digital's stock price closed Friday at $3.10. The company ranks 25th on this year's *Times* list of top-performing public companies.

Digital also has put in place new accounting practices that, Zwan says, will prevent past problems from recurring.

"The facts and circumstances . . . associated with that era have all been dealt with quite completely," Zwan said. "We're really a different company than we were four years ago."

As for the turbulent last four years:

- The SEC imposed a $10,000 fine on Zwan in settling its case last fall. There was no admission of wrongdoing.

  To one former SEC attorney, Zwan's penalty seems benign. "If one assumes that 50 percent or even 25 percent of what is alleged is true, a $10,000 settlement to me sounds like a gift," said New York lawyer Jeffrey Plotkin, who reviewed Zwan's deal at the request of the *Times*. "It sounds to me . . . that the SEC, when it got its feet put to the fire, couldn't come up with the goods."

  The SEC had hoped to develop Licciardi as a witness against Zwan. The agency interviewed her in 1999 but could not find her as it prepared for trial.

- The *Times* likewise could not find Licciardi. A *Times* reporter visited several times a residence listed on Licciardi's driver's license, mailed her letters and sought interviews through her mother and Gerald Gentile, whom she married after leaving Digital. Reporters also left an interview request at a Scientology Mission in Belleair Bluffs, where she is said to work.

- Chastelet lives in St. Petersburg and sits on the boards of several technology companies.

- Joseph, who declined to be interviewed for this story, works at a Miami law firm. Digital has not paid him the $3.8 million award, and is appealing.

    His case, though, resulted in a strong rebuke from Miami lawyer Stanley Beiley, the arbitrator who heard Joseph's complaint.

    Digital shareholders should have been told, Beiley wrote, that "senior management knew that Denise Licciardi admitted to significant inventory falsifications and yet rewarded her by permitting her to resign, rather than firing her."

- Brian Haney sold his toy company and is a venture capitalist. He also runs a Christian charity organization out of his home in Columbus. Haney and Zwan settled their suit in 2000. Terms are confidential.

- Zwan, now Digital's chairman, CEO and president, recently upped his stake in the company to 60 percent. He insists Scientology plays no part in Digital's operations. He says no more than three Scientologists work there today.

    His grand plan for the future: introduce a "worldwide incredible product" by year's end.

    "Digital Lightwave," Zwan promises, "has embarked on a whole new reinvention of itself."

Times *researcher Kitty Bennett contributed to this report.*

The U.S. Catholic Church faced financial problems before its sex scandal became front-page news. William C. Symonds of *Business-Week*, who carefully researched the church's funding and hierarchy, describes a decentralized system that is often lacking in financial controls and oversight.

William C. Symonds

The Economic Strain on the Church

AS THE U.S. CATHOLIC CHURCH battles the most sordid scandal in its history, it is fighting to preserve its moral and spiritual authority as the largest nongovernmental institution in American life. Yet even as it does so, another catastrophe looms—one that is not about sex abuse and priests but about money and management. The fierce scrutiny that is piercing the Church's veil of secrecy over sex is also beginning to reveal the largely hidden state of its finances. As the institution's legal and moral crisis builds, so too do the threats to its economic foundation—a foundation already under enormous strain. "If there is anything that is kept more secret in the Church than sex, it is finance," says former priest and activist A. W. Richard Sipe.

The cascade of legal claims may just be starting. Plaintiffs' lawyers say as much as $1 billion in settlements, many of them secret, has already been paid since the first big sex-abuse case surfaced in Louisiana in 1985. And more payouts, sparked by incensed juries, are likely in the future. Cases filed to date "are just the tip of the iceberg, and it will be a multibillion-dollar problem before it ends," says Roderick MacLeish Jr., a Boston attorney who has represented more than 100 victims in the past decade. Church attorneys dismiss such sums as exaggerated. But they concede that because much of its insurance is either inadequate or exhausted, the Church increasingly will be forced to sell land and other assets to pay claims. Ultimately, some dioceses "might be pushed into bankruptcy," warns Patrick Schiltz, dean at the University of St. Thomas School of Law in St. Paul.

In turn, that poses a growing threat to the myriad good works the Church performs in its vast network of schools, colleges, hospitals, and charities. If the scandal cuts into donations, as many fear, "that would create a whole new class of victims—the kids in our inner cities," worries David W. Smith, director of finance for the Archdiocese of Boston.

Most appalling to many Catholics has been the insensitive way Church officials have handled the crisis, putting the protection of well over 1,000 of its priests above the interests of the victims. On a scale of 1 to 10, "this is an 11," says former Hill & Knowlton Chairman Robert L. Dilenschneider, who has helped manage such crises as Three Mile Island. "The Church has been hit by a truck and permitted the truck to back over it several times," he says. "The quickest way to deal with a crisis is to tell it all and tell it fast." Instead, the Church's hierarchy helped fuel the crisis by dealing with abusive priests in-house, often reassigning them to new parishes, and by insisting that victims sign confidentiality agreements before receiving settlements.

Now a groundswell is building for radical reforms—among them optional celibacy, changes in the strict dogma about sex, and the ordination of women. At the same time, there is a growing call for more financial disclosure and corporate-style discipline for the billions on the Church's books. "The Church consists of the people, so the people ought to know what is going on," says William B. Friend, bishop of the Diocese of Shreveport, Louisiana, who worked in banking before becoming a priest.

Indeed, because the Church depends nearly entirely on contributions from parishioners, experts say such reforms are necessary before donors will be assured that the practice of covering up sex-suit settlements funded with the collection plate has ended. Already, Catholics give half as much as Protestants as a percentage of income. And a March 27 Gallup poll found that 30% of Catholics are now thinking of cutting off contributions.

To regain parishioners' confidence, the Church should start acting like a corporation, says R. Scott Appleby, director of the Cushwa Center for the Study of American Catholicism at Notre Dame. "The way to restore integrity," he argues, "is to become perfectly transparent financially, to submit financial reports, and to become exemplary in best practices." If you do this, adds Bishop Friend, "the money comes in."

The Church can ill afford diminished contributions, operating as it does on donations. A common perception of the Church is that it is an ancient treasure chest with deep pockets, replete with opulent basilicas, a world-class art collection, and trophy properties like New York's St. Patrick's Cathedral. Yet the glittering holdings and the enormous reach of its institutions mask serious, systemic operating problems.

For one thing, there is a startling lack of financial controls and oversight—an omission that experts say has allowed bishops from California to Philadelphia to misuse Church funds. What's astounding to some is that even though billions of dollars are at stake, bishops have almost free rein over funds and virtually no supervision. Moreover, some of the nation's largest dioceses are confronting worrisome structural problems—including rising labor costs and deteriorating school buildings and churches, as well as its more tightfisted parishioners. The red ink is already spilling. Boston's archdiocese is "facing a financial squeeze," says financial director Smith, and will run a deficit of about $5 million this year. The Archdiocese of New York has a budget gap of about $20 million. In Chicago, which publishes perhaps the most complete financial reports of any large U.S. archdiocese, the Church saw its operating deficit for parishes and schools soar 63% last

CATHOLIC INSTITUTIONS

Schools The Church is the largest operator of private schools in the U.S., with over 2.6 million students enrolled in its 6,900 elementary schools and some 1,200 high schools, costing roughly $10 billion a year. Most of the elementary schools are attached to local parishes, while high schools are often run by a Catholic religious order, such as the Jesuits or Christian Brothers. Although tuition has been rising sharply, schools still receive large subsidies from the Church.

Universities There are 230 Catholic colleges and universities with a combined total of 670,000 students. Most colleges are sponsored by a religious congregation, like the Jesuits, who have 28 colleges—including Georgetown, Boston College, and Holy Cross. Just 11 are sponsored by a diocese, and only Catholic University in Washington is sponsored by the Church. There are few direct finanacial ties between most Catholic colleges and the Church. Most are run by a lay board of trustees. Like other private colleges, tuition is the primary source of revenue, though some have sizable endowments, like Notre Dame's $2.8 billion.

Health Care The nonprofit health-care system includes 637 hospitals, accounting for 17% of all U.S. hospital admissions. The Church also runs 122 home health-care agencies and nearly 700 other service providers, including assisted living, adult day care, and senior housing. The hospitals alone have annual expenses of $65 billion and account for 5% of U.S. health-care spending.

Charities Catholic Charities USA consists of 1,400 agencies that run soup kitchens, temporary shelters, child care, and refugee resettlement. In 1999, Catholic Charities had collective revenues of $2.34 billion. Most of that comes from state and local governments and from program fees. The Church accounts for only about 12% of income.

year, to $23.3 million. But it's far from insolvent, with $790 million in assets, most of which is in real estate.

Damage to the rest of the Church's empire is also a concern. The U.S. Catholic Church is by far the largest operator of private schools, with 2.6 million students. An additional 670,000 students attend the 230 Catholic colleges and universities. The nation's Catholic hospitals account for 17% of all hospital admissions, while Catholic Charities USA—which collectively spends $2.3 billion annually—provides everything from soup kitchens to child care to refugee resettlement (see chart on Catholic Institutions).

By no means would all of these institutions be vulnerable to billion-dollar legal settlements. Nor can the Church be likened to a unified corporation or a conglomerate. In the U.S., its members and assets are divided along geographical lines into 194 dioceses, each of which is legally separate (see chart on how the U.S. Catholic Church works).

THE U.S. CATHOLIC CHURCH: HOW IT WORKS

The Roman Catholic Church, with some 64 million members and thousands of affiliated operations, is the largest and most influential nongovernment organization in the U.S. But the Church is not a unified corporation: It is a decentralized organization with thousands of legally and financially separate entities. Its 20,000 Catholic churches raise some $7.5 billion annually. A primer on the Church's hierarchy:

The Pope The Pope appoints the bishops who run the U.S. Church and sets policies—including rules on who may become a priest. The U.S. is one of the wealthiest Catholic countries and a top contributor to the Vatican. Legally, the Vatican is a sovereign state, beyond the reach of U.S. law.

The Papal Nuncio The Nuncio, who cannot be an American, is the Papal representative to the U.S. Based in Washington, he reviews all U.S. priests nominated for bishop before forwarding names to Rome for final approval.

The U.S. Conference of Catholic Bishops The Conference is a kind of steering committee for the U.S. Church, made up of the 375 U.S. bishops. With a budget of some $150 million, it speaks for the U.S. Church on policy matters such as abortion and welfare and has committees on everything from worship to domestic policy. The Conference, funded by the dioceses, does not have any authority over them.

Cardinals These so-called princes of the Church have the ultimate power over its future, since they elect the Pope. But the U.S. has a small role in the College of Cardinals.

Dioceses The key administrative unit of the Church, it is comprised of many local parishes and headed by a bishop, archbishop, or cardinal. Everything from ordinations of priests to education is run at the diocesan level. There are 194 in the U.S. Although each diocese is a separate legal entity, abusive priests shuffled from parish to parish may extend the trail of liability.

Parishes The U.S. has some 20,000 parishes, and each individual church depends on its members' weekly donations, the major source of funding. Congregations are growing larger, averaging 3,000 members, even as the number of priests is falling, straining resources. At the same time, the ranks of U.S. Catholics are increasing with the arrival of new immigrants.

Data: Center for Applied Research in the Apostolate at Georgetown University; National Catholic Educational Association; Catholic Health Association; U.S. Conference of Catholic Bishops; Catholic Charities USA

This fragmentation cuts two ways. It is one of the Church's strongest defenses in the current legal firestorm, making it all but impossible for plaintiffs to go after the Church as a whole. The Vatican's bank accounts are also out of reach: As a sovereign state, it cannot be sued. Similarly, most of the Church's educational, medical, and charitable agencies are walled off. Although Boston College has a $1 billion endowment, for example, it is owned by a lay board of trustees, with no ties to the Archdiocese of Boston.

But the financial web that ties together the Church's massive network could be weakened if more big jury awards and settlements materialize. Churches, dioceses, and even the Vatican have an essentially symbiotic financial relationship—one that is largely hand-to-mouth and doesn't include large cash reserves. Joseph Harris, financial officer for the St. Vincent de Paul Society in Seattle and a student of Church finances, estimates that the nation's nearly 20,000 parishes had revenues of $7.5 billion in 2000. About $6.5 billion went to cover direct expenses, and much of the remaining $1 billion was used to subsidize Catholic schools.

These parishes also support the dioceses' operations, which in turn funnel money to other needy parishes, schools, or charitable programs. The dioceses also send money up the hierarchy. They contribute to the U.S. Conference of Catholic Bishops (USCCB) and also the Holy See. "Rome doesn't usually offer to help distressed dioceses," says Bishop Joseph Galante of Dallas.

In fact, it's the reverse. The U.S. and German dioceses are the top two contributors to the Holy See, which in 2000 reported total revenues of $209 million. After years of deficits, the Holy See named then-Detroit Cardinal Edmund C. Szoka the effective budget director in 1990.

Within two years, Szoka had used management basics to reverse 23 years of deficits. He trimmed overhead, boosted investment return, tripled contributions from dioceses, and even began publishing a consolidated balance sheet. Still, because the Vatican depends so heavily on U.S. contributions, a few financially crippling jury awards at the parish level could send a ripple effect all the way to Rome.

Even with so much at stake, most bishops and cardinals have little financial training and follow no Church-mandated accounting or auditing procedures, though some have professional advice as well as boards of advisers. "Every bishop is responsible for his own diocese—he doesn't have to send Rome a financial statement," says Szoka. This leads to wide variation. In New York, for instance, the late Cardinal John O'Connor, though beloved by his flock, had a reputation for being a terrible financial administrator. He was ill at ease with wealthy donors who could have pumped up Church coffers. Yet he loved to bail out money-losing schools and parishes, and blew through virtually the entire endowment.

Some believe Pope John Paul II chose Cardinal Edward Egan to succeed O'Connor in part because of Egan's strong record as a money mastermind. Egan mopped up a financial mess in the Archdiocese of Bridgeport and counts former General Electric Chairman Jack Welch as a trusted adviser. He's so adept at tackling costs with layoffs and school closings that he's known among some Archdiocese insiders as "Edward Scissorhands."

Yet even with the Papacy's growing awareness of the need for financial discipline, the system has no checks and balances, making it vulnerable to abuse. In 1998, the *National Catholic Reporter* revealed that Philadelphia's Cardinal Anthony Bevilacqua had sunk $5 million into renovating his mansion, a seaside villa, and other properties in the early '90s, even as he closed money-losing parishes in impoverished North Philadelphia. Parishioners were so outraged that they took to the streets with signs depicting Bevilacqua as Darth Vader. In a more shocking case, the then-bishop of the diocese of Santa Rosa, California, resigned in 1999 after he allegedly forced a priest to have sex with him in exchange for covering up the priest's embezzlement of church funds. Only later did the laity learn the bishop had also incurred enormous losses through mismanagement, including offshore investments. And in Fort Lauderdale, local law enforcement authorities are now investigating $800,000 in missing funds at a local Catholic parish. Getting the financial documents "has not been easy," says a spokesman for the Archdiocese of Miami.

So far, many of the doors that could reveal a true picture of the Church's finances remain tightly sealed. Kenneth Korotky, chief financial officer of the USCCB, says the U.S. Church has not even attempted to prepare a consolidated financial statement. Although Chicago, Detroit, Shreveport, and other dioceses do disclose their numbers, some of the largest—including New York and Philadelphia—refuse to release financial reports to their members. Charles E. Zech, an economics professor at Villanova University, in Villanova, Pennsylvania, says 38% of Catholics don't know how parish donations are being spent.

The same secrecy has obscured just how much the Church has

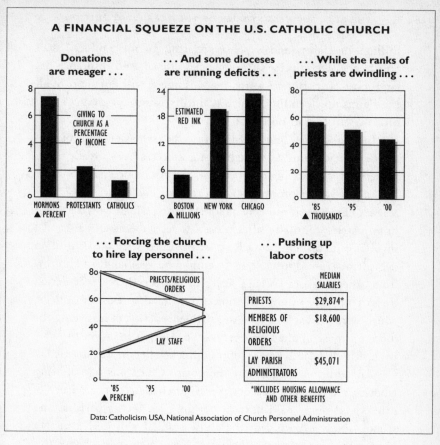

A FINANCIAL SQUEEZE ON THE U.S. CATHOLIC CHURCH

Donations are meager . . .

GIVING TO CHURCH AS A PERCENTAGE OF INCOME

MORMONS PROTESTANTS CATHOLICS
▲ PERCENT

. . . And some dioceses are running deficits . . .

ESTIMATED RED INK

BOSTON NEW YORK CHICAGO
▲ MILLIONS

. . . While the ranks of priests are dwindling . . .

'85 '95 '00
▲ THOUSANDS

. . . Forcing the church to hire lay personnel . . .

PRIESTS/RELIGIOUS ORDERS

LAY STAFF

'85 '95 '00
▲ PERCENT

. . . Pushing up labor costs

	MEDIAN SALARIES
PRIESTS	$29,874*
MEMBERS OF RELIGIOUS ORDERS	$18,600
LAY PARISH ADMINISTRATORS	$45,071

*INCLUDES HOUSING ALLOWANCE AND OTHER BENEFITS

Data: Catholicism USA, National Association of Church Personnel Administration

paid out so far in settlements and how much more could be on the line. Mark Chopko, general counsel at the USCCB, says he "doesn't know the total volume of settlements" because many were sealed but estimates that $350 million has been paid to victims so far. But plaintiffs' lawyers insist the amount is close to $1 billion. Moreover, the legal climate is tilting against the Church, warns law dean Schiltz, who has defended both Protestant and Catholic churches against almost 500 sexual misconduct suits. Given the volume of damning media coverage, Schiltz predicts legislators in some states eventually will make it easier to sue the Church.

At the same time, the Church faces "an increasingly grim insurance situation," adds Schiltz. What little coverage it has is being exhausted. In Boston, "we have paid out just less than $30 million in claims and expenses relating to misconduct," says Smith, the Archdiocese's top financial official, and insurance has paid most of it. But he warns that insurance will fall short of all the claims now pending, which plaintiffs' attorneys predict could hit $100 million in Boston alone.

Inevitably, the Church will be forced to sell assets and cut programs to pay claims, as some hard-hit dioceses have already done. To settle 187 suits in the mid-'90s, the Archdiocese of Santa Fe had to sell vacant properties and a retreat center, says CEO Tony Salgado. Even so, it ran deficits for six years, which halted growth in ministries. Similarly, after sex-abuse settlements and a scandal involving its bishop, Santa Rosa was saddled with a $16 million debt. It was forced to ax 50 of 75 employees, sell land, and borrow from other dioceses. What's next? In Boston, there's speculation the Archdiocese might sell some prized land to Boston College, which wants to expand. And in Providence, lawyers are eyeing the diocese's most opulent property—the Aldrich mansion in Warwick, Rhode Island, where John D. Rockefeller Jr. was married.

An additional strain on the entire Church is a mounting labor-cost crisis. For decades, the Church relied on an army of priests and nuns, paid next to nothing, to run its parishes and schools. Now experts fear the abuse scandal will deal a further blow to the priesthood, since even fewer men will choose this vocation—at least until the chastity rule is relaxed.

Meanwhile, with the average priest now 60 years old, "the number of active priests will shrink" as retirements pick up, says Brian Froehle, head of the Center for Applied Research in the Apostolate. Add to that the decline in the ranks of nuns—whose numbers have dropped from 174,000 in 1965 to less than half that now—and the Church will have to rely more on lay workers, who are far more costly. The median salary for a diocesan priest is about $13,600, plus $16,000 in living expenses, says Sister Ellen Doyle, executive director of the National Association of Church Personnel Administrators. In contrast, parish administrators— often hired to do work once done by priests—are paid around

$45,000, says Doyle. That's not to mention the need to increase the notoriously low salaries paid to teachers in most Catholic schools. But inner-city Catholic schools are in no position to hike salaries. As it is, "affording tuition [of $2,300] is a big problem" for parents sending their kids to McKinley Park Catholic School on Chicago's Southwest Side, says the Reverend James Hyland. Enrollment in Chicago as a whole dropped 3.4% in the current school year, the most in a decade, leading the Archdiocese to announce it would close 16 elementary schools.

Catholic charities could also be hurt. In Boston, Catholic Charities—the no. 2 provider of social services after the state—is already planning a 15% reduction in its central staff and is bailing out of some of its programs. Mostly that's because of reduced government funds, which provide 54% of its budget. But in the wake of the abuse scandal, fund-raising could also suffer. Health care won't be directly hit by the scandals, argues the Reverend Michael D. Place, CEO of the Catholic Health Association, because much of its funding comes from government or private insurance. Even so, he concedes that "the current financial status of the ministry is challenged."

If anyone can see good coming out of so much bad, it's the Catholic faithful. Sister Jane Kelly, a 71-year-old nun who exposed sexual and financial abuse in Santa Rosa, figures the scandals can be an opportunity for reform. "Sexual misconduct of clerics has been an abscess on the Body of Christ for centuries," she says. And to its credit, the Church is moving toward more forceful measures to prevent further cases of sex abuse by priests—a subject the U.S. bishops will address at their June meeting.

But there are few signs the bishops—or the Pope, who has the ultimate say—are about to heed the will of reformers. "I don't see a major change coming in celibacy" right now, says Bishop Galante. Nor does the Church appear to be moving toward requirements for a more transparent system of financial reporting. "Our mission is to preach the Gospel," says Cardinal Szoka, who urges bishops to publish finances but dismisses American calls for financial reforms as a result of "secularization." The Church "is not an empire. It's not a financial entity. That's secular talk."

It's all a forceful reminder that, after 2,000 years of history, the Catholic Church isn't a democracy. But for the U.S. Church, the stakes have never been this high. Further delays and missteps may only increase the price it must pay—in money, in prestige, and ultimately, in power.

With Michelle Conlin in New York, Gail Edmondson in Vatican City,
Ann Therese Palmer in Chicago, Christopher Palmeri in Los Angeles,
and Aixa M. Pascual in Atlanta

An increasing number of brand-name U.S. companies are trading their corporate citizenship for a flag of convenience and a tax break in Bermuda, according to Hal Lux of *Institutional Investor*. Although such firms use outmoded U.S. tax laws as their excuse, Lux believes there's still the nagging issue of patriotism.

Hal Lux

Nationalities of Convenience

"There is nothing sinister in so arranging one's affairs as to keep taxes as low as possible. Taxes are enforced exactions, not voluntary contributions. To demand more in the name of morals is mere cant." —*Judge Learned Hand*

ON NOVEMBER 5, 2001, less than two months after the terrorist attacks on America, Martin Huddart, general manager of Ingersoll-Rand Co.'s Recognition Systems subsidiary, submitted prepared testimony to the U.S. Senate's aviation subcommittee meeting in Morgantown, West Virginia. Chaired by West Virginia Democrat Jay Rockefeller, the subcommittee was meeting to discuss technological methods for improving safety at U.S. airports.

"As our nation moves forward following the tragic events of September 11," Huddart instructed, "the overriding security issue will be to better manage people and access within the complex environment of a commercial airport."

"Our nation"? Maybe not. What Huddart neglected to mention, while subtly pitching his company's expertise, was that venerable Ingersoll-Rand would be leaving the good old U.S.A.—on paper, anyway—to avoid paying taxes on income earned overseas.

Incorporated in New Jersey in 1905, the Woodcliff Lake-based company has played more than a passing role in the pageant of American history. Ingersoll-Rand jackhammers carved out the presidential faces on Mount Rushmore. Its Thermo King refrigeration trucks made possible the rise of the American frozen food industry. And Ingersoll's New York Stock Exchange listing is one of the ten oldest on the Big Board.

But on October 16 Ingersoll's board of directors had voted to become a Bermuda corporation. The reincorporation took effect on December 31.

Ingersoll isn't actually moving to the island nation. The company's headquarters and CEO, Herbert Henkel, will stay in New Jersey. The industrial conglomerate will continue to employ 35,000 people in 24 states. As for Ingersoll's balmy new domicile, three weeks after the company reincorporated, its Web site directory listed phone numbers for Bosnia and Cambodia but not for Bermuda. Still, Ingersoll is now a full-fledged Bermuda company, which is a fortuitous thing to be when tax time rolls around in the United States of America.

American companies, like individual citizens, have to pay taxes. And like American citizens, companies try to minimize what they pay, through whatever means they can manage. Paying taxes on domestic earnings is a fairly simple matter. It gets trickier with income earned overseas.

America is rare among nations in taxing individuals and companies on income that they earn anywhere in the world. The U.S. government gives American companies credits for taxes they have already paid to foreign governments, but the system is complicated and flawed. For example, companies must allocate interest expenses against foreign income, even if the capital isn't being deployed overseas. That requirement can wipe out a company's foreign tax credit for an entire country. So Ingersoll-Rand, which earns 40 percent of its income outside the U.S., can end up paying more than it should have to. Many tax experts say the U.S. laws are so unfair that American companies have a right, maybe even a duty to their shareholders, to look for ways to cut their taxes. "It arguably doesn't make sense to impose U.S. corporate-level tax on income that has already been taxed once in a foreign country and will be taxed again when it is distributed to U.S. shareholders," says David Hariton, a tax partner at Sullivan & Cromwell. "Three taxes makes a crowd."

But there is an easy way out. A U.S. corporation can create a shell holding company that is incorporated in Bermuda, "transfer" its overseas operations to the Bermuda company and merge its U.S. company into the Bermuda shell. What was an American company is now, on paper, Bermudan. And Bermuda companies don't pay U.S. taxes on their international income.

Companies relocate all the time to cut taxes. They move from state to state in return for a break on local taxes or to take advantage of some favorable corporate regulation or court system. New York City has offered numerous tax breaks to Wall Street firms to fend off a predatory New Jersey. Boeing Co. recently moved its headquarters from Seattle to Chicago after securing a large tax break. For some time hedge funds and insurance companies have been quietly slipping off to Bermuda for tax reasons. But the hedge funds are private entities managing offshore money, and so far only a handful of small reinsurance companies have gone to Bermuda.

What is happening now appears to be a movement of another order. The companies that are moving are mainstream, heart-land names. Foster Wheeler Corp., an engineering company and builder of large gas and oil field projects, founded in New York City in 1927, reincorporated as a Bermuda corporation in May. In January Houston-based oil drilling contractor Nabors Industries, a Standard & Poor's 500 company with a $4 billion market cap and 18,000 employees, said it would reincorporate in Bermuda later this year. Then there's Houston-based Cooper Industries, which traces its origins to an 1830s Ohio iron foundry: In June Cooper announced plans to leave for Bermuda, but the move was postponed because of an unsolicited takeover offer from Danaher Corp. The takeover fell through, and Cooper may still go.

Experts expect more companies to follow. "It will start out as a trickle," predicts Monitor Group consultant Michael Jensen, a former Harvard Business School professor who has analyzed relocations for corporate governance issues within the U.S. "It always does. And then it will be a rush."

Leaving the country for a tax break sure seems to carry a bad taste now, when many American businesses are conspicuously wrapping themselves in the flag. Insurance companies have been lobbying Congress for a federal backstop to cover claims related to terrorist acts. At the same time, they've been investing billions in start-up reinsurance companies that hope to profit from soaring policy rates. The reinsurers have been set up in Bermuda and won't pay U.S. taxes.

Companies say American tax laws are outdated, even nutty, in the era of globalization. And Ingersoll says that its decision to shed its U.S. citizenship was wrenching. "We thought very long and hard about it," says chief financial officer David Devonshire. "Our main domicile will still be the U.S. We have no intention of moving our operations to Bermuda. At the end of the day, we were dealing with a competitive disadvantage, and we have a duty to shareholders."

But critics say there are plenty of strange laws and nutty taxes on the books in the U.S. What these companies are doing is essentially trading their corporate citizenship for a flag of convenience— and a tax break. Ingersoll will save $40 million to $50 million per year on taxes. And, according to one analyst's projections, Nabors will cut $40 million to $70 million.

Companies can rationalize these moves legally. They can rationalize them financially. But some critics say there are greater values and principles at stake than saving a few million in taxes. As more and more companies do this, and as these moves become better known to the public and politicians, especially at a time of war, the tactic seems likely to set off a fiery debate. Because in the end, patriotism is not about reason. It is a gut-level attachment to home, place and familiar values.

Even sophisticated capitalists can be outraged when they hear about companies relocating to pare their taxes. "I find it appalling. I think the term 'Benedict Arnold' is appropriate," says Jack Bogle, founder of Vanguard Group, the country's second-largest mutual fund company, and a renowned corporate cost-cutter himself. "I think it's outrageous when American individuals say they're not Americans for tax purposes, and I think it's outrageous when companies do it."

Even discussing such moves gets people angry. Former Intel Corp. tax chief Robert Perlman got himself into hot water two years ago when he told the Senate Finance Committee: "If I had known at Intel's founding [in 1968] what I know today about the international tax rules, I would have advised that the parent company be established outside the U.S. Our tax code competitively disadvantages multinationals simply because the parent is a U.S. corporation." When Perlman suggested the company could have set up shop in the Cayman Islands, New York's then-Senator Daniel Patrick Moynihan, a former ambassador to India and the United Nations, upbraided the Intel executive, asking Perlman if he expected the Marines to show up in the Caymans in case of trouble. Says an unrepentant Perlman, "I should have said 'Ireland.'"

For the most part, however, these corporate moves have occurred without publicity or scrutiny. "Ingersoll-Rand is a significant event," says a senior congressional tax aide. "Until now you've just had insurance companies doing this. Now you have a big mainline company reincorporating. People in Washington aren't paying attention to this. But they should be."

Ingersoll's timing certainly stinks. While it was becoming officially Bermudan, the company, a leader in airport security technology, was pitching the U.S. government for business. In November it even got California Representative Adam Schiff to demonstrate a handprint-reading device at a multicompany showcase at the Burbank-Glendale-Pasadena Airport. Did Schiff care, or know, about the company's reincorporation? He didn't respond to a request for comment.

These moves raise the question of what it means to be a corporate citizen, especially in an era of globalization. For companies reincorporating in Bermuda, there are few day-to-day changes. Bermuda has respected laws and courts; in the U.S. the companies still get the same access to roads, infrastructure and police—and government business. Last summer a government agency looking to redesign its Web site selected Accenture (the consulting firm spun off from Andersen), which has its CEO in Dallas but was incorporated in Bermuda when the company went public last July. The agency? The Internal Revenue Service.

Sensitivities, however, are a different matter. "Companies get benefits from being in the U.S., whether it's roads or defense. There are a lot of people in Congress who think that if you go offshore just to cut taxes, 'a pox on your house,'" says Jonathan Talisman, who oversaw tax matters as acting assistant Treasury secretary in the Clinton administration. "'If Argentina decides to freeze your assets, we're not coming to help you.'"

Part of what angers many is that the companies are not really leaving. "I've told my competitors [that] if they want to move offshore, just have at it," says C. Robert Palmer, chairman of Houston-based Rowan Cos., an NYSE-listed oil services company with rivals that have moved offshore. "These companies are saying they're in Bermuda, which, of course, is not true. All the management of the companies are still in Texas."

It might interest the public to know that some administration policy makers don't have hard feelings about these moves. "These transactions do evoke a strong reaction—that these companies are somehow abandoning the U.S.," concedes Barbara Angus, international tax counsel at the Treasury Department. "We need to understand if there are aspects of our tax system that are driving companies to consider these transactions."

Most companies are not going to reincorporate. Many U.S. companies pay no tax on foreign income, because they're able to take advantage of tax credits and other rules. And for some companies, leaving wouldn't make financial sense. The IRS now imposes a onetime "toll charge," which can be substantial for companies with longtime shareholders or high stock prices.

Other companies would probably never risk the public relations black eye: Coca-Cola Co., for example, which earns 72 percent of its income abroad, or McDonald's Corp., which gets 55 percent of its income from outside the U.S. Their American identity is central to their branding. "Companies have to consider the potential stigma," says Lehman Brothers tax specialist Robert Willens. "It does seem unpatriotic to people. There is a lot of emotional baggage that comes with this transaction."

For decades corporate America mostly stayed put. Millions of U.S. jobs moved overseas, but few companies relinquished their American corporate identities, even though the favorable tax consequences have long been available and understood. Although no one tracks the number of U.S. companies moving offshore, bankers say that the first American company to reincorporate overseas in recent memory was a New Orleans-based oil company, McDermott International, which changed its legal domicile to Panama in 1982. McDermott has a $750 million market cap and an NYSE listing, and it still operates out of the U.S.

In 1994 Helen of Troy, an El Paso, Texas-based beauty supply company, announced plans to reincorporate in Bermuda. The IRS, fearing that many more companies would follow, laid down new regulations, since dubbed the Helen of Troy rules, that require shareholders and companies to pay a onetime toll charge in the form of an immediate capital gains tax on the transfer of the assets and stock. (Ingersoll-Rand paid no toll charge on the corporate level, but the company's shareholders were stuck with a $100 million capital gains hit, according to a shareholder lawsuit that has since been settled.) The toll charge is steep enough that expatriating wouldn't make sense for many companies. But a bad economy and stock market can whittle away most of the toll charge for a company and its shareholders. "If a company has a couple of bad years in a row, it gets attractive," says former Intel tax chief Perlman. "That's why you're seeing companies do this now."

Bermuda is especially attractive for relocators. "It's like having Greenwich in the middle of the Caribbean," says a private equity banker. The success of large Bermuda insurance companies like

Ace and XL Capital in recent years has made a Bermuda domicile seem safe to much larger U.S. corporations. Even so, Lehman's Willens—who has worked on corporate expatriations—estimates that since the Helen of Troy rules, only 25 to 30 companies have reincorporated offshore to take advantage of taxes.

"There is definitely a perception of a stigma," says an investment banker who has worked on these transactions. "But it's hard to know whether there's an actual stigma, because what high-profile companies have tried it?"

The biggest company to move to Bermuda has been a success. In 1997 conglomerate Tyco International acquired Bermuda-based security system company ADT Security Services in a reverse merger that shifted Tyco to Bermuda. It seems clear that the reason for the reverse merger was to reduce taxes. Some shareholders complained about having to pay the capital gains tax, but the company sliced its effective tax rate from 36 percent to 25 percent. "There doesn't seem to be a stigma about Tyco being in Bermuda," says UBS Warburg analyst David Bleustein. Tyco didn't buy ADT for tax reasons, however, and the parent company is not exactly a household name.

Corporate governance experts say that making companies act like citizens will just lead to runaway taxation and angry shareholders. "Companies are not citizens," says Monitor Group consultant Jensen. "We don't want them to be. It's like saying we should have only one car company. You want competition among localities to provide services." Being angry at Ingersoll-Rand for leaving after September would be an example of "irrational patriotism," he adds.

Some tax policy experts are also concerned that a debate about patriotism will obscure more fundamental issues related to ducking the country's overseas tax rules. "The real issue is that this is disastrous if you believe in keeping manufacturing jobs in this country," notes one tax lawyer. "The unions haven't caught on to this, but if your top company is now offshore, you have a lot more economic incentive to build your next plant in Asia."

After the ascendancy of free-market economics and years of

cross-border mergers that routinely change the nationality of parent companies (including *Institutional Investor,* which was acquired by Euromoney, a British publishing company, in 1997), many business types seem startled to be asked about the patriotic angle on taxes. "As a shareholder, I would be steamed if a company changed a business decision because of September 11," says University of Chicago law professor David Weisbach.

Moreoever, almost every business uses tax havens in some way. In May 2001, at the urging of a group of U.S. insurers, two members of the House—Massachusetts Democrat Richard Neal and Connecticut Republican Nancy Johnson—introduced legislation aimed at foiling Bermuda tax ploys by insurance companies. "We think the system is broken," says Robert Marzocchi, chief tax executive of Chubb Insurance Co., which has been lobbying Congress to crack down on reincorporations in the reinsurance business. "At some point Congress is going to get tired of the *Fortune* 500 moving to Bermuda."

But it's hard to resist that country's allure. Although Chubb itself may be staying put in Hartford, it has invested in a reinsurer called Allied World Assurance Co. It's in Bermuda.

How do average Americans feel about these actions? That's hard to say. Ingersoll's reincorporation received little publicity except on the Yahoo! message board for the company, where those who posted were split but very emotional. "Bad time to kiss off the U.S. and evade taxes," said one anonymous writer.

Corporate identities will grow increasingly blurry in an age of multinational business and borderless capitalism. But even some very sober tax experts believe that the appeal of grass-roots patriotism should not be dismissed by Wall Street sophisticates. "I think it's a reasonable question," says Reuven Avi-Yonah, a former Wall Street lawyer who is now a professor of international tax law at the University of Michigan Law School. "This is more than just a tax question. It goes to the issue of whether multinational companies still have a nationality. I think the common intuition has a point here."

Here's a surprise: You may have chatted with someone in New Delhi the last time you placed a call to a technical support center for help with your computer. The various calculated steps taken to "Americanize" staffers working at call centers in India are recounted here by *Newsday*'s S. Mitra Kalita.

S. Mitra Kalita

India Calling

NEW DELHI, INDIA—At 10 P.M., as most Indians end dinner and prepare for bed, a grand four-story building in a dusty industrial park comes alive with chatter about the weather, the Yankees and Hollywood's latest.

Twentysomethings dressed in trendy gear, from Levi's jeans to three-inch platforms, log on to work stations and throw on headsets. Against the hum of air conditioners fighting the heat, they check the weather report for temperatures so low they haven't felt them in months. Kanika becomes Kelly and Siddharth becomes Sid.

Business with America can now begin.

The shop floor of Spectramind, as this call center is known, bustles with voices and movement. Technical support staff shift from foot to foot as the customer on the other end waits for a computer to reboot. Others frantically simulate the problems of callers on desktop computers with reminders of the time zone they are talking to.

"How did you get that window, ma'am?" asks one worker.

"Do you have a floppy disk, ma'am?" asks another.

On the other side of the room, a call agent remains just as polite, but clearly agitated: "Sir, please don't use such abusive language."

By all appearances, the scene at this call center mirrors that of thousands across the world. Calls placed, calls fielded, credit denied, credit granted, tempers flared and subsided. But most of these agents have never been to the countries at the other end of the line. Some boast MBAs or master's degrees. And they place thousands of calls a week from a country where telephones still remain a luxury.

"I've always wanted to go to America," said Sharley Juneja, 21. "If I'm not going there right now, I'll at least speak to them. At least, some part of my dream is happening."

Indeed, call center jobs provide workers the chance to not only talk to Americans, but to earn more than $200 monthly, more than five times the average Indian's salary. And unlike Americans, for whom telemarketing carries a stigma of part-time and unskilled grunt work, Indians view the job as a legitimate profession, even a career they can advance in.

"There's a big thing with Asians about not working with our hands, but working in an office," said Upendra Singh, vice president of operations.

For evidence, look no further than Spectramind's waiting room, filled with applicants in suits and saris. Spectramind employs 400 and expects to hire hundreds more in coming months.

During the last decade, India's information technology sector has boomed in the outsourcing model, exporting billions of dollars in software services to the world. Now a new industry has sprung up, handling tasks from medical transcription to payroll processing to telemarketing.

"Telecom is becoming so much more open," said Jacqueline Armitage, chief operating officer of Minerva Telelink here. "Talking to India or Timbuktu becomes superfluous to the call."

Last year, India's call centers raked in an estimated $183.9 million, according to the National Association of Software and Service Companies in New Delhi. By 2008, that's projected to more than double. Association chairman Phiroz Vandrevala estimated about 50 call centers operate in India.

"It's new, it's happening, it has a future," said Padmini Misra, Spectramind's vice president for training and development. "It's not exhausted like medicine or engineering."

Call center recruits generally consider themselves fairly Americanized. Trisha Sharma, 24, counts Russell Crowe among her favorite actors and *Friends* and *Ally McBeal* among her favorite TV shows.

"As a consumer, I'd rather watch an American movie over a Hindi movie," said Sharma. "I feel like I know a lot about the U.S. The culture is so common out here."

That wasn't always the case. In 1991, India began a series of economic reforms that eased restrictions on imports, introducing the world's second most populated country to McDonald's, MTV and M&M's.

Despite their ease with American culture, call center workers undergo rigorous training after they're hired. Those handling American clients learn American English, rather than the British English taught in school—a throwback to India's colonial history. They learn to say "garbage" instead of "dustbin," "elevator" instead of "lift." They are quizzed on Michael Jordan and George W. Bush. And trainees' favorite part of a workday: They watch American movies and TV shows over and over.

On a recent afternoon, new hires at CustomerAsset, a call and e-mail process center in Bangalore, watched *Chicken Run,* an animated comedy set on a 1950s English farm, their laughter audible from several rooms away. In a downstairs classroom, an instructor taught recruits handling British customers the intricacies of that country's accent.

Many associates change their name—conjuring a U.S. identity to go along—to make it easier for the customer on the other end, but also because the companies that outsource to India would prefer to keep that under wraps.

"I live in Brooklyn, New York," said Riaz Basha, a.k.a. Allan Douglas. "The zip code is 11224."

In reality, Basha has never been to Brooklyn and lives in Bangalore, a southern Indian city. But he said telling people he went to New York University and has a dog, Boozo, at home makes them feel more at ease.

Indian call centers say they don't outright encourage lying among employees, but tell them to do whatever it takes to warm up to a customer. And associates say conjuring identities and role-playing is fun.

"When a customer rings in, they need to feel they are talking to the company," said Armitage, a native of Australia. "If anybody believes I am going to take a bunch of Indians and change their Indian accents, I don't think anybody could do that. But we want to give them idioms and phraseology and then accent doesn't become an issue."

A typical shift at a call center in India begins with a summary of the day's news and a look at the weather in various U.S. regions. Each week, agents meet with their team leaders and "share experiences," from the nasty names they were called to the cultural lexicons that posed stumbling blocks.

At CustomerAsset in Bangalore, Basha said he learned much about American culture from comedians. "Have you heard of Jeff Foxworthy?" he asked. "We used to listen to a lot of jokes and laugh . . . jokes about rednecks, too."

India's call center industry boasts many multinationals, namely American Express, General Electric and British Airways, which has been downsizing its Jackson Heights office and beefing up business in India. Large computer companies are also relocating help desks and tech support to India, citing a significantly cheaper talent pool. Manhattan-based Juno Online Services Inc. handles some of its e-mail customer support operations from its Hyderabad office.

Larger call centers in India have U.S. operations to manage sales and marketing. From an office in Bellmore, about a half-dozen employees drum up business for Caretel, a New Delhi-based call center.

"Companies are very hesitant to work with companies based out of India," said Veeral Lakhani, executive manager of the Bellmore office. "We have to prove we're a bona fide call center."

At Spectramind, too, managers recount skeptical U.S. clients who've asked to inspect their equipment and wiring. "It's a big leap of faith," said Malhotra. "Some people still think of snake charmers and the Taj Mahal."

Yet some stereotypes work to its advantage. "Lots of Indians in the States run tech help desks," said Srinivas R. Pingali, an assistant vice president. "Sometimes customers feel better hearing the accent."

Besides an English-speaking and highly educated population, India's technology and telecommunications companies also have time on their side. For example, U.S. doctors can send dictation at the end of their day to be transcribed in India as they sleep. By the time they awake—the end of the workday in India—transcription is generally complete. The same scenario occurs for U.S. customers in need of tech support or instruction via e-mail.

But for the business of telemarketing to the United States, there's no escaping the overnight shift. Associates need to catch American consumers as they get home from work—about 4 A.M. in India.

"A lot of these guys are youngsters and would be out partying anyway," reasoned Pingali of Spectramind. "Here, you get paid for partying."

In some cases, that's true. Cognizant of how many telemarketers abroad burn out quickly, call centers strive to make their workplaces fun—from the bright colors they paint rooms to the weekly meetings over pizza to birthday parties in the cafeteria.

After a long day of fielding complaints and troubleshooting, call center agents ran through CustomerAsset's offices recently, screaming, laughing and carrying lists of clues. "It's a treasure hunt . . . to keep the atmosphere light," said marketing manager Brian Carvalho. "People never call a company to tell them their service was lovely."

DROPPING THE "SIR" CULTURE

Bombay, India—Ram Ramadorai of Tata Consultancy Services used to begin memos to employees with the words: "Office orders."

Earlier this year, that changed to "From the CEO's desk."

Still, the chief of corporate communications wants to order new stationery.

"I'm trying to get him to change it to 'Ram Speaks,'" said Atul Takle.

Welcome to the modern Indian workplace. Multinationals and homegrown software companies are helping this former British colony say goodbye to the days of calling bosses "sir" and office assistants "peons."

In 1991, India embarked on a series of reforms that paved the way for foreign investment and imports. In many ways, entering companies helped transform the workplace, making air-conditioning and wall-to-wall carpeting commonplace. But business experts say the nature of high-tech firms and their young workforces also have had a liberalizing effect—similar to the laid-back atmosphere of dot-coms in the United States.

"If you have an idea, you can implement it now," said Prashant Tyagi, a software consultant in New Delhi. "We show our ideas to the vice president and he says, 'Fine, go ahead.' Before, you had to go through the hierarchy of project manager to head leader."

Yet workplace experts say the drawbacks of a Westernized workplace are more stress and the threat of layoffs. Layoffs have been rare in India, a country where most banks are unionized.

"You need to constantly run to stand where you are," said Suresh Bethavandu, a human resources manager in Madras. "Every day is a day where you deliver."

Getting rid of the old has not been easy for all. At Tata, India's largest conglomerate and maker of everything from tea to trucks, workplace traditions often date back to the founding of the company 123 years ago, such as standing when senior managers enter the room or calling them "sir."

On a recent afternoon, Tata's Takle sat at a table, a spread of colorful slogans before him. Signs and T-shirts displayed phrases like: "Boss is what I call my best buddy." Another said: "Paradigm Shift. TCS: Reboot Your Life."

"We have a lot of legacy," Takle admitted. "But we've dropped the 'sir' culture."

During orientation at Spectramind, a telemarketing and e-mail processing center in New Delhi, the head of human resources collects 10 rupees—about 25 cents—from each recruit who slips and calls him "sir." The money is placed in a big jar in the front of the room and used to buy candy at the end of the day.

"All employees from a fresh recruit to a VP call me by my first name—Baru," said Baru S. Rao, chief executive of Syntel India Ltd., a software services company in Mumbai.

Rao, who once lived in Flushing, said living in the United States initially exposed him to less formal work environments.

Indeed, returnees from the West are triggering some changes. That is, the doctors, software engineers and business leaders who left India—often in pursuit of the American Dream—only to return home.

"It takes a few days to get used to," said Vineet Malhotra, a relationship manager at Spectramind who used to live in New Jersey. "But we lived most of our life here. We get used to things."

Moments later, when the electricity went out and backup generators took over, Malhotra didn't even flinch. He continued describing the shade of blue that workers had just voted to paint the cafeteria.

Slavery didn't end with the Civil War. Corporations "leased" a total of 40,000 or more Alabama convicts as workers over a period that lasted until 1928. Many were minor offenders, most were black, and thousands died in reprehensible conditions. Douglas A. Blackmon of *The Wall Street* Journal relates individual stories and points out the lack of reparations for the convicts' descendants.

Douglas A. Blackmon

Hard Time

BIRMINGHAM, ALABAMA—On March 30, 1908, Green Cottenham was arrested by the Shelby County, Alabama, sheriff and charged with vagrancy. After three days in the county jail, the 22-year-old African-American was sentenced to an unspecified term of hard labor. The next day, he was handed over to a unit of U.S. Steel Corp. and put to work with hundreds of other convicts in the notorious Pratt Mines complex on the outskirts of Birmingham. Four months later, he was still at the coal mines when tuberculosis killed him.

Born two decades after the end of slavery in America, Green Cottenham died a slave in all but name. The facts are dutifully entered in the handwritten registry of prisoners in Shelby County and in other state and local government records.

In the early decades of the 20th century, tens of thousands of convicts—most of them, like Mr. Cottenham, indigent black men—were snared in a largely forgotten justice system rooted in racism and nurtured by economic expedience. Until nearly 1930, decades after most other Southern states had abolished similar programs, Alabama was providing convicts to businesses hungry for hands to work in farm fields, lumber camps, railroad construction gangs and, especially in later years, mines. For state and local officials, the incentive was money; for many years, convict leasing was one of Alabama's largest sources of funding.

Most of the convicts were charged with minor offenses or violations of "Black Code" statutes passed to reassert white control in the aftermath of the Civil War. Mr. Cottenham was one of more than 40 Shelby County men shipped to the Pratt Mines in the winter of 1908, nearly half of them serving time for jumping a freight train, according to the Shelby County jail log. George Roberson was sent on a conviction for "assault with a stick," the log says. Lou William was in for adultery. John Jones for gambling.

Subjected to squalid living conditions, poor medical treatment, scant food and frequent floggings, thousands died. Entries on a typical page from a 1918 state report on causes of death among leased convicts include: "Killed by Convict, Asphyxia from Explosion, Tuberculosis, Burned by Gas Explosion, Pneumonia, Shot by Foreman, Gangrenous Appendicitis, Paralysis." Mr. Cottenham was one of dozens of convicts who died at the Pratt Mines complex in 1908.

This form of government and corporate forced labor ended in 1928 and slipped into the murk of history, discussed little outside the circles of sociologists and penal historians. But the story of Alabama's trade in human labor endures in minute detail in tens of thousands of pages of government records stored in archives, record rooms and courthouses across Alabama.

These documents chronicle another chapter in the history of corporate involvement in racial abuses of the last century. A $4.5 billion fund set up by German corporations, after lawsuits and intense diplomatic pressure from the U.S. and others, began making payments last month to the victims of Nazi slave-labor programs during the 1930s and 1940s. Japanese manufacturers have come under criticism for their alleged use of forced labor during the same period. Swiss banks agreed in 1998 to a $1.25 billion settlement of claims related to the seizure of Jewish assets during the Holocaust.

In the U.S., many companies—real-estate agents that helped maintain rigid housing segregation, insurers and other financial-services companies that red-lined minority areas as off-limits, employers of all stripes that discriminated in hiring—helped maintain traditions of segregation for a century after the end of the Civil War. But in the U.S., recurrent calls for reparations to the descendants of pre-Civil War slaves have made little headway. And there has been scant debate over compensating victims of 20th-century racial abuses involving businesses.

The biggest user of forced labor in Alabama at the turn of the century was Tennessee Coal, Iron & Railroad Co., the U.S. Steel unit that owned the mine where Mr. Cottenham died. Dozens of other companies used convicts, too, many of them now defunct or absorbed into larger businesses. Executives at some of the corporate descendants say they shouldn't be asked to bear responsibility for the actions of executives long dead or the practices of businesses acquired decades ago.

U.S. Steel says it can find no evidence to suggest that the company ever abused or caused the deaths of convicts in Alabama. U.S. Steel spokesman Thomas R. Ferrall says that concerns voiced about convict leasing by Elbert H. Gary, the company's chairman at the time, helped set the stage for "knocking the props out from under" the system. "We think U.S. Steel proper was a positive player in this history . . . was a force for good," Mr. Ferrall says.

The company's early presence in Alabama is still evident a few miles from downtown Birmingham. There, on a hillside over-grown with brush, hundreds of sunken graves litter the ground in haphazard rows. A few plots bear stones. No other sign or path marks the place. Only a muddy scar in the earth—the recently filled-in mouth of a spent coal mine—suggests that this is the cemetery of the Pratt Mines complex.

"The convicts were buried out there," says Willie Clark, an 82-year-old retired coal miner. He grew up in a house that overlooked the cemetery and the sprawling mine operation that once surrounded it. "I heard my daddy talking about how they would beat the convicts with pick handles. If they didn't like them, they would kill them."

He and other older people living in the ramshackle "Pratt City" neighborhood surrounding the old mining site still call the graveyard the "U.S. Steel cemetery." There are no records of those buried on the hillside. Mr. Cottenham could be among them.

When Mr. Cottenham died in 1908, U.S. Steel was still new to convict leasing. But by then, the system was decades old and a well-oiled machine.

After the Civil War, most Southern states set up similar penal systems, involving tens of thousands of African-Americans. In those years, the Southern economy was in ruins. State officials had few resources, and county governments had even fewer. Leasing prisoners to private individuals or companies provided revenue and eliminated the need to build prisons. Forcing convicts to work as part of their punishment was entirely legal; the 13th amendment to the U.S. Constitution, adopted in 1865, outlaws involuntary servitude—except for "duly convicted" prisoners.

Convict leasing in other states never reached the scale of Alabama's program. By the turn of the century, most states had ended the practice or soon would because of opposition on humanitarian grounds and from organized labor. Convict leasing also wasn't well suited to the still largely agrarian economies of most Southern states.

But in Alabama, industrialization was generating a ravenous appetite for the state's coal and iron ore. Production was booming, and unions were attempting to organize free miners. Convicts provided an ideal captive workforce: cheap, usually docile, unable to organize and available when free laborers went on strike.

Under the convict-leasing system, government officials agreed with a company such as Tennessee Coal to provide a specific number of prisoners for labor. State officials signed contracts to supply companies with large blocks of men—often hundreds at a time—who had committed felonies. Companies entered into separate deals with county sheriffs to obtain thousands more prisoners who had been convicted of misdemeanors. Of the 67 counties in Alabama, 51 actively leased their convicts, according to one contemporary newspaper report. The companies built their own prisons, fed and clothed the convicts and supplied guards as they saw fit.

In Barbour County, in the cotton country of southern Alabama, nearly 700 men were leased between June 1891 and November 1903, most for $6 a month, according to the leather-bound Convict Record still kept in the courthouse basement. Most were sent to mines operated by Tennessee Coal or Sloss-Sheffield Steel & Iron Co., another major industrial presence in Birmingham.

Sheriffs, deputies and some court officials derived most of their compensation from fees charged to convicts for each step in their own arrest, conviction and shipment to a private company. That gave sheriffs an incentive to arrest and obtain convictions of as many people as possible. They also had an incentive to feed the prisoners as little as possible, since they could pocket the difference between what the state paid them and what they spent to maintain the convicts while in their custody. Some convicts had enough money to pay the fees themselves and gain their freedom; the many who didn't were instead put to work. Company lease payments for the convicts' time at hard labor then were used to cover the fees.

In 1902 and 1903, the only period for which a complete prisoner ledger survives for Jefferson County, where Birmingham is located, local officials prosecuted more than 3,000 misdemeanor cases, the great majority of them yielding a convict to work in a Sloss-Sheffield mine.

One of those convicts was John Clarke, a black miner convicted of "gaming" on April 11, 1903. Unable to pay, he ended up at the Sloss-Sheffield mines. Working off the fine would take 10 days. Fees for the sheriff, the county clerk and even the witnesses who testified in the case required that Mr. Clarke serve an additional 104 days in the mines. Sloss-Sheffield acquired him at a rate of $9 a month, Jefferson County records show. One month and three days later, he was dead, crushed by "falling rock," according to the Alabama Board of Inspectors of Convicts, the agency that monitored the system.

In an 1898 convict-board report, the largest category in a table listing charges on which county convicts were imprisoned was "Not given." In a 1902 report, one man was in the mines for "disturbing females on railroad car." More than a dozen were incarcerated for "abusive and obscene language." Twenty convicts were digging coal for adultery, 29 for gambling. At any given time, the convict board's reports show dozens of prisoners at labor for riding a freight train without paying for a ticket. In 1914, convict-board records show, five black men were in prison for allegedly having sex with white women.

In 1895, Thomas Parke, the health officer for Jefferson County, investigated conditions at Sloss-Sheffield's Coalburg prison mine. There, Dr. Parke found 1,926 prisoners at toil. Hundreds had been charged with vagrancy, gambling, carrying a concealed weapon or other minor offenses, he reported. In many cases, no specific charges were recorded at all. Dr. Parke observed that many convicts had been arrested for minor infractions, fined $5 or $10 and, unable to pay, leased for 20 days to Sloss-Sheffield to cover the fine. Like Mr. Clarke, most of those prisoners then had another year or more tacked on to their sentences to cover fees owed to the sheriff, the clerk and the witnesses involved in prosecuting them.

"The largest portion of the prisoners are sentenced for slight offenses and sent to prison for want of money to pay the fines and costs. . . . They are not criminals," Dr. Parke wrote in his formal report. He asked whether "a sovereign state can afford to send her citizens, for slight offenses, to a prison where, in the nature of things, a large number are condemned to die."

The company's explanation for the lethal conditions in its convict mines: "The negro dies faster," Sloss-Sheffield's president wrote in a letter to local officials a month later.

At Sloss-Sheffield's Flat Top mine a few miles north of Birmingham, convicts reached the mine by shuffling through a long, low-ceilinged shaft extending from inside the walls of their prison compound, according to a 1904 map of the site. A special committee of the Alabama Legislature studying the convict system in 1889 reported that "many convicts in the coal mines . . . have not seen the sun shine for months." Another state inspector reported that at the Flat Top mine prison, which had 165 inmates, there were 137 "floggings" with a whip in one month of 1899.

In a 1904 report to acting Gov. Russell Cunningham, the state's top prison official, J.M. Carmichael, reported that Sloss-Sheffield had been "required to move its prison" at the Flat Top mine to a new location "because of the death rate at the prison formerly occupied by them." Mr. Carmichael added: "Hundreds and hundreds of persons are taken before the inferior courts of the country, tried and sentenced to hard labor for the county, who would never be arrested except for the matter of fees involved. This is a condition inexcusable, not to say shameful."

At the Pratt Mines complex where Mr. Cottenham later died, an observer for a special Alabama legislative committee in 1897 wrote a report describing 1,117 convicts, many "wholly unfit for the work," at labor in the shaft. The men worked standing in pools of putrid water. Gas from the miners' headlamps and smoke from blasts of dynamite and gun powder choked the mine.

The convict board's death registers show that in the final decade of the 19th century, large numbers of men died when diarrhea and dysentery periodically swept through the Pratt Mines. Citing inadequate food, beatings of miners and unsanitary conditions, state inspectors periodically issued reports criticizing the mine's operators, initially Pratt Coal & Coke Co. and later Tennessee Coal, which acquired Pratt Coal in the late 1800s. An 1889 report by Alabama legislators reported an "immense amount of whipping" of inmates at Pratt and other prison mines. An 1890 report from the convict inspectors board described "more sickness" at the Pratt Mines "than any other place."

Men were priced depending on their health and their ability to dig coal. Under state rules adopted in 1901, a "first class" prisoner had to cut and load into mine cars four tons of coal a day to avoid being whipped. The weakest inmates, labeled "fourth class" or "dead hands," were required to produce at least one ton a day. A first-class state convict cost Tennessee Coal $18.50 a month in 1897, according to a prison board financial report. A dead hand cost $9. Twenty years later, the monthly rates had risen to $93.12 per month for the strongest workers and $63.12 for the weakest.

As revenue from the lease system rose, companies took over nearly all the penal functions of the state. The Alabama legislature enacted elaborate statutes in the late 1800s regulating convict leases. The rules required companies to pay a fine of $150 a head for escapees. Company guards were empowered to shoot prisoners attempting to flee and, well into the 20th century, to strip disobedient convicts naked and whip them. State regulations mandated that a company "decently" inter any corpse not claimed by the prisoner's family at a mine cemetery.

"The demand for labor and fees has become so great that most of them now go to the mines where many of them are unfit for such labor; consequently it is not long before they pass from this earth," wrote Shirley Bragg, president of the Board of Inspectors of Convicts, in a September 1906 report to Alabama's governor. "Is it not the duty of the State to see that proper treatment is accorded these poor defenseless creatures, many of whom ought never have been arrested and tried at all?"

This is the world U.S. Steel entered in 1907 when it bought Tennessee Coal. It was a big deal, engineered by Wall Street banker J. Pierpont Morgan and requiring the personal approval of President Theodore Roosevelt. Tennessee Coal was a huge enterprise that had used slaves to operate its mines in Tennessee during the Civil War, according to a 1966 doctoral thesis on the company written by Justin Fuller, an Alabama historian.

U.S. Steel Chairman Elbert H. Gary was widely regarded at the time as a leader in progressive labor practices and business ethics. A former county judge after whom the steel city of Gary, Indiana, was named, Mr. Gary told the author of a 1925 biography that he ordered an immediate end to the use of convicts as soon as he learned of the practice. "Think of that!" Mr. Gary says in *The Story of Steel,* by Ida Tarbell. "I, an Abolitionist from childhood, at the head of a concern working negroes in a chain gang. . . . I won't stand for it."

Mr. Gary moved quickly to assert control over Tennessee Coal, installing his own president of the unit. In testimony during a 1913 investigation into alleged corruption in Alabama's convict-leasing bureaucracy, U.S. Steel executives, who weren't the subject of the investigation, said Mr. Gary had directed them to abandon convict leasing "as soon as possible." "Judge Gary said whether the hire of convicts was a good thing or a bad thing that he didn't care to be connected with the penal system of the State of Alabama," Walker Percy, then division counsel for Tennessee Coal, testified.

Still, according to state records and an internal company memo provided by U.S. Steel, the company continued to use more than 700 convicts already in the custody of Tennessee Coal under state and county contracts that weren't scheduled to expire for four more years. The company also entered into unspecified new convict-labor contracts after 1907, according to the company memo, written in 1913.

It isn't clear—and U.S. Steel today says it doesn't know—why the chairman's order to stop using forced labor in Alabama wasn't carried out promptly. Newspaper accounts and state records from the time indicate that Alabama officials were aware that Tennessee Coal was considering abandoning the practice, beginning immediately after the merger with U.S. Steel. In testimony from the 1913 inquiry, company executives cited the costs and logistics of recruiting and building housing for free miners as impediments to ending the use of convicts.

Whatever the reason, J.L. Walthall, the Shelby County sheriff who arrested Mr. Cottenham, and other law-enforcement officials continued regularly to ship convicts to the Pratt Mines. On

November 2, 1907, Sheriff Walthall received $373.50 from fees related to 65 cases, according to a county ledger. Adjusted for inflation, that figure would equal about $7,000 today.

The following February, a wave of pneumonia and tuberculosis killed nine miners at the Pratt Mines. When Mr. Cottenham arrived from the Shelby County jail in April, Sheriff Walthall had already shipped more than 60 convicts to the Pratt Mines in the previous 12 months, according to his records, now stored in a county building a few blocks from the old stone courthouse in Columbiana. In March, six more convicts died of tuberculosis, including Mr. Roberson, the Shelby County man convicted of "assault with a stick."

Mr. Cottenham, the youngest of nine children born to a widowed former slave named Mary Cottenham, died August 15, after a 13-day illness, according to his death certificate. Nine others were killed at the mine on November 16. The cause listed in convict-board records was "asphyxiation." A newspaper report at the time said 50 black convicts had set fire to the mine and attempted to escape during the ensuing chaos. Flames and collapsing coal trapped scores of convicts as the fire incinerated timbers holding up the roof of the mine. Those who died were "roasted and suffocated," the paper reported.

By the end of the year—the first full year of U.S. Steel control—58 convicts had died in the Pratt Mines.

Mortality rates gradually declined at the U.S. Steel operations as the company improved conditions. U.S. Steel continued to run a recently constructed, more sanitary prison for its no. 12 mine, where only convicts worked. State inspectors rated one U.S. Steel prison the "best in the state." In 1911, the number of deaths fell to 18.

But despite Judge Gary's pronouncements, nothing in the records indicates that U.S. Steel took any direct action to end its involvement in convict leasing. In the middle of 1911, for reasons that aren't specified in extant documents, Alabama officials began cutting the number of men convicted of state crimes that it supplied to U.S. Steel. Based on testimony in the 1913 investigation and a series of letters and memos transcribed into the record of that inquiry, U.S. Steel resisted giving up the prisoners under its control in the mines.

In a November 24, 1911, letter to the convict board that was copied to Alabama Gov. Braxton Comer, George C. Crawford, president of Tennessee Coal, said the company's past treatment of convicts "reflects credit upon the humanity and intelligence" of those in charge of the prisoners. The company planned to end its use of convicts eventually, he wrote, but couldn't yet do so "without detriment to our operations." Mr. Crawford added that U.S. Steel's "chief inducement for the hiring of convicts was the certainty of a supply of coal for our manufacturing operations in the contingency of labor troubles."

In June, when the number of convicts under lease from the state fell below the 400 men Alabama was obligated to provide at any one time, Tennessee Coal Vice President F.H. Crockard wrote convict bureau President James Oakley to complain, "asking him for 30 or 40 more men," according to testimony during the 1913 inquiry. When the number of state prisoners at the company's disposal fell below 300 later that summer, the company's general mine superintendent, E.H. Coxe, paid a personal visit to Mr. Oakley to demand more convicts, according to the records.

As the end of Tennessee Coal's convict lease with the state approached in 1911, the company told Alabama officials that it wanted to begin negotiations to extend the contract for at least another year. The state responded that it intended to lease all the convicts to another mining company, ostensibly because it believed the other company would pay more for the prisoners.

"I wish to enter a very vigorous protest against this action, as it is manifestly unfair to us to take the men from us," wrote Mr. Coxe in a September 25, 1911, letter to the official in charge of convicts. "We are paying the State a great big price for these convicts, and it is certainly a hardship on us to deplete our organization."

State officials were unswayed. On January 1, 1912, state convicts held at the Pratt Mines were marched out under guard and turned over to overseers at Pratt Consolidated, an unrelated mining company, and immediately sent into that company's Banner mine. There, nine months earlier, a giant explosion and fire had killed nearly 130 convicts, all but a dozen of whom were black, according to the state's death records for that year.

The end of U.S. Steel's convict leases with the state in effect marked the beginning of the end of the company's involvement in the system. The records show that at least until late 1912, the company was using some county convicts. But after that year, no prisoners appear to have been leased by U.S. Steel. The Pratt Mines stayed open, worked by free miners.

Convict leasing, however, persisted. By 1910, as many as 5,000 state and county prisoners were under lease in Alabama at any given time. Thousands of African-American men sentenced to terms of less than a year were being cycled through the system. The threat of arrest and forced labor had become a fixture of black life in many rural areas of Alabama.

In Barbour County, that threat took the form of brothers William M. and Robert B. Teal. In 1911, when term-limit law forced William to give up his job as sheriff, Robert was elected to the job, and William became chief deputy. "The brothers just swapped places," according to the local newspaper.

Based on jail records the brothers kept, the Teals typically arrested fewer than 20 people a month. Then suddenly, every few months, dozens of minor offenders were rounded up over a few days, charged with vagrancy, alcohol violations or other minor offenses. Nearly all were sentenced to hard labor and shipped to a mine within 10 days.

One day in the summer of 1912, Edwin Collins was being held in the county jail on the charge of eavesdropping. Another black man, Josia Marcia, was in for allegedly having sexual relations with a white woman. Louis Denham was jailed for vagrancy. Housed with them were Ad Rumph, Henry Demas, Jackson Daniels and Peter Ford, four African-American men accused in the murder of a sharecropper named George Blue.

Whatever evidence was presented against the various defendants has been lost, along with any record of their trials or whether the men had access to attorneys. By fall, though, all had been convicted and sentenced to varying terms of hard labor. Each of the accused murderers received between 20 years and life. Mr. Collins, the eavesdropper, received six months of hard labor; Mr. Denham, the vagrant, got five months. No sentence was recorded for Mr. Marcia.

The African-American men in the Barbour County jail bore all the outward signs of grinding poverty. Will Miller, charged with a separate murder, was logged into the state's Descriptive Record as having "one good tooth on top," "shot through top of right shoulder," "badly burnt on back left leg." Mr. Demas, 5-foot-9 and 150 pounds, bore scars across his frame—the most prominent a six-inch gash stretching from above his left eye down the side of his face.

Messrs. Collins and Denham apparently survived their terms; convict-board death records don't mention them. Mr. Miller died the following April in a Pratt Consolidated mine, "killed by convict," according to convict-board records. In November 1916, Mr. Rumph died of tuberculosis in a state prison hospital. Mr. Demas died the following month of pneumonia, at Pratt Consolidated's Banner mine. Mr. Daniels was killed July 27, 1917, while attempting to escape from the Sloss-Sheffield mine at Flat Top.

By the 1920s, state officials, under growing humanitarian and union pressures, were moving to end the worst abuses of the convict-leasing system, eventually taking more direct control of the supervision and punishment of convicts, though the convicts continued to work for companies. Despite the state's attempted reforms, monthly memos written by Glenn Andrews, a state medical inspector, record scores of lashings for offenses such as cursing, failure to dig the daily quota of coal and "disobedience." In one entry, two black inmates, Ernest Hallman and R.B. Green, received five lashes each on March 12, 1925, for "disobedience." Others were put in chains and given up to a dozen lashes for "not working."

Reforms were often cursory, such as requiring that men be

clothed during their lashings. The fee system remained in force. "Our jails are money-making machines," wrote state prison inspector W.H. Oates, in a 1922 report.

In 1924, a white convict named James Knox died shortly after he was leased to Sloss-Sheffield to work in the mines. The cause of death stated on his death certificate was suicide. Later, a series of newspaper reports alleged that a coroner had determined that Mr. Knox died of heart failure while being tortured by guards, who held him upside down in a barrel of water. The resulting public outrage finally pushed state officials to ban the use of leased convict labor entirely in 1928, roughly six decades after it began.

Tallying the total number of convicts leased to companies in Alabama during the 60 years the system prevailed is impossible. Record-keeping deteriorated in the system's last decade, as much larger numbers of men were arrested. State officials took a complete head count of prisoners only once every four years, meaning tens of thousands of prisoners entered and left the forced-labor system without ever being added to the totals.

Records of the head counts, compiled in the convict board's periodic reports, show that at least 40,000 state prisoners were leased to private enterprises, most of them between 1900 and 1922. The relatively few records the convict board kept on the county system show that more than 20,000 additional prisoners were leased from local jails between 1890 and 1914. In the years that followed, the number of arrests by sheriffs ballooned—averaging 30,000 a year in 1924, 1925 and 1926—though state-prison-inspector records don't indicate how many of those prisoners were leased to companies. In the end, the total number of those sent into the mines over the 60-year span of the system probably far exceeded 100,000.

The number of convicts who died while in the custody of private companies is more difficult to determine. The convict-board records show nearly 4,000 fatalities in the years leading up to 1918. Complete death records weren't maintained after that. Based on the numbers that do exist, annual mortality rates among the prisoners ranged from 3% to more than 25%.

The convict board's records show that Alabama's forced-labor system generated nearly $17 million for the state government alone—or between $225 million and $285 million in today's dollars—in the first two decades of the century. The total amount collected by counties isn't known. A Birmingham newspaper reported in 1908 that U.S. Steel's unit in Alabama paid Jefferson County about $60,000 ($1.1 million in today's dollars) for county convicts in that year, under a four-year contract between the company and local officials.

Sloss-Sheffield continued leasing convicts until at least 1926. In 1952, the company was merged into U.S. Pipe & Foundry, another Birmingham industrial group, which was in turn acquired in 1969 by Jim Walter Corp., a Tampa, Florida, industrial company. Now called Walter Industries, the company is best known as a manufacturer of inexpensive prefabricated homes.

"Obviously, this was a dark chapter for U.S. business," says Kyle Parks, a spokesman for Walter Industries. "Certainly no company today could even conceive of this kind of practice."

Pratt Consolidated used convict labor until the abolition of the system. By then, the company had merged with Alabama By-Products Corp. The combined entity merged 60 years later with what is now Drummond Coal Co., a privately held coal and real-estate company based in Jasper, Alabama, with mining operations in Alabama and South America. "I don't know how we could be tied back to something that happened in the early part of the century," says Drummond spokesman Mike Tracy. "Drummond wasn't even founded then."

U.S. Steel executives say that whatever happened at the company's Alabama mines long ago, it would be impossible to appropriately assign responsibility for any corporation's actions in so remote an era. "Is it fair in fact to punish people who are living today, who have certain assets they might have inherited from others, or corporate assets that have been passed on?" says Richard F. Lerach, U.S. Steel's assistant general counsel. "You can get to a situation where there is such a passage of time that it simply doesn't make sense and is not fair."

The company says it knows almost nothing about the "U.S. Steel cemetery" near where Willie Clark, the retired miner, grew up. U.S. Steel still owns the burial ground, and it obtained a cemetery property-tax exemption on the site in 1997. But officials say they are unable to locate records of burials there or of the company prison that once stood nearby. The only reference to the graveyard in surviving corporate documents, they say, is a map of the property marked with the notation "Negro Cemetery." Company officials theorize that the graveyard was an informal burial area used by African-American families living nearby, with no formal connection to U.S. Steel.

"Are there convicts on that site? Possibly, quite possibly," says Mr. Ferrall, the company spokesman. "But I am unable to tell you that there are."

Over the decades, Birmingham spread to surround the site: low-rent apartments on one side, shabby storefronts on another, an industrial site, a city park. In 1994, industrial archaeologist Jack Bergstresser stumbled across the cemetery while conducting a survey for the federal government to map the remains of nearby coke ovens, mine shafts and railroad lines.

Mr. Clark says that as a boy, he and other youngsters played among the unmarked graves, picking blackberries from the thorny vines that grew wild between the plots. Burials were rare by then. The older graves had begun to collapse, he says, exposing jumbles of human bones.

Though in his ninth decade, Mr. Clark, more than 6 feet tall, can still walk to the site from his home nearby and point out where the old mine shafts reached the surface and where dozens of company houses once stood.

"What can you do about it now?" he says, stepping gingerly through the trees and undergrowth. "But the company . . . ought to clean that land up, or turn it back over to the city or somebody else who can make some use of it, take care of it."

Asbestos lawyers have filled the courts with an avalanche of suits
on behalf of people who are minimally injured or uninjured,
thereby delaying consideration of the seriously ill. Roger Parloff of
Fortune believes that if this debacle is to end, judges, legislators, and
attorneys must all move toward tougher standards on cases being
allowed into court.

Roger Parloff

The $200 Billion Miscarriage of Justice

"YOU INDICATED that you walked three or four miles a
day?" a defense lawyer asked plaintiff James Curry this past October in a rural courthouse in Lexington, Mississippi.

"Correct," answered Curry, a 65-year-old former railroad
worker in seemingly good health. Curry and five co-plaintiffs were
in court seeking compensation for exceedingly mild cases of asbestosis and other "asbestos-related conditions." Such conditions—scars,
marks, opacities, and other imperfections in the lungs that show
up in X-rays—are not necessarily accompanied by any impairment
or symptom severe enough to spur someone to see a doctor. Nevertheless, most state courts recognize these conditions as "compens-
able injuries," that is, the proper subject of lawsuits.

Like most asbestos plaintiffs today, Curry and his co-plaintiffs
were never asbestos workers per se. They were, rather, laborers,
janitors, plant workers, or general maintenance men who, once in
a while during their long working lives, allegedly either handled

asbestos-containing products or worked in the general vicinity of others who did.

"And you also jog?" the defense lawyer asked Curry.

"No, I don't jog anymore. . . . I stopped after '96."

"Did you tell them at your deposition [in March 2001] that you jog?"

"Possibility that I did. . . . Just made a mistake."

This past October 26 the jury returned a verdict for Curry and his five co-plaintiffs against three defendant corporations of $150 million—$25 million per plaintiff—in compensatory (not punitive) damages. Four defense doctors had testified that none of the plaintiffs suffered from any asbestos-related condition whatsoever, but the plaintiffs' doctor, a Jackson pulmonologist, had disagreed. None of the plaintiffs claimed to have incurred any medical expenses or to have ever lost a day of work due to asbestos exposure.

The prospect of winning verdicts like Curry's has turned the original mass tort—asbestos litigation—into the ultimate mass farce. There are now about 49,000 asbestos plaintiffs awaiting trial in Lexington, Fayette, Port Gibson, Pascagoula, and other propitious plaintiffs' venues in Mississippi, and at least 200,000 more cases nationwide—mainly concentrated in other favorable plaintiffs' locales sprinkled across such states as Texas, Louisiana, West Virginia, New York, and California. The nation's dockets are now so jammed with asbestos suits being brought on behalf of minimally injured people that lawyers who represent the truly ill are teaming up with asbestos *defendants* to demand reform. They fear that the marginally impaired plaintiffs will drive so many defendants bankrupt that the genuinely sick and dying will have no one left to collect from.

Total corporate asbestos liability to U.S. plaintiffs is now expected to reach $200 billion. Insurers worldwide will soak up $122 billion of that sum, according to actuarial firm Tillinghast–Towers Perrin, while the defendant corporations themselves will disgorge the remaining $78 billion. Though as recently as 15 years ago dispassionate experts predicted that a total of 100,000 people might eventually file asbestos-related claims, the most recent forecasts predict between 1.3 million and 3.1 million claims, of which only about 570,000 have yet been filed.

Until very recently, most Americans regarded asbestos litigation as a problem of the distant past. And with good reason. It has now been more than 35 years since Dr. Irving Selikoff published his medical studies definitively establishing that asbestos dust was causing horrendous diseases among asbestos workers. It has been more than 30 years since the government began imposing strict limits on workplace exposure to asbestos dust. It has likewise been at least 30 years since labor unions came to understand the dangers of asbestos dust and began warning their members to take precautions. It has been 20 to 30 years since most asbestos-containing products were phased out of production completely. As a result, instances of serious asbestosis began declining many years ago. The 1994 edition of the medical text *Occupational Lung Disorders* describes asbestosis as a "disappearing disease."

But while asbestosis may be disappearing from America's hospitals, it is precipitously on the rise in America's courthouses, with the rate of new filings against some defendants having nearly tripled in the past two years. Filings against one defendant surged from 31,000 in 1999, to 58,000 in 2000, to more than 91,000 last year. Almost all of that surge occurred among claimants alleging nonmalignant asbestos-related conditions like Curry's—the most subjective and least serious diagnoses.

The filings by workers in so-called nontraditional industries— industries in which employees seldom come anywhere near asbestos dust—have skyrocketed. Filings in the textile industry, for instance, jumped more than 721% in the past two years, according to one defendant's records; in the pulp and paper industries, 296%; in the food and beverage industries, 284%. Companies like Chiquita Brands, General Electric, and Sears Roebuck have all been hit with asbestos suits.

The avalanche of new claims being brought by ever less impaired plaintiffs alleging ever more marginal medical conditions caused by ever more fleeting exposures to asbestos dust has triggered a new wave of bankruptcies. Since January 2000, 16 asbestos defendants have entered Chapter 11, including boiler-maker Babcock & Wilcox; glassmaker Pittsburgh Corning; insulation maker Owens Corning; floor manufacturer Armstrong World Industries; roofing-materials company G-I Holdings (formerly GAF Corp.); chemical giant W. R. Grace; construction-materials manufacturer USG Corp.; and auto-parts conglomerate Federal-Mogul Corp. Adding them to at least 39 other asbestos defendants that have sought bankruptcy protection since 1979 brings the momentary total to 55.

Each newly bankrupt company will eventually turn over most of its already dissipated shareholder value to a trust that will then divvy it up, mainly among minimally impaired claimants and their lawyers. Like the employees of Enron, employees of these reorganizing companies have seen their retirement savings vanish in a flash. At the time of Federal-Mogul's bankruptcy filing this past October, all-too-loyal employees held 16% of the company's stock, which had lost 99% of its value since January 1999. About 14% of Owens Corning's shares—which lost 97% of their value in the two years before its filing—were owned by employees. But those employees' losses have thus far gone unbemoaned by Congress.

Each time another company seeks bankruptcy protection, the prospects for all the remaining companies worsen, since the bankrupt company passes most of its liability along to them, under the ancient principle of tort law known as joint and several liability.

"The last man standing gets to pay the entire liability," summarizes Frank Macher, who became Federal-Mogul's CEO in January 2001, nine months before its Chapter 11 filing. What proved fatal to his company, he says, was its 1998 acquisition of T&N plc, a British manufacturer that carried what had seemed at the time a manageable level of U.S. asbestos liability. But as each new domino fell—Babcock & Wilcox, Owens Corning, Grace, USG—plaintiffs lawyers' demands on Federal-Mogul increased correspondingly. "Within four years," says Macher, "settlement costs went from $80 million a year to $350 million [in 2000], to a projected $400 million [in 2001]." Inundated beneath 360,000 active cases, Macher's company entered Chapter 11 in October.

Companies that once barely gave their modest asbestos liability a second thought are now trying to reassure shareholders that they can survive. The stock of oil-field supplier Halliburton Corp. fell 42% on December 7 after the company, now battling 275,000 asbestos cases, sustained the latest in a series of stunning, adverse jury verdicts. In January, Moody's Investors Service began reviewing the debt rating of Georgia-Pacific, the forest-products company, due to its 62,000 cases. Dow Chemical shares fell 7.5% in a day that month, as jittery shareholders absorbed news of an asbestos settlement paid by its recently acquired Union Carbide subsidiary. Ford Motor, General Motors, and DaimlerChrysler are now defending more than 15,000 cases, and that number could rise, since claims alleging injury from asbestos in brakes and clutches increased 1,634% over the past two years.

In fact, more than 1,000 American corporations have now been named as asbestos defendants, according to a report issued last August by the RAND Institute for Civil Justice. Those companies are scattered across 44 of the 82 industrial categories used by the U.S. Department of Commerce, meaning that employers across more than half of the American economy now face asbestos liability.

How did so many American businesses find themselves hurtling toward this $200 billion black hole? Can anything be done to deflect their path?

The course of asbestos litigation over the past 30 years has been shaped less by the law of torts than by the law of unintended consequences. At every turn, well-intentioned court rulings have, in the fullness of time, backfired.

Few people doubt that the unprecedented scale of today's corporate asbestos liability stems ultimately from the unprecedented scale of yesterday's corporate wrongdoing. In the 1920s and '30s, at least some American corporate officials—now long deceased—knowingly concealed evidence that asbestos dust could cause horrendous, fatal diseases. When the first asbestos suits were filed in the 1960s, the plaintiffs were usually asbestos workers suffering from grave and crippling maladies. The most common were mesothelioma, a 100% fatal cancer; lung cancer; and severe asbestosis. Though nonmalignant, severe asbestosis may have been the most torturous of all. Its asphyxiating symptoms could drag on for years, often ending only when the victim finally suffocated to death.

Because workers were usually barred from suing their employers for occupational disease—being restricted by state law to modest workmen's compensation benefits—lawyers framed these cases as product-liability suits against the asbestos manufacturers. Once that legal theory won the imprimatur of a federal appellate court in 1973, filings picked up momentum. In the late 1970s plaintiffs lawyers began unearthing smoking-gun corporate documents showing that corporate officials had concealed asbestos's perils. As a result, by the early 1980s plaintiffs had begun to win punitive-damages verdicts, magnifying the allure of such suits to other contingent-fee plaintiffs lawyers.

As defendants tried to stanch the rising tide of cases by raising statute-of-limitations defenses, plaintiffs lawyers responded by filing cases as soon as their clients manifested the slightest trace of exposure, even if the client had not yet developed a disabling disease. Most judges allowed those suits to go forward, concerned that if the plaintiffs waited till their conditions grew worse, their cases might be dismissed for tardiness. Increasingly mild asbestosis cases were brought, as were suits on behalf of plaintiffs suffering only from pleural plaques—a scarring of the lungs that most doctors regard as harmless.

In 1982, Ronald Motley, a young plaintiffs lawyer from

Charleston, South Carolina, won about $1 million in Pascagoula, Mississippi, for a shipyard worker suffering from moderate asbestosis. Motley, who would ride the crest of the asbestos wave to become the premier mass tort trial lawyer in the country, had argued that the plaintiff in that case should be compensated for his fear of developing cancer. Though awards for fear of cancer are legally controversial, many judges permit them—either overtly or covertly—out of concern that a plaintiff who later does get cancer might be either legally barred from bringing a second suit or might have no one left to collect from, the defendants having all gone bankrupt by then.

As the number of asymptomatic plaintiffs rose, a handful of jurisdictions started either rejecting them or deferring them until the plaintiffs developed disabling conditions. But liberal venue rules usually permitted plaintiffs lawyers to avoid those jurisdictions by filing their so-called unimpaireds elsewhere.

Since asymptomatic cases had become valuable, plaintiffs lawyers began seeking them out. By the mid-1980s they were organizing mass screenings, often with the cooperation of labor unions. A van equipped with radiographic equipment—an "examobile," as some were called—would roll up to a factory door, and all workers over a certain age would be invited to receive a free chest X-ray. Just before the exam, the worker would typically be asked to sign a retainer agreement, promising to be represented by a certain law firm if the X-ray came back positive for asbestos-related disease. The X-rays would then be collected and sent to a single radiologist—a credentialed specialist, albeit one working for the plaintiffs lawyer—who would sift through them, assembly-line style, looking for arguable cases of asbestosis, pleural plaques, or cancer.

There was nothing illegal or unethical in itself about staging mass screenings, and plaintiffs lawyers straightfacedly claimed that they provided a benefit to society. "I think it's a wonderful thing," says Fred Baron, the past president of the Association of Trial Lawyers of America and the head of Dallas-based Baron &

Budd, which now handles about 12,000 asbestos cases. "If I have a disease, I want to know about it, and I want to be able to seek treatment for it."

Nevertheless, the purported medical benefits of screening were always dubious; asbestosis and mesothelioma are untreatable, and National Cancer Institute studies have suggested that X-rays catch lung cancer too late to reduce mortality rates. The opportunities for abuse, on the other hand, were legion. The X-rays of hundreds of screened tire workers who submitted claims in the mid-1980s to one now-bankrupt asbestos defendant were subsequently reevaluated by independent academic researchers in a paper published in November 1990. The researchers concluded that "possibly 16, but more realistically 11 of the 439 tire workers evaluated may have a condition consistent with exposure to an asbestiform mineral." A Kansas federal judge, reviewing the evidence involving the tire workers, commented that screening procedures in that case had produced "a mockery of the practices of law and medicine."

As asbestos manufacturers desperately groped for defenses against the then-unfamiliar phenomenon of mass tort liability, they adopted a variety of strategies. In retrospect it has become clear that the most culpable defendant, Johns-Manville Corp., chose the shrewdest approach: early departure from the tort system. In 1982, that company, already defending 16,000 suits, shocked the business community by filing for bankruptcy protection. Then ranked 181st on the *Fortune* 500 list, with 1981 revenues of more than $2.2 billion, Johns-Manville was the largest and most vibrant industrial corporation ever to seek Chapter 11 protection. Because it had been the biggest asbestos manufacturer, plaintiffs lawyers had until then regarded it as the primary target, and had looked to it for at least 30% of their recoveries. But with the filing, Johns-Manville's treasury was lost to plaintiffs for most of the next 13 years, while the bankruptcy litigation played out, and it never fully returned.

In what would become the model followed by most asbestos defendants who later filed for reorganization in Chapter 11, Johns-Manville split into two units: the reorganized company, which went forward minus its asbestos operations and liabilities, and a trust. The trust's funds were invested so that the proceeds could be used to pay the company's asbestos victims. Most such trusts, including the Manville Trust, ultimately set up administrative processes whereby claimants, after submitting minimal proofs of exposure and an asbestos-related condition, would be paid set sums for designated medical conditions. Most trusts also paid, however, only at a greatly discounted rate—in Johns-Manville's case, 10 cents on the dollar.

With Johns-Manville effectively out of the picture by 1982, plaintiffs lawyers looked to the remaining manufacturers and distributors to make up the difference. Most of those companies turned to settlements as the most rational way of coping. Like the trusts, they essentially developed grid schedules, whereby they would offer X amount for a mesothelioma case, Y amount for a pleural plaque case, and so on. Looking back ruefully, many defendants now believe that by settling so readily for so many years they unwittingly encouraged the filing of increasingly marginal and dubious claims.

If defendants were making asbestos recoveries tantalizingly easy for plaintiffs, so were the courts. Since it was difficult, for instance, for plaintiffs to recall precisely which products they had worked with 40 years earlier, or to guess which of many asbestos products might have ultimately caused their injuries, courts relaxed the standards of proof required to link any one asbestos defendant to a plaintiff's injury. Even if a plaintiff could not recall using a defendant's product, he could sue that defendant if a co-worker remembered seeing that defendant's products at a work site.

Perhaps the most dramatic slackening of the rules came in the procedural realm, where judges increasingly joined plaintiffs and defendants in large cases and trials to keep up with their exploding asbestos dockets. Though such consolidations created grave doubts about the ability of jurors to keep the unique circumstances of each plaintiff or defendant clear in their minds, trial judges increasingly saw no alternatives. Within just two years after one federal appeals court in 1985 very cautiously okayed the joinder of four plaintiffs into one case—explaining that all four had served on the same work crew and that two were brothers—a federal trial judge consolidated 3,031 plaintiffs into a single case in Beaumont, Texas. That judge announced his plan to hold trials for representative plaintiffs, and then statistically to extrapolate those verdicts to thousands of co-plaintiffs.

Though a federal appeals court later blocked that plan, the so-called jumbo consolidation—in which as many as 11,000 plaintiffs and scores of defendants were joined in a single case—was soon common practice in the state courts of Texas, West Virginia, Maryland, Massachusetts, and Mississippi. Courts in West Virginia, Texas, and Mississippi allowed out-of-state plaintiffs to join those suits, even if they had never lived or worked in the forum state. As a result, by July 1999 some 9,100 asbestos plaintiffs all over the country were suing in rural Jefferson County, Mississippi—about 700 more asbestos plaintiffs than there were county residents.

Though judges turned to jumbo consolidations in an effort to get out from under their groaning caseloads, they may have unwittingly exacerbated the problem. "You think you're clearing your docket," says David Bernick, a litigator at Chicago's Kirkland & Ellis who represents three bankrupt asbestos defendants, "but what you're doing is you're widening the pipeline to the courthouse."

In the jumbo cases, a sampling of illustrative cases would typically go to trial together—in a "bouquet" trial, as it became known—and the judges would then hope that thousands of co-plaintiffs' claims could then be settled based roughly on the verdicts awarded the representative plaintiffs. But, academics have since concluded, the bouquet trials overcompensated the least injured plaintiffs by allowing them to benefit from "sympathy by association" or "the piggyback effect." In addition, jumbo consolidations tended to coerce settlements from asbestos defendants by presenting them with the so-called Armageddon scenario. Going to trial in a jumbo case was a bet-the-company proposition, one that few defendants were willing to risk.

Wanting to avoid these bouquet trials, defendants were often willing to settle the malignant cases, but plaintiffs lawyers frequently refused unless the defendants would settle the firm's nonmalignant cases as well. Much as a movie studio might refuse to rent out a blockbuster film unless an exhibitor agrees to take five clinkers along with it, the plaintiffs lawyers held their malignant clients hostage to fetch a higher price for their nonmalignants. Though the ratios vary widely by jurisdiction, in some states nonmalignant cases now outnumber cancer cases by margins as wide as 47 to 1.

Through the 1990s, plaintiffs lawyers continued using mass screenings to conscript fresh armies of asbestos plaintiffs. Just eight screening doctors accounted for more than 70% of all the claims filed with the Manville Trust between January 1995 and April 1998. Concerned about the reliability of such diagnoses, the trust had begun auditing claims in 1995, having independent doctors reevaluate claimants' X-rays. Its doctors concluded that 38% of all the asbestosis claimants audited in 1996 suffered from no asbestos-related condition at all, while another 28% had conditions milder than had been asserted. The audits were discontinued after plaintiffs firms sued to stop them. David Austern, president of the trust's claims-paying arm, says that the high audit-failure rates probably do not reflect fraud on anyone's part, but rather the intrinsic subjectivity of X-ray interpretation, especially when the alleged diseases are so mild. "It's more art form than science," Austern says.

Many of the men now being screened held numerous jobs in their lifetimes—sandblasting, welding, painting—each of which carries its own hazards to the lungs. Consequently, asbestos defendants are very likely now paying compensation for every occupational disease known to man. Incipient or marginal asbestosis, as picked up on an X-ray, bears at least a superficial resemblance to more than 130 other lung inflammations, including scores caused by various airborne particles.

The asbestos mass tort has proven more resistant to comprehensive settlement than any other, because the class of people exposed is so enormous, the injuries so ill defined, and the pool of potential defendants so bottomless. But the most vexing problem has been that so many asbestos-related injuries will not occur for decades. How do you negotiate a settlement with plaintiffs who don't yet exist?

An intrepid group of lawyers tried to do just that in 1993, when they announced the so-called *Georgine* settlement. In an agreement between about 20 asbestos defendants and many of the country's leading asbestos-plaintiffs firms—including Ron Motley's Ness Motley Loadholt Richardson and Poole—the companies settled a backlog of 14,000 cases in exchange for the plaintiffs firms' agreement to set up an administrative claim process for adjudicating all future claims. Under the new regime, future unimpaireds would got nothing unless they came down with a real illness, as defined by objective medical criteria.

But the deal, which was framed as a highly unorthodox class action settlement, needed judicial approval. And since the settling lawyers were, in effect, trying to alter the tort laws of all 50 states, the arrangement raised serious constitutional issues.

In June 1997 the U.S. Supreme Court struck down *Georgine* on procedural grounds, not addressing the constitutional issues. After the Court rejected a second proposed asbestos settlement in 1999, the prospect of ever hammering out a court-sanctioned, negotiated solution was laid to rest.

"We should've filed bankruptcy on the day after the *Georgine* settlement was overturned by the Supreme Court," says the CEO of one now-bankrupt asbestos defendant. "Every asbestos defendant should've done the same thing."

Since the most obvious asbestos defendants were, by that time, mostly out of the picture, the second- and third-tier defendants began to bear the brunt of the litigation. "The concept is picking low-hanging fruit," explains Steven Kazan, an Oakland, California, plaintiffs lawyer who represents almost exclusively mesothelioma victims. "In the early days of the litigation, you had Manville. Manville goes away. Next in line are the regional distributors. If they go away, next in line are the contractors who bought from them. If those guys disappear, there are cases where we very legitimately are suing the neighborhood hardware store, because that's where the guy bought asbestos joint compound, or the lumberyard where he bought asbestos shingles, or the floor company where he bought floor tiles. They say, 'All of a sudden, why me?' One answer is: 'Consider yourself lucky that we left you alone for 20 years.' We're now higher in the tree." Defense lawyers see it differently. "It's the search for the solvent bystander," says John Aldock, chairman of Shea & Gardner.

No matter how many major asbestos defendants succumbed to bankruptcy, plaintiffs always seemed able to identify the products of ever more peripheral defendants as having been present at their work sites. In fact, plaintiffs usually managed to convince juries that these afterthought defendants, who never used to be sued at all, were actually the guiltiest parties. In railroad worker Curry's case, for instance, the jury apportioned 80% of his $25 million award between the two defendants who were left in his case after scores of others had already settled before trial. (Dozens of other key potential defendants had never even been named in the suit, of course, since they had already gone bankrupt.) Specifically, the jury ordered that 60% of Curry's award be paid by ACandS Inc., a tiny Lancaster, Pennsylvania, insulation contractor that never had offices in Mississippi, never performed contracts at any of the sites where the plaintiffs worked, and sold few asbestos-containing products anywhere. For all six plaintiffs in the case, ACandS's liability came to $83.75 million, which was more than ten times the company's net asset or equity value, and more than the firm's total cumulative earnings in its 43 years of existence. (ACandS would like to appeal, according to a spokesman, but is not certain it can afford the bond required by law to do so.)

During the summer of 1997 the mysteries of the so-called product-identification phase of asbestos litigation came under scrutiny when a 20-page memo prepared by a paralegal at Baron & Budd was inadvertently turned over to defense lawyers at a deposition. The memo provided startlingly candid advice to asbestos plaintiffs about how to prepare for their depositions:

> You must be able to pronounce the product name correctly and know WHICH products are pipe covering, WHICH are insulating cements, and WHICH are plastic cements. . . . Have a family member quiz you until you know ALL the product names listed on your Work History Sheets by heart. . . .
>
> Do NOT mention product names that are not listed on your Work History Sheets. The defense attorneys will jump at a chance to blame your asbestos exposure on companies that were not sued in your case.
>
> You may be asked how you are able to recall so many product names. The best answer is to say that you recall seeing the names on the containers or on the product itself. The more you thought about it, the more you remembered. . . .

When the memo surfaced, Baron said that neither he nor any lawyer at his firm had ever seen it before. A Baron & Budd paralegal eventually signed an affidavit in which she took sole responsibility for writing it. (She is still employed at Baron & Budd.) Nevertheless, Baron also argues in an interview that the memo doesn't actually counsel anything improper, especially when taken in context with other materials the firm provided to plaintiffs, which advised them, for instance, to tell the truth.

Judicial reactions to the memo ranged widely. One state district judge referred the memo to a Dallas County grand jury for criminal investigation, but the inquiry died. Meanwhile, in civil proceedings, a panel of the state's appellate court concluded that the memo, while "heavy-handed," was not fraudulent. In fact, the court found, it was protected by the attorney-client privilege, so the asbestos defendants were barred from making any further inquiries about it.

In May 1998, a watershed trial took place in Fayette, Mississippi, the county seat of rural Jefferson County. An array of twelve plaintiffs went to trial, having been selected from among the more than 1,700 then joined in a jumbo consolidation known as *David Cosey*. That June the jury returned a verdict of $48.5 million in compensatory damages for just those 12 individuals—including $2 million for each of at least five seemingly healthy plaintiffs. "He reported no respiratory symptoms," the plaintiffs' expert had testified about one of the men. "He had normal pulmonary function tests in all ways."

The *Cosey* case, as it then played out, became an unusually vivid illustration of the dreaded "Armageddon scenario." With the same jury deliberating whether to impose punitive damages on top of the $48.5 million already assessed, most defendants settled those 12 individuals' claims, many agreeing to pay every penny of the verdict, according to one lawyer familiar with the case. When a few defendants balked, however, circuit judge Lamar Pickard telephoned their representatives, according to affidavits later filed in the case. He allegedly advised those defendants that if they did not settle the remaining 1,700 co-plaintiff's claims within 30 days, he was considering reconvening the same jury that had just ruled and having it set damages for all of their claims as well. He then allegedly implied that the defendants would not be able to appeal the resulting aggregate verdict to the Mississippi Supreme Court, because they would not be able to afford the appeal bond required under Mississippi law, which, at the time, had to cover 125% of the total judgment. The defendants settled the 12 individual claims that afternoon. They still balked, however, at settling the rest of the co-plaintiffs'claims.

Though Judge Pickard did not proceed with a trial of all 1,700 remaining co-plaintiffs, he did schedule a group trial of 63 more plaintiffs' claims for October. Five days before that trial was scheduled to begin, and after the Mississippi Supreme Court denied the defendants' emergency petition seeking, among other things, to disqualify Judge Pickard for bias, the defendants agreed to settle all the remaining 1,700 claims. (Judge Pickard declines to comment, on the grounds that a piece of the *Cosey* case is still pending. Mississippi relaxed its appellate bonding rules in 2001, but it is unclear whether the changes are sufficient to make much difference in practice.)

Owens Corning's share of the June 1998 *Cosey* verdict came to about $27 million. That blow struck the company just a few months after a new general counsel, Maura Abeln Smith, had joined it. "We looked at our position," Smith recalls, "and said, 'We can't be paying $27 million to $30 million for ten to 12 individual plaintiffs'—even if they were sick. That would be an incredible amount of money to have to pay out per person for a company that was trying to meet its obligations to hundreds of thousands of people."

As a result, Smith and CEO Glen Hiner launched the company's National Settlement Program, whereby Owens Corning eventually reached agreements with 120 plaintiffs firms, including Ness Motley and Baron & Budd. In a sense, it was Owens Corning's own private *Georgine,* except that it could not be forced upon anyone. The company agreed to pay all outstanding claims for amounts listed in a grid schedule, and the plaintiffs firms, in turn, promised to recommend that their future unimpaired clients not seek reimbursement until they became sick.

Owens Corning settled about 245,000 cases through the program, over and above the roughly 200,000 it had already resolved previously. "We thought we had gone over the hump," Smith recounts.

But as claims filings rose throughout 1999 and 2000, Owens Corning's program proved unable to save the company. Periodic windfall verdicts like the one in *Cosey* ensured that there would always be new plaintiffs attorneys—typically the younger lawyers who had not yet made their fortunes—who insisted on taking cases to trial.

"It was the spin-offs we were having difficulty with," says CEO Hiner, referring to start-up firms formed by lawyers who left more established firms and were not bound by those firms' agreements to participate in Owens Corning's settlement program.

The situation worsened in February 2000, when Babcock & Wilcox entered bankruptcy, the first of a new line of dominoes. As each fell, plaintiffs firms ratcheted up their settlement demands on all the defendants left in the tort system. After two more defendants entered Chapter 11—and with an ominous trial date looming in Beaumont, Texas—Owens Corning sought bankruptcy protection in October 2000.

Though Hiner and Smith had guessed wrong about their settlement program, they had guessed right about ducking the Beaumont case. In February 2001 that jury returned a $35.2 million verdict for 22 modestly injured workers—$1.6 million each—which the jury predictably apportioned primarily between the two defendants still left in the case: USG and Federal-Mogul. When USG went bankrupt in June, Federal-Mogul was left on the hook for the entire sum under the principle of joint and several liability. Federal-Mogul filed in October.

Gazing across this desolate landscape, two colonies of unbowed reformers are now plotting parallel avenues of attack upon the indomitable asbestos dragon. Though the leaders of each band profess optimism about their own prospects, they are disconcertingly skeptical about the prospects of the other camp.

One group is led by litigator Bernick, who hopes to entice federal judges presiding over bankruptcies to lead the way out of the quagmire. Now representing Babcock & Wilcox and Grace, among others, Bernick wants federal judges to appoint panels of medical experts to evaluate what he believes to be dubious scientific theories underpinning many asbestos claims today—a tactic that bore fruit for Bernick a few years ago when he was national defense counsel for Dow Corning during its breast implant litigation. Bernick believes, for instance, that independent experts will agree that the fleeting occupational exposures that form the basis of most claims today cannot really cause asbestosis. In Bernick's grand vision, the conclusions of these panels would then have a far-reaching, persuasive impact on judges throughout the country.

But while other asbestos defense lawyers would be delighted to see Bernick succeed, many consider his strategy quixotic. If nothing else, Bernick's goal of using federal bankruptcy courts to dismiss thousands of tort claims that would be permitted in the state courts where they were brought raises at least as many legal and constitutional red flags as did the *Georgine* settlement, which the Supreme Court felt constrained to strike down.

Accordingly, other defense lawyers place their hopes in a legislative solution. But while some still reflexively call for sweeping tort reform, most now forswear that rallying cry. "We need to save ourselves from the people who would like to do tort reform again," says Aldock, "because you never get it." Surveying 30 years of failed asbestos reform bills, Aldock and others believe that the only hope for legislative success lies in seeking very narrow fixes. Prototype legislation embodying this strategy is now being proposed by the Asbestos Alliance, a group led by the National Association of Manufacturers, but also supported by a group of plaintiffs firms that specialize in representing mesothelioma and other cancer victims.

Because of the dwindling number of plausible, solvent asbestos defendants, tension has built between the firms that represent only very sick plaintiffs, like Steve Kazan's, and larger firms that represent all plaintiffs, including the unimpaireds. "I happen to believe," says Kazan, "that the interests of the unimpaired clients in fact are better served by giving them nothing or very little now, but making sure that if they were to get sick later on there will be money for them."

In February 2000, when the most recent wave of bankruptcies began, Kazan and others with practices like his decided that their clients' interests could no longer be adequately protected by plaintiffs creditors' committees composed predominantly of lawyers like Baron. They formed a committee of their own to make sure that their point of view would be heard. That group now also supports the Asbestos Alliance's legislative approach.

The alliance proposes leaving asbestos litigation in the courts rather than trying to replace it with an administrative claims process, and it would not attempt to bar punitive damages or cap attorneys' fees—as failed initiatives of the recent past have tried to do. Instead, the alliance proposes legislation that would establish minimum objective medical criteria of actual injury that a plaintiff would have to prove before he could file suit anywhere in the country. In addition, its bill would ban jumbo consolidations and bar plaintiffs from suing outside the states where they live or were exposed.

Though most defense lawyers would favor such a bill, many are highly skeptical that it will ever pass—as anyone has to be, given the wretched history of such initiatives. Furthermore, many note, any asbestos reform supported by the Bush Administration will almost inevitably be derided as a bailout for Halliburton— Vice President Dick Cheney's old firm.

Unless the alliance can enlist mainstream plaintiffs firms like Ness Motley into their cause—bringing them support from labor unions and victims groups—its efforts certainly seem doomed. Still, such recruitments may not be impossible. Those firms consented once to the idea of establishing minimal medical criteria— in the context of the *Georgine* settlement in 1993—and, conceivably, they could be coaxed back into the reform camp again.

The other thing legislation may have going for it today is the unusual zeitgeist—the bipartisanship of the post–September 11 Congress combined with the palpable sense that the wheels are simply coming off the asbestos wagon.

In November, for instance, the federal judge overseeing the Manville Trust demanded that the trust's leadership advise him on whether he should order fundamental changes in its rules. He was responding to the fact that in light of ever-multiplying claims, the trust had been forced to halve its payments on claims from 10 cents on the dollar to just 5 cents last June, and was in danger of having to shave them further, possibly to as little as 2 cents on the dollar.

Then, in January 2002, another federal judge, presiding over the consolidated pretrial proceedings of all federal asbestos cases nationwide, ordered that all nonmalignant cases initiated through mass screenings would henceforth be subject to dismissal unless the plaintiff could show independent evidence of asbestos exposure and disease.

A legible message is coming into focus. Judges, legislators, and even plaintiffs lawyers may finally be converging on an overdue consensus. After 30 years of watching lawyers game the system until they have turned it inside out, it's time to try some narrow, targeted, legislative reform.

Enough is enough.

Reporter Associate Ellen Florian

Like the Roman Empire, Saul Steinberg's Reliance Insurance empire, born in the late 1960s, was not destined to last forever. Here Joseph N. DiStefano paints a colorful picture of Steinberg's earliest days of conquest. This was the first part of a three-part series that appeared in *Inquirer*, the Sunday magazine of *The Philadelphia Inquirer*.

Joseph N. DiStefano

The Empire Builder

IN HIS SECRET corporate takeover plans, Saul P. Steinberg used to code-name his targets after famous actresses.

New York's snooty Chemical Bank was "Faye," for icy Faye Dunaway. Philadelphia's cash-rich Reliance Insurance Co. was "Raquel," for amply endowed Raquel Welch.

Faye fought him off. But after a short struggle, Raquel succumbed.

And for 33 years, Steinberg used Reliance's prized assets—its thousands of employees, millions of customers, and billions of dollars in customer payments and borrowing power—to support his princely Manhattan lifestyle; to bankroll his pet causes, including the University of Pennsylvania's Wharton School; to finance his career as a bargain-hunting investor and corporate raider; and, finally, to fund his attempts to construct a global Internet financial-services empire.

Fast and funny, talking with his hands and rolling his eyes, fat-faced and squeaky-voiced, grandiose and self-deprecating, Steinberg exuded confidence in early interviews.

How did it feel to be the nation's richest businessman under age 30? "I'll own the world. I could even be the first Jewish president." Why did he want to buy Disney and cut it in pieces against management's wishes? "I have always had a fondness for children." How did it feel to be rebuffed by Chemical and excoriated on the floor of the United States Senate? "I always knew there was an establishment—I just thought I was part of it."

"He was ahead of his time. He was very aggressive—a visionary," said one of his former board members, retired Philadelphia banker Samuel H. Ballam Jr. "He did scare people."

But instead of owning the world, Steinberg indulged himself—and overreached. His empire has turned to ashes, leaving investors, banks, employees, the Commonwealth of Pennsylvania, and insurance policyholders across the nation to pay the cost, which reaches into the as-yet-uncounted billions of dollars.

"There's no question he was hoping very much to be a benevolent despot," said Abraham Briloff, a retired accounting professor at Queens College in New York. "Only trouble was, there was too much greed on behalf of himself and his family. And there's a certain limit to which any empire can be sucked." Briloff, who in 1977 won in a libel lawsuit that Steinberg filed against him, has written academic and business-press exposés of Steinberg's accounting methods over the last 30 years.

To support his grand vision and lifestyle, Steinberg ran Reliance deep into debt—and into high-risk ventures that went disastrously wrong.

The money ran out last spring, and the Pennsylvania Department of Insurance was finally obliged to take Reliance away from Steinberg. More than $5 billion in cash reserves, stock-market value, and loan and bond payments had vaporized during the company's final 24 months.

Steinberg's empire became the biggest insurance company failure in U.S. history.

In October, Pennsylvania Insurance Commissioner Diane Koken abandoned efforts to "rehabilitate" the company. Reliance, she said, will have to be liquidated—and it will be months, or years, before her department can figure out the cost of it all, she predicted.

The wreckage includes workers who have lost jobs and severance pay, individuals and institutions whose stock investments collapsed, banks and bondholders that Reliance stopped paying last year, insurers who depended on Reliance's financial support, and consumers, who will pay higher premiums because of lessened competition and the costs of an industry-funded Reliance bailout.

Perhaps, in the end, the former billionaire himself may be asked to pay for some of the damages.

In his long, dramatic reign over the Reliance cash machine, Steinberg both heralded and exploited the powerful forces that transformed the American economy—and Philadelphia.

His unsolicited 1968 bid for Reliance signaled the beginning of the end of Philadelphia's old business aristocracy, and the city's conversion from a major financial center into just another branch-office town.

Likewise, Steinberg personified the rise of a swashbuckling era of billion-dollar mergers and junk finance, when the people who run America's biggest companies don't dare make a move without considering how Wall Street investors will react.

Steinberg's dominion spanned a generation. It arose in the computer tech-stock bubble of the late 1960s and blew away amid the implosion of the Internet tech-stock bubble in the last two years.

Along the way, Steinberg hired the nation's boldest and most powerful financiers, including junk-bond king Michael Milken and the visionary investment firm (Carter, Berlind & Weill) run by future Citigroup chairman Sanford I. Weill, the world's most powerful banker.

Later, in the crucial years when he was gearing up for the disastrous expansion that destroyed Reliance, two of Steinberg's lieutenants were put in charge of two state watchdog agencies that were supposed to prevent insurers from taking on too much risk. In 1994, after an expensive election campaign supported by Steinberg and other Reliance figures, Pennsylvania Gov. Tom Ridge named a Steinberg lieutenant, Reliance assistant general counsel Linda Kaiser, insurance commissioner. The same year, another beneficiary of Steinberg's campaign cash, New York Gov. George Pataki, put another Steinberg aide, Reliance senior vice president Edward J. Muhl, in charge of regulating that state's insurers—including Reliance's most aggressive subsidiary, Reliance National Insurance Co.

Why did the regulators responsible for ensuring that Reliance stayed solvent allow Steinberg and his family to take millions in dividends, stock options, and executive pay from the company—more than $150 million during the 1990s alone—even though the company was hundreds of millions of dollars in debt?

Pennsylvania's current insurance commissioner, a former insurance lawyer who took office in 1997, defends her agency and her predecessors. "We did everything that could be done, when we could, as soon as we could," insisted Commissioner Koken, who finally shut Reliance down—after it ran out of money.

Longtime observers say it didn't have to end this way.

"I look back with regret for Saul," said Philadelphia investor Paul F. Miller Jr., a former Reliance director who fought and then collaborated with Steinberg, and later saw millions in Steinberg largesse go to the University of Pennsylvania while he was chairman of its trustees.

"When he made the Reliance acquisition, he had a hell of a good asset he could have exploited very, very well as a serious business," Miller said. Indeed, during the Steinberg years, two old Reliance rivals, Travelers and American International, grew into Citigroup and AIG, the biggest and most profitable financial companies in the world—something accomplished "with good management and good underwriting," according to Miller.

By contrast, Steinberg "did a piss-poor job of it," Miller said.

"Reliance was a great company, and he killed it. Saul was always too impatient to get the buck in the till."

By his own account, Saul Steinberg "didn't leave a ripple" at the Wharton School when he finished his studies in 1959, at the age of 20.

At the time, Wharton enrolled its share of immigrants' sons—many of them, like Steinberg, the children and grandchildren of Russian Jewish immigrants who thought of themselves as poor and outside the nation's white Protestant business mainstream, even if, like Steinberg, their parents were successful businesspeople.

"We both came from very modest and humble backgrounds. Everyone doubted him, but he has always been a pioneer in creative thinking," said Steinberg's classmate Jon M. Huntsman, the Idaho-born head of Huntsman Cos., which calls itself the world's biggest privately owned chemical company. As one of Wharton's few Mormons, Huntsman also thought of himself as an outsider, and he and Steinberg became close friends.

Steinberg's most often-told story about his Wharton days concerned the nameless instructor who he said pushed him to write a paper about "The Decline and Fall of IBM."

Steinberg said his research showed that IBM wasn't really in danger: It was a money machine that enjoyed high profits, in part because it rented and serviced computers—large mainframe units in the pre-PC era—through expensive four-year leases instead of selling them at more modest market prices.

Yet Steinberg also figured IBM could be outflanked—and that he could do it—by purchasing its used computers after the leases expired, re-leasing them to smaller companies at more affordable rates, and extending IBM's four-year equipment depreciation charge to an additional eight years, long enough to claim generous federal tax benefits.

Steinberg went back to Brooklyn, where his father and uncle operated the Ideal Rubber Products Co., which made bath mats. They lent him $25,000 to start Ideal Leasing Co., where he put his Wharton-hatched ideas to work.

That graduation loan was the basis of Steinberg's eventual billion-dollar fortune. It also marks one of the few times Steinberg or anyone in his family put their own money into his moneymaking enterprises.

By 1967, the name had become Leasco, Steinberg had raised $750,000 at an initial public stock offering, and the company could claim 800 employees and $74 million in assets. It didn't lease just computers. "Shipping containers—that's what we used to finance," said Roger Hillas, former head of one of Leasco's main lenders, Philadelphia's Provident Bank. "And that's how Leasco made its money."

But shipping containers weren't sexy. In public statements, Steinberg declared big plans for his computer business. Leasco quickly became a darling of Wall Street pitchmen and the national business press: In 1967 Merrill Lynch put Leasco alongside IBM and General Electric among 50 major tech stocks—just as Merrill would equate ephemeral stocks such as Internet Capital Group with GE and Microsoft during the Internet stock mania a generation later.

At a time when popular culture was obsessed with youth and took for granted the easy money of an economic boom, Steinberg represented both.

But that wasn't enough for Steinberg.

He wanted to build an empire. And he knew Leasco alone wasn't big enough to make that happen. Thanks to a visionary analysis published the same year, Steinberg found a vehicle: Reliance Insurance Co.

Why would a hot-stock operator like Steinberg want a Philadelphia insurer?

"Insurance is accounting. Its profitability is in the manipulation of reserves. You can get away with all kinds of things until the house of cards falls apart," said Hillas, the banker. "It's unbelievable what you can do with the insurance world—even with all the regulators."

Dominic Frederico, chairman of Philadelphia-based Ace INA,

which traces its roots to the Colonial-era Insurance Co. of North America, offers a similar take on the industry. "I work in the insurance industry because, as a balance-sheet guy, there's a lot of junk you can play with," he told a Philadelphia insurers' group this fall.

"If you work in manufacturing, there's only projecting obsolescence. If you work in banking, there's only the loan loss reserve. But insurance has referring agency costs, loss reserves," and many other categories that can be subjectively reported, he said. "The fun you can engineer into an insurance company's balance sheet is a lot more fun than some others."

The "fun" was just beginning when Saul Steinberg set out on his novel quest to build a financial empire on the back of an insurance company.

In the 1930s, Congress blamed the Great Depression on rampant speculation by banks and insurers in the stock market and industrial companies. The Glass-Steagall Act enforced separation of banking, insurance, investment, and industrial companies. Three decades later, America was a country of more than 10,000 local banks and thousands of state-regulated insurance companies whose investment portfolios were swelling in a bull stock market— but these companies were strictly forbidden from controlling non-financial firms.

In 1967, a young Wall Street analyst, Edward Netter of Carter, Berlind & Weill, wrote a report asking: What if a non-financial holding company could take over a financial company— and then redeploy its investments into new businesses?

Netter suggested the creation of holding companies that would offer "a one-stop, comprehensive financial institution servicing all of the consumer's financial needs," funded by the cash generated by property and casualty insurers like Reliance. For Reliance and other insurers, he even estimated the millions in "surplus" investment cash available to be tapped by creative new owners.

The Netter report, "The Financial Service Holding Company," ignited a frenzy of attempts by financiers to acquire insurance-company assets. It turned out to be a remarkably accurate blue-print for Citigroup, AIG, Chubb, Berkshire Hathaway, and other giant financial-service companies, all of which have grown from insurers into multipurpose financial and investment companies.

Among the early readers of Netter's report was Steinberg, who had his staff draft a "Confidential Analysis of a Fire and Casualty Company." It focused on one of Netter's potential targets: Reliance Insurance Co. Netter estimated that Reliance had built up an extra-cash surplus of $60 million. Steinberg's report estimated that more than twice as much—$125 million—could be raised from Reliance.

Another man who read the Netter report was Reliance's chairman, A. Addison Roberts.

Steinberg brought his dream of financial empire to Philadelphia at the start of the tense summer of 1968 as a brainy, cheerful and utterly unwelcome ambassador from the future.

Like the Black Power and Vietnam War protesters who threatened the nation's political establishment that summer, Steinberg saw himself as a representative of a new era. There was, he announced, "a whole new financial establishment being formed in this country."

There was, of course, also an old financial establishment in Philadelphia, largely Episcopalian, Presbyterian, and Quaker, which initially gave Steinberg the kind of welcome that a gang of drunken halfball players might expect on barging into the Merion Cricket Club.

"In those days, there really was a Philadelphia business establishment. They played golf together, they ate lunch together at the clubs, they knew each other," said Miller, who ran what was then the old Philadelphia investment bank of Drexel Harriman Ripley. "We fought like hell to keep [Steinberg] out."

When Steinberg made his move in 1968, Reliance's board looked like a Who's Who of corporate Philadelphia, and a museum of 19th-century commerce.

There were the bankers: Ballam of Fidelity Bank, William G.

Foulke of Provident National, and William B. Walker of First Pennsylvania. There was Miller, the investment banker, and John B. Prizer, general counsel of the Pennsylvania & New York Central Transportation Co., the nation's biggest railroad, formed by the mighty but ailing Pennsylvania Railroad's recent purchase of its Manhattan-based archrival.

All those institutions traced their roots to the pre–Civil War Republic. And all of them would be sold to out-of-town interests and vanish from Philadelphia before Steinberg was done with Reliance.

As chairman of Reliance, the Virginia-born Roberts had brought an outsider's vigor and energy to the corner office even as he recruited board members from the city's best clubs. He joined the company in 1938 and took the top job in 1964, pledging to grow and diversify what was already a national property, auto and business insurer.

By 1968, Reliance had bought 22 companies over the previous 20 years. Yet the deal-making had ground to a halt because of the company's weak—and vulnerable—share price. (Roberts blamed the slump on "property destruction in the previous summer's racial rioting" and on hurricanes and other uncontrollable events.)

Roberts continued to meet with New York investment bankers, looking for deals. That's how he learned, in February 1968, that his own company was being stalked. Steinberg's interest had become an open secret on Wall Street. By May, "many mutual funds were buying this stock" in the belief "we were going to be raided," Roberts, who died in 1992, later told a federal judge investigating the Reliance deal.

Five months later, at Reliance's Four Penn Center headquarters, Steinberg unveiled a radical plan to take over the company—with $400 million borrowed from its own shareholders.

Speaking fast, high and with his hands, the 29-year-old New Yorker assured Roberts that Reliance's 8,000 workers would be more productive, its 13,000 shareholders would be more prosperous, and its $125 million in extra cash would be put to better use if they were part of Steinberg's own tiny company, Leasco Data Processing Inc.

Roberts—who was given to writing anti-Communist tracts and praising Confederate battle tactics while lunching under the portraits of Northern generals at the Union League—gave his visitor a "rather abrasive" initial reception, he later recalled in court.

Indeed, by the numbers, it looked as if Steinberg's flea were trying to take over Roberts's dog. Reliance was a multinational giant, one of the biggest American insurers of homes, cars, and businesses. Leasco's main business was leasing used computers at cut-rate prices. It was one-tenth Reliance's size and nowhere near as profitable.

Yet Roberts couldn't brush Steinberg away: In a runaway stock market whose obsession with unproven computer companies presaged the Internet bubble of 30 years later, Leasco was a hot stock, having been dubbed a "computer industry leader" by Merrill Lynch.

Never mind that Leasco relied heavily on a dubious depreciation schedule and tax write-offs. Or that Steinberg had no special knowledge of computers, having dealt in newsstands and shipping containers before applying his Wharton-concocted idea to rent out secondhand IBM machines cheaply.

With investors seduced not only by Steinberg's growth projections but also by glowing profiles in the hero-worshiping business press, Leasco's stock-market value rose like an Apollo rocket, giving Steinberg the financial leverage to go far beyond used computers if he chose.

Under Steinberg's plan, Reliance shareholders would be given not cash or stock, but certificates payable from future Leasco and Reliance profits, at a price 50 percent higher than what Reliance had lately been worth.

To Reliance, "the market for computer leasing looked pretty phony," and Steinberg's debt-financed takeover plan looked pretty shaky, recalled Miller of Drexel Harriman Ripley.

Yet Roberts noted with mounting concern that a significant

segment of Reliance's shareholders—mutual funds and their managers—was receptive to Steinberg's offer. They believed it would push the stock price higher than Roberts's own expansion plans.

In proposing to take over Reliance, Steinberg threatened more than its tight-knit, elite directors: He threatened Roberts's job.

"He was a king, and we were about to make him a baron," Steinberg later explained to a federal judge investigating the deal. "It wasn't friendly; we were taking over his company."

To prevent the unwelcome takeover, Roberts tapped allies on every side. During the final week of July, the chairman:

- Mailed a letter to Reliance shareholders dismissing Steinberg's Leasco as a "highly speculative" little company whose "long-term prospects are by no means as good" as its inflated share price would make it seem.
- Sent Reliance lawyers' into federal court, accusing Steinberg's company and his investment bankers—including Sandy Weill, future head of the world's biggest bank, and Arthur Levitt, later President Bill Clinton's top securities regulator—of "conspiring" to "manipulate" Reliance's stock price based on "false and misleading information."
- Secured the support of the most powerful Pennsylvanian on Capitol Hill, Senate GOP leader Hugh Scott, who denounced Steinberg-allied investors from the Senate floor for "touting" Reliance in "a highly questionable manner."

The state government had already done its part by issuing regulations that then Insurance Commissioner David O. Maxwell told *The Inquirer* "would undoubtedly put a damper" on unwelcome insurer takeovers.

Roberts had even gone so far as to open competing merger talks with a Leasco rival—Data Processing Financial & General Corp. DPF wasn't any less ephemeral than Leasco later turned out to be—it was eventually folded into the company that makes Wonder Bread and Twinkies—but under the weird conditions of

1968, Roberts for a moment considered it, with its inflated stock, as a white knight in the battle against Steinberg.

To observers such as Maxwell, all these defenses looked formidable, even forbidding.

But on August 1, Roberts surrendered.

On that day, Roberts stopped his lawsuit, called off his allies, and sent stockholders another letter, making plain that he was stacking his weapons, standing aside, and letting Steinberg take over.

He had cut a deal.

What had happened?

Three years later, ruling in favor of a complaint by a small group of angry Reliance shareholders, Judge Jack Weinstein concluded: "Peace was made on that date at a considerable financial gain to Roberts." The chairman had made a personal deal with the buyer he was publicly resisting.

That wasn't what Roberts told shareholders at the time. Instead, he announced that a modified offer by Steinberg represented a better deal for them.

Indeed, the new offer appeared to be worth slightly more—$412 million, versus the original $400 million. But the new offer—in preferred stock instead of bonds—was taxable. For private investors, it actually wasn't as good a deal as the original offer, though it remained above the going price for Reliance stock.

But the new deal had major benefits for Roberts. Steinberg promised to leave him and his team in control and not to interfere with the management of Reliance's insurance business for the next five years.

Roberts also got an option to buy Leasco stock at a 70 percent discount (which he exercised, for a quick profit of $435,000) and a 25 percent raise in his base salary, to $100,000 a year, among other sweeteners.

Having accepted Steinberg's offer, "Roberts was no longer concerned with details such as tax consequences to [Reliance's] own shareholders," Weinstein wrote.

The chairman's "tacit abandonment of his duty to shareholders [came] in return for personal benefits," he said. Roberts had come to believe "it was better to acquiesce—advancing his personal fortune in the process—than to incur the displeasure of the raiders."

Weinstein also found that Roberts and Steinberg had both hidden from Reliance shareholders a key reason for the takeover: $125 million in Reliance cash, which would now be available for Steinberg to invest. If they'd known, Weinberg ruled, investors might have held out for a better offer.

He ordered Steinberg's company to pay a belated 12 percent takeover bonus to Reliance shareholders who had sold their shares between Leasco's 1968 takeover and the stock-market collapse the following year.

But Weinstein's ruling came in 1971—far too late to affect the course of the deal.

"It's the story of Philadelphia in recent years," says Ballam, who now lives in a Main Line retirement community where his neighbors include the heirs to the John Wanamaker and Quaker Lace fortunes, two more local stalwarts sold to outsiders.

"I guess that we were not aggressive enough to get our [share prices] up to defend ourselves," Ballam said. "Those people who are investment bankers are always looking at wounded ducks!"

Philadelphia "is a nice place to live . . . but it does not have the reputation of being a growth city," Ballam added. "You know the saying, 'Corrupt and contented.' That's how they see us."

As it was, in 1968 Steinberg was a hero. He had made more money by age 30 than anyone else in America, according to *Forbes* magazine. And he'd done it through computers—the business of the future.

If it was good to own an insurer, Steinberg and his advisers reasoned, it would be great to own a bank.

At the beginning of 1969 he settled on Chemical Bank New York Corp.—which boasted more than 10 times the combined assets of Leasco and Reliance.

But Reliance had been 10 times bigger than Leasco, and "the minnow had swallowed the whale," as insurance observer David Schiff put it.

Bank shares were slumping, as insurance stocks had been when Steinberg bought Reliance. As with Reliance, he prepared to offer convertible securities in return for a 30 percent premium on Chemical's stock.

Like Philadelphia's Reliance, New York's Chemical was big, traditional, and undervalued by recent stock-market trends.

Like Reliance's Roberts, Chemical chairman William Shyrock Renchard came out swinging, once news of the bid was leaked to the press. "We intend to resist this with all the means at our command," he announced. "And these might turn out to be considerable."

In Chemical's case, the means included allies such as New York Gov. Nelson Rockefeller and U.S. Sen. John Sparkman of Alabama, both of whom promptly proposed antitakeover laws.

Steinberg wasn't cowed, and Leasco went on buying Chemical stock—most of it through Reliance, which already owned 1 percent of the New York bank before bidding began.

But if Steinberg thought Chemical would fold the way Reliance did, he had misjudged his prey.

"It was very, very close," says Maurice Hartigan, a young Chemical officer at the time, and currently head of the Philadelphia-based Risk Management Association. The Princeton-educated Renchard "led a mighty battle. He lined us up and said, 'I'm going out to run the war. I want you to stay inside and run the bank.'"

Steinberg, for his part, rolled out a new weapon—Reliance's A. Addison Roberts, who, having cut his deal, set his past criticism aside and went to work lobbying Chemical on Steinberg's behalf.

Roberts called on Renchard, as a Philadelphia executive talking to his New York equal, to suggest the benefits of a takeover by Saul Steinberg.

But Renchard was not interested.

"I told [Roberts] he was off his rocker," Renchard later told *The New Yorker*. "I said computer leasing had nothing to do with banking. He said the Leasco-Reliance merger hadn't hurt Reliance. I was disappointed in him."

Around that time, Leasco shares began dropping dramatically, cutting deeply into the value of Steinberg's offer for Chemical. The drop remains mysterious; Steinberg later told a congressional committee that he suspected but could never prove that Chemical had urged its Wall Street friends to dump the stock.

The U.S. Department of Justice began inquiring into Steinberg's plans. Federal Reserve Chairman William McChesney Martin and several members of the Senate Banking Committee condemned the deal.

In February, even before he completed his formal bid, Steinberg surrendered, renouncing any interest in Chemical. For the moment, he had reached a limit on his powers of persuasion.

Chemical went on to prosper over the next generation. It would ultimately acquire a string of its powerful rivals, appropriating the names as well as the assets of J.P. Morgan and Chase Manhattan.

And Reliance resumed its colorful march under Steinberg.

Steinberg's first career as the progenitor of a new kind of financial empire had ended with the wreck of the Chemical deal and the relentless waning of the 1960s bull market that had propped up Leasco.

But if Steinberg saw it, he refused to admit it, at first.

In April 1969, he returned to Philadelphia. Meeting with investment managers at the Barclay Hotel, he had the crowd chuckling, thanks to his self-deprecating humor and uplifting pronouncements.

"The common complaint seems to be that I am too ambitious," he told the crowd. "Why, that's one of the qualities that made this nation great—we'd have never gone past the Appalachians without it."

To the mostly sympathetic audience of Philadelphia money

managers, Steinberg made great claims for Leasco and said he'd need to invest more money in expansion.

Instead, in August, Steinberg took one of his first steps in separating Reliance Insurance from its extra cash, declaring a special bonus dividend to shareholders. As the biggest shareholder, he was the biggest beneficiary of that dividend. For all of 1969, Reliance dividends to shareholders jumped to $52 million, from $10 million the year earlier.

Steinberg had pledged he'd use Leasco's cash for acquisitions that would expand both his computer business and his insurance business. He told investors he planned to offer time shares on his computers—and to take the business international.

But somehow Steinberg never found the time or opportunity to make the big investments that he acknowledged a successful expansion would require.

Insurance companies make most of their money from investments. With the stock market down, Leasco and Reliance lost $61 million on investments in 1971.

Yet Reliance continued paying dividends. And Steinberg continued to spend money—even if it wasn't on his companies' operations: He moved his headquarters from Long Island to Park Avenue. And he moved his wife and their three young children to a 29-room Long Island mansion. He decorated the walls with Picassos.

Meanwhile Leasco's original business was running out of gas.

Steinberg was one of the first and most spectacular victims of Moore's Law—the principle, enunciated by Intel Corp. founder and computer-chip pioneer Gordon Moore, that computer power doubles every year or two, thanks to rapid advances in hardware technology.

Through the 1960s, IBM estimated its machines had a four-year life span for tax purposes.

Steinberg had built Leasco on the proposition that IBM was being too conservative. He bet IBM machines could be leased over an eight-year period, allowing him to claim extended depreciation and federal tax benefits.

But by 1973, with ever-more-powerful and cheaper IBM machines flooding a market depressed by the oil crisis, Leasco was having an increasingly tough time renting its machines.

Its stock price plunged, dragging Reliance down with it.

The following year, Steinberg wrote off $14 million in computers. Losses mounted as Leasco wrote off more computers each year. Steinberg still had Reliance, but the company was battered by inflation and the weak investment market. The value of his personal stake plunged from $60 million to an estimated $9 million in 1975, *Forbes* reported.

Steinberg's marriage broke up. His children's school sued him for nonpayment of a promised donation. He married again, but that union dissolved in tabloid accusations of misbehavior.

But Steinberg had learned some powerful lessons from his spectacular and highly public failure to buy Chemical Bank.

The next time he went after a company that didn't want him, he had no intention of going away without a profit.

Let's say you daydream about settling down one day to own a happy and profitable Krispy Kreme store. Sweet deal, right? There's much more to it than meets the eye. Carlye Adler of *Fortune Small Business* tabulates the high cost of getting into the doughnut business—and whether it's worth it.

Carlye Adler

Would You Pay $2 Million for This Franchise?

IN A FEW MONTHS, the new Krispy Kreme store in West Palm Beach, Florida, will open, and until then James A. Cosentino is counting the seconds. Cosentino, a native of Buffalo, is part-owner of that store, and because he already owns two other Krispy Kreme locations, he has a pretty good idea of what he can expect come opening day. At 5:30 that morning, he'll let in a mob of people who've been waiting outside for hours for the warm doughnuts streaming from his ovens at a rate of 2,640 per hour. The event will probably be covered by a TV news crew—most Krispy Kreme openings are—and in his first week Cosentino will take in almost as much in revenue as the typical Dunkin' Donuts store makes in a year.

In case you haven't noticed—Dunkin' Donuts likely has— North Carolina-based Krispy Kreme has become a full-fledged phenomenon in the food business. Launched in 1937 by Vernon Rudolph, a Southern entrepreneur with a secret French doughnut recipe and a Pontiac, the company went unnoticed for decades before it expanded nationally in the mid-1990s, in part through franchised locations like the ones Cosentino owns. It held a public offering in April 2000, and since then its stock is up about 300%. For fiscal 2002, the chain took in $394 million in revenue, and sales for locations open at least 18 months were up almost 13%, impressive in the fast-food or any other retail business. No wonder Cosentino is impatient for the Florida store to open.

But if you think the doughnuts are popular, you should see the line of people trying to get a piece of the business. Krispy Kreme isn't signing on any new franchisees right now (it plans to in the next 18 to 24 months), yet about 500 people call or e-mail each week to ask for applications. That's even more surprising when you realize how much the stores cost—almost $2 million on average, which is an order of magnitude more than other fast-food places. Even McDonald's, the McDaddy of all franchises, costs far less, topping out at about $750,000 per location. And assuming you have $2 million to open a Krispy Kreme, and the required restaurant experience, you still have to campaign like a Senate candidate to get accepted. Cosentino has worked in the restaurant industry for 30 years and owns 19 T.G.I. Friday's and six Dennys locations. Even so, it took him two years and three trips to the company headquarters before he finally got the nod. Kevin Gordon, an ex-banker who specialized in lending to franchisees, called every business day for six months before winning a contract to open nine stores in his hometown of Houston.

All of which makes you wonder—do these people really know what they're doing? Can any doughnut shop, even one this popular, actually be worth $2 million? To find out, we spoke to dozens of franchising experts and went through the numbers ourselves, comparing Krispy Kreme's initial investment and operating expenses with those of similar franchises. The answer? Yes, it really is worth that much—for now, at least.

All companies are required by the Federal Trade Commission to tell prospective franchisees exactly how their businesses operate, through a phone-book-sized document called a uniform franchising offering circular (UFOC). In the Krispy Kreme UFOC, some of the requirements aren't too surprising. For example, the company charges a nonrefundable $40,000 fee that's akin to membership dues—it gives you the rights to a specific location for 15 years. Dunkin' Donuts charges $40,000, and Tim Horton's, a Canadian doughnut franchise owned by Wendy's Corp., charges $35,000. The Krispy Kreme contract also requires that all franchisees give the company 4.5% of their total sales as a royalty fee, plus 2% to help pay for brand development and public relations costs. In the franchise business such fees are fairly standard.

But other aspects of the Krispy Kreme application are more daunting. For example, you need $5 million in net worth to apply, and you also need "ownership and operating experience of multi-unit food service operations." So forget the archetypal franchisee—the middle manager who took early retirement from Xerox. In addition, the company wants only "area developers," mega-franchisees who commit to opening at least ten stores in a given region. (Outback Steakhouse uses a similar arrangement.) In part, that allows the company to expand more quickly. Its 23 current area developers are contractually bound to open 250 stores by 2007. But there's another reason. "Krispy Kreme is doing so well, they don't want to take the chance of giving it to a mom-and-pop," says George A. Naddaff, former chairman of Boston Chicken, who now invests in early-stage franchise companies.

If your application is approved, you can expect to pay about $1.35 million to open a Krispy Kreme, which covers furniture and fixtures, the doughnut-making equipment, and your initial inventory (sacks of things like dough conditioner and malted barley flour). That's about five times what the International Franchise Association considers standard for most operations, and it doesn't even include the real estate. That will tack on another $500,000 or so, depending on what city you're building in, which brings the total to nearly $2 million per location, making Krispy Kreme the costliest food franchise available. The doughnut equipment alone costs $350,000—for that amount of money you can buy a Dunkin' Donuts, a Cinnabon, or two Manhattan Bagels stores.

Once you open the doors, though, the flow of money reverses course—and fast. Gerard Centioli, an area developer in the Pacific Northwest, holds the record for highest first-week sales in the U.S.; his Issaquah, Washington, store took in $454,000. But because the stores are so wildly popular right now, just about every new location that opens resets the record. Krispy Kreme COO John W. Tate says there's typically a 12-month honeymoon period, and after that the business starts to settle to a pace that's more manageable but still impressive: In its 2001 annual report, Krispy Kreme says the average week for a franchise is $43,000 in revenue, which works out to $2.2 million a year. The 2002 annual report was not released by press time, but Tate says the per-store revenues for area developers have gotten higher, averaging $60,000 to $70,000 a week, or $3.4 million a year, and one store outside Denver did $8 million.

"Those are big numbers," says Timothy Bates, an economics professor who studies franchising at Wayne State University in Detroit. "They're on the extreme high end of fast-food franchises." The typical McDonald's takes in about $1.5 million a year, according to industry experts. Dunkin' Donuts averages $744,000; Cinnabon posts $408,000 per site; and Auntie Anne's (a pretzel store) averages $395,000.

In addition to the volume, though, Krispy Kreme tends to have higher profit margins than other fast-food businesses. Michael Shepardson, the president of CNL Advisory Services, a boutique investment bank in Orlando that helps restaurant owners, says the typical chain has cash-flow margins of 10% to 15%, but at Krispy Kreme the number is more like mid-20s. That's because just about every store does both retail and wholesale business, explains Krispy Kreme CEO Scott A. Livengood, who says he considers the stores more like manufacturing plants than bakeries. They're running 24 hours a day, and they're built to produce enough doughnuts for walk-in customers, plus wholesale distribution to places like supermarkets and convenience stores. "Like any other manufacturer, idle equipment is not profitable," says Livengood, whose name is probably apt right new.

It's a formula of high volume plus high margins, and to understand the end result, consider Jim Morrissey, who has an impressive background even in the rarefied air of Krispy Kreme developers. Morrissey has spent 27 years in the restaurant business, and until a few years ago he co-owned nearly 100 franchises, including Bruegger's Bagels, KFC, and Godfather's Pizza restaurants. After getting a contract to open 15 Krispy Kremes in six states, he sold all the others. "It was an easy decision," he says. "I still shake my head over the sales-per-unit numbers. I've never seen anything like it." Think of it this way: Morrissey pegs his revenues at about $3.5 million to $4.5 million per store. Assuming margins of 20% (that's conservative), his stores take in $700,000 in profit every year. For 15 stores, that's $10.5 million. Of course, this is only a back-of-the-napkin calculation, but it underscores why investors like Morrissey or Cosentino have no problem signing on to open ten or more stores in a region.

Before you head down to North Carolina to camp out in front of the company's headquarters, realize that there are a few catches. For one thing, you'll have a partner: Krispy Kreme Doughnuts Inc. Until a few years ago, it seems even the company itself didn't realize how profitable the franchise locations could be. But that has recently changed, and Krispy Kreme now takes an ownership stake in all new franchises, claiming anywhere from 33% to 75%, according to Philip R. S. Waugh, senior vice president of franchising. The company currently has joint venture deals with nine area developers, and it owns a majority stake in three markets: Northern California, New England, and Philadelphia.

Other franchisees typically own their business outright, but not always. McDonald's started offering similar joint venture deals in the mid-1990s. The parent companies engage in such partnerships because they lead to higher earnings and faster expansion (though in this case, Krispy Kreme franchisees have the money and desire to open as many stores as the company will allow). Fundamentally, however, the reason Krispy Kreme operates this way is, well, because it can. "If it's the only way to get more territory, we'll do it," says Morrissey.

That joint-partnership structure has already led to a lawsuit. According to court filings, two partners, Kevin Boylan and Bruce Newberg, claim they entered into a deal where they would open stores in Northern California and own 44% of the overall business. They were set to hand over their portion of the start-up costs, but they say Livengood, the CEO, then decided that he wanted a significant cut for his personal investments. The terms of the deal were changed so that Livengood would own 26% of the holding company, and Boylan and Newberg's stake was cut in half. They filed a breach-of-contract lawsuit, asking for $10 million in damages. Through their lawyer, the two declined to comment, and the case could go to an arbitration hearing in the next few months. In response, Livengood says they never had a contract and declined to comment further.

Similarly, 35 Krispy Kreme executives (not the corporation) formed an equity fund in 2000 to invest in franchise stores, something they'd started doing before the company went public. But in the wake of the Enron scandal, management took steps to ensure that no individual's personal gain would conflict with the overall good of the company. It paid about $1 million this past March to buy out the equity fund. According to Waugh, Krispy Kreme executives no longer hold personal investments in the franchise stores.

Of course, the company may take less of an interest in specific franchises if the novelty factor wears off. What Krispy Kreme is selling, after all, is only a doughnut (granted, it's a smaller, sweeter one). Livengood says he's not worried. There are still just 217 locations in the country, compared with 5,500 Dunkin' Donuts and 30,000 McDonald's locations. And although the company plans to open about 750 Krispy Kremes—at least 250 under franchise contracts in the next five years—that's still not a lot in the fast-food business. Subway opens nearly 1,000 restaurants annually.

The bottom line? Two million dollars may sound steep, but

it's actually a fair price for a Krispy Kreme store right now. Sure, tastes change, and there's a decent chance the country could go on another health kick (in which case those glazed calorie bombs may not seem so appetizing). But for the foreseeable future, people will still continue to line up, especially whenever a Krispy Kreme store turns on its hot light—a neon sign that glows whenever warm, fresh doughnuts are ready. Every location has one. "It's like a big bug zapper," says Miami attorney Robert M. Einhorn, who specializes in franchise law. "Humans are attracted to that light."

In assessing the value of today's sports teams, the team itself has become an add-on. Media deals are what drive value in the market. A team of *Forbes* writers explains why paying hundreds of millions of dollars for a money-losing team now makes perfectly good financial sense.

Kurt Badenhausen, Cecily Fluke, Lesley Kump, and Michael K. Ozanian

Double Play

IF YOU WANT TO UNDERSTAND what drives the economics of baseball these days, just look at the recent sale of the Boston Red Sox.

The Red Sox haven't won the World Series since 1918, a year before they sold Babe Ruth to the New York Yankees. Boston's home, Fenway Park, was built in 1912 and is the smallest in the majors. And last season the team had an operating loss of $11.4 million.

Yet in February a group led by John Henry, then-owner of baseball's Florida Marlins, paid $700 million for the team, more than twice the previous record sale price (the $323 million Larry Dolan paid for the Cleveland Indians in 2000) and $550 million more than Henry paid for the Marlins just three years ago. What gives?

Along with the team and ballpark, Henry also got an 80% interest in the New England Sports Network (hockey's Boston

337

Bruins own the remaining 20%). Lawrence Lucchino, president of the team and a minority owner, says: "The value of the Red Sox and NESN combined is far more than the value of the two entities separately."

Here's why. Prior to Henry's purchase, NESN, which is broadcasting 86 Red Sox games and 54 Bruins games this season, struck deals with all the major cable providers in eastern Massachusetts to move the channel to their basic cable lineup. Switching NESN to basic cable pushed its reach to 3.8 million homes across New England, more than double the number of subscribers who paid to watch Red Sox games when NESN was available only as a premium channel.

The Red Sox and Bruins provide NESN with plenty of guaranteed prime-time programming in the nation's sixth-largest media market. And, unlike ratings for baseball on national TV (which have been declining), those on cable have remained high because fans always get to see the home team.

The Red Sox in particular have a very loyal fan base. Last year an average of 400,000 households tuned in to each Red Sox game on NESN. There are few baseball teams that do as well on cable. Only New York's Yankees and Mets—in a much bigger market—draw more viewers. This year NESN's revenue will be close to $90 million versus $75 million in 2001, according to John Mansell of Kagan World Media. Pretax cash flow (in the sense of net income plus depreciation) should be around $20 million, $5 million higher.

The additional revenue the Red Sox owners rake in from NESN will never increase enough to equal that of the New York Yankees, who play in baseball's biggest market and have started their own cable sports network. But the Red Sox will surely have the money to sign enough star players to challenge their hated Bronx rivals on the diamond. Our calculations show the Red Sox increasing 26% in value, to $426 million.

And NESN, which shows heaps of other sports programming—such as college basketball and football, boxing and bowling—is likely to increase revenue much more. Among the new owners is Thomas Werner, who has experience both as a baseball owner (San Diego Padres) and in television (developing several sitcom megahits, including *The Cosby Show* and *Roseanne*).

Werner told *Forbes* he plans on increasing advertising revenue by bidding for major sporting events as they become available, as well as partnering with other regional cable networks. "The goal is to not just make it [NESN] essential for Red Sox and Bruins fans, but for all New England sports," he says. Red Sox executives believe that NESN alone is worth $400 million.

If you think this is a pipe dream, keep in mind that Cablevision Chairman Charles Dolan, Larry Dolan's brother, offered to pay $790 million for the Red Sox and NESN but was rebuffed in favor of Henry's group. (Insiders say the league didn't want to have two brothers each owning a team.)

Of course, using a baseball team to build a media asset isn't new. Ted Turner used the Atlanta Braves to build TBS into the first superstation starting in the late 1970s. Tribune Co. did the same thing with the Chicago Cubs in the 1980s. But the value of cross-ownership is much greater today because Baseball Commissioner Bud Selig is making a big push to increase the sport's revenue sharing, from 20% of local media revenue to 50%. Teams with cross-ownership will have a lot of leeway in what they report for cable fees.

Says sports economist Andrew Zimbalist of Smith College: "If you own the baseball team and the sports network, you can put the team's revenues into the sports network and not subject it to revenue sharing. The more revenue sharing you have in baseball, the more advantageous it is to a team to own its own sports network." Last season baseball's richest teams gave $167 million to the poorest franchises to keep the league competitive.

The impact of cross-ownership is reflected in our ranking of baseball teams. Of the five most valuable teams, four (New York Yankees, Los Angeles Dodgers, Boston Red Sox and Atlanta Braves) either own cable networks or are owned by a media company. An even more telling statistic: These four teams are worth an average of $504 million, versus a league average of $286 million.

For the fifth consecutive year the Yankees take the top spot. This year the Bronx Bombers rose 15% in value to $730 million. Owner George Steinbrenner had a deal with Cablevision's MSG Network that would have paid him more than $50 million this season. The Boss, who also controls New Jersey's pro basketball and hockey teams, the Nets and the Devils, thought that figure was too low and paid the cable outfit $30 million to get out of the contract.

Instead Steinbrenner is starting his own sports channel, the Yankees Entertainment & Sports Network. This year YES will show the Yankees and the Nets; the Devils will be added in 2007. The network is looking to charge cable companies $1.85 a month per subscriber to carry the channel on their local systems. With 8.6 million TV households in the New York area, YES has the potential to generate close to $200 million in subscriber fees alone. The value of the YES Network is already pegged at a minimum of $850 million.

The Dodgers surged 14% in value, to $435 million, to overtake the Braves as the third-most-valuable team. In 1998 News Corp. paid a then-record $311 million for the Los Angeles Dodgers. Rupert Murdoch realized that Walt Disney, which had purchased stakes in the Anaheim Angels and hockey's Mighty Ducks during the mid-1990s, planned on using its teams to launch a southern California cable sports channel. Buying the Dodgers helped Murdoch solidify his second cable sports channel in southern California and thwart Disney's efforts.

Yes, the Dodgers lost $29.6 million last year because they have the third-highest payroll in baseball after signing stars like pitcher Kevin Brown and outfielder Shawn Green. But the Dodgers are worth every penny. Marc Ganis, president of Sportscorp, believes that launching the two Fox Sports Net regional networks in southern California and securing the broadcast rights to the Dodgers has added over $200 million to the value of Murdoch's broadcast holdings.

In Canada, Rogers Communications, the country's largest cable outfit, bought 80% of the Toronto Blue Jays from Belgian brewer Interbrew in late 2000 for $112 million. Last year the team had an operating loss of $20.6 million. But the increased value to Rogers of being able to carry the Blue Jays' programming has been enough to increase the team's total worth to $182 million. After broadcasting 31 games on its cable channel Sportsnet last season, Rogers plans to broadcast 106 games in 2002.

The national pastime has become so attractive for cable—football is shown almost exclusively on network TV, while basketball and hockey schedules have half the number of games as baseball—that sometimes just the threat of a team's starting its own cable channel is enough to land it a fat cable deal.

Last season the local media revenues for the Seattle Mariners were the largest of any team outside of New York, Atlanta or Chicago—$28.8 million—despite playing in the 12th-largest media market. Fox Sports Net signed a ten-year deal with the Mariners in 2000 for $288 million, in large part because the team's cable rights hit the market at the same time Paul Allen and Barry Ackerley were contemplating the launch of their own regional sports networks. Seattle went up in value 12% to $373 million.

With NESN the Red Sox will certainly have the cash to be a financial success. But to erase the Curse of the Bambino, the Red Sox still have to win a World Series someday.

PERMISSIONS ACKNOWLEDGMENTS